Overseas Press Club

COOKBOOK

Overseas Press Club

COOKBOOK

EDITED BY

Sigrid Schultz

DOUBLEDAY & COMPANY, INC.
GARDEN CITY, NEW YORK • 1962

Contents

INTRODUCTION

We, the members of the Overseas Press Club, hope that the recipes in this book will prove good additions to the home chef's menus, either in their fancy versions or the simpler ones.

Some may wonder why contributors to this book have strayed from their usual field of weighty reports and discussions on World Affairs. The truth is that our "Book Committee" under the chairmanship of Will H. Yolen was sitting in solemn conclave weighing the pros and cons of a possible new tome on international politics. The roster of its members is an impressive one: Ted Amussen, Simon Michael Bessie, Bill Doerflinger, Dickson Hartwell, Charles Hurd, Ken McCormick, James Parton, John Lowell Pratt, Eleanor S. Rawson, Quentin Reynolds, J. Wendell Sether, Donald Wayne, Victor Weybright. They had a good laugh when confronted with the suggestion that a collection of anecdotes, centering around memorable meals and backed by tried-out recipes, might prove interesting and possibly stimulating. Then, remembering some of their own experiences, they paved the way for the publication of stories and recipes that shed light on some of the lighter moments in correspondents' lives, when the inner man gets his due, wherever he be.

If anybody gathers from this book that gala banquets and fancy little dinners are the regular fare of overseas correspondents, let me state most emphatically that this is not

the case. When covering big stories, watching literally day
and night for the news break and trying to get our messages
home ahead of the competition, most of us have gone
through stretches when a soggy sandwich or a hot dog
wrinkled with age proved lifesavers. Most of our tribe
would rather go without food than miss "the" story, be it
that of the day or the year.

But it does not take a correspondent long to discover,
while traveling from country to country, that the alert politicians, officials and businessmen worth knowing as news
sources generally take their eating seriously. They have
favorite hangouts famed for special dishes and drinks, rang-
ing from little bistros or their equivalent to fancy restaurants. You get more news and acquire a better insight into
the thinking of people who count by sharing a meal with
them, as host or as guest, than at the best staged press conference. Therefore it is almost a professional necessity to
try to become an amateur epicure, though the auditor in
the home office may not always share that view.

There was the auditor of the Chicago *Daily News* who
felt that the word "caviar" appeared too frequently on the
expense account of Junius Wood when he was stationed in
Moscow. He cabled his disapproval. Junius cabled back:
"Eggs is eggs"—and that settled the matter. In fact, once
you become a part-time member in the caviar, lobster,
champagne and fancy-dish circuit, the number of news-
worthy people you can buttonhole increases. The drawback
is that at times you must sit through banquets and listen to
good oratorical "snow jobs" of tycoons or statesmen. There
are occasions when the fanciest food seems to stick in your
throat. That happens when you have to listen to propaganda speeches that make you madder by the minute and
you have to keep on smiling, as if you were as dumb as the
speaker and his cohorts think you are. Instead of enjoying
the food, you keep on thinking of questions you'll have to

ask to catch the propagandists off guard and get a story to justify the time wasted listening to them.

But given enough experience most correspondents reach the point where they can enjoy the meal spiced with news —or the hope for news—and give it a gourmet's proper appreciation. We have collected stories about just such experiences and recipes discovered while hunting for "the inside dope" or the spectacular scoop.

Of necessity this is an eclectic collection. A great variety of cooking schools are represented, though we have resisted the temptation of including a dinner with the head hunters or stewed monkeys cooked in the jungle. You'll hear from believers in short cuts, from gourmets who follow the Cordon Bleu teachings, from believers in mathematical precision to others who operate more freely.

None of the prescriptions will be quite as artistic as those of the chef of the last Sultan of Turkey. His Majesty was entertaining the Kaiser of Germany, Wilhelm II. His Imperial Majesty relished the rice dishes and asked for permission to have gentlemen of his staff interview the Sultan's chefs. The permission was granted. The German officials arrived in the Sultan's kitchens. After the traditional mocha was served, the guests ordered the aide, who was acting as secretary, to get out pen and paper to write down the exact figures for the Turkish rice recipes.

The Turkish chef was taken aback. "But," said he, "there are no exact figures when it comes to cooking rice. Everything depends on the kind of rice we have just received. We study each new batch. We try it out and only then can we decide on the best way of using this special shipment, whether it be as a pilaf or as a dessert. You must know your rice."

Matters are simpler in these days of standardization— yet the truth is that the flavor, the strength, the texture, the quality of our ingredients vary. Being amateur epicures we can indulge in the sport of taking the basic suggestions offered and adapting them to our personal taste, to give those 132,000 taste buds provided by nature a chance to act as final arbiters.

Part I

HIGHEST ECHELON BANQUETING

From Chequers to the Kremlin

QUENTIN REYNOLDS

THOUGH experts and near experts have worked out new, fine-sounding theories about "mass communications" and "news media," I doubt whether they have solved one baffling mystery about overseas correspondents.

The mystery centers around two questions: How do some of them succeed in almost always securing personal interviews with the most important men in the countries where they travel? How do they almost always manage to turn up just in time to cover the most important events, stirring the imagination of the American public, whether they write their reports or broadcast them?

Psychologists and news specialists interested in these problems might well study the records and adventures of some of these masters of our craft. There is, for instance, our friend and colleague Quentin Reynolds.

Ever since he first turned up as a young correspondent in London and Berlin in the early thirties, he has rarely failed to meet and interview the leaders of the day and convey an alert impression of their personalities and their colorful background. Thanks to these experiences he can take us to dinner at the country residence of Mr. Churchill in Chequers and to the pageantry of a banquet in the Kremlin at the height of World War II. He writes:

Yᴏᴜ don't always remember memorable dinners just because of the food that was served.

For instance, in 1943 I had dinner with Winston Churchill at Chequers, his summer residence. It was an ordinary meal, but naturally, I will never forget it.

The other guests were Averell Harriman and Harry Hopkins. Mrs. Churchill and young Mary were also present.

The dinner consisted of smoked salmon, and there isn't much of anything better than that. Then we had what Mrs. Churchill said was lamb as a main course. Churchill grunted after he tasted it and said: "This isn't lamb, it's mutton, Clemmie. Can't you get us better meat than this?" Mrs. Churchill looked at him sweetly and said: "Remember, Winston, there's a war on."

With the lamb, or mutton, we had smooth brown potatoes and a dish of purée of Brussels sprouts, well seasoned. Hopkins asked what the dish was, and Churchill said he would tell him after he had finished it. Hopkins liked it enormously, and Churchill roared with laughter. He turned to me and said: "Harry has told me he hated Brussels sprouts and asked me never to serve them at Chequers when he came. But Clemmie fooled him. She made a purée and added a lot of spices and Harry never knew the difference."

Incidentally, with the lamb we had a great Johannisberger. Churchill growled and said to me: "It's incredible to me how barbarians like the Germans can make such a wonderful wine."

Our dessert was nothing but good Stilton cheese with crackers. At this point, the butler passed around port, a drink which I wouldn't put into my automobile. Churchill also refused, but the others all had a portion. When he saw I didn't take any he turned and asked me why. I was honest and said I didn't like it and added: "However, because I don't like port doesn't make me anti-English. I'm an Irishman, and if there's one thing I hate, it's Irish whisky." Churchill chuckled mischievously and said: "I don't like port either. Let Harry and Averell have the port. You and I will have brandy." So we had brandy.

I might add that during the whole dinner Churchill never stopped talking, and this was the greatest conversation I had ever heard. By most standards, this was a pretty ordinary meal, but I will always remember it because of Churchill's running commentary.

Once at the Kremlin I had dinner with Stalin. I and about a hundred others. It was a dinner for Beaverbrook and Harriman who were there on a mission in 1941. They slipped me into Moscow as their press attaché. I could not get a visa as a press correspondent. After they left, I stayed on for nine or ten months more, but this dinner was the most fantastic I ever had.

There were twenty-three courses. The three high spots, I think, were the mushrooms fried in sour cream, the sturgeon in champagne, and the pilaf of quail. In front of each man there were three bottles of vodka, white, yellow and red, with peppers in it. The waiters were also constantly passing bottles of Ukrainian white wine, and toward the end of the meal they started serving Russian champagne, which was much like the German champagne which you and I drank in Berlin. I am enclosing the menu.

The highlight of the dinner was a toast by Stalin, translated by Litvinov. He gave a toast to President Roosevelt and he ended by saying: "May God help Roosevelt in his most difficult task." It was an amazing moment to hear Stalin, who was so anti-Christ, asking for help for Roosevelt.

Menu of banquet given by Stalin in 1941—enjoyed and reported by Quentin Reynolds:

COLD HORS D'OEUVRES:

Fresh caviar, pressed caviar
Smoked sturgeon, salmon
Kertch herrings
Cold ham, sausages *assortis*
Cold pork with horse-radish
Tomato salad, tomatoes
Game with mayonnaise
Fresh cucumbers
Caucasian cucumbers
Cheese of various kinds

HOT HORS D'OEUVRES:

Tartelettes de volaille
Mushrooms in sour cream
Sturgeon in champagne

DINNER

Chicken crème
Meat pies
Borstchok (cabbage soup with beets)
White fish *bouilli,* with Sauce Mousseline
Turkey and romaine salad
Chicken—Hazel hen-grouse
Pilaf of quail
Cauliflower and asparagus

Parfait of nuts—Petits fours
Coffee
Liqueurs and wines
Fruits
Almonds

Notes from the Editor and Our Cooking Experts

No long treatise could illustrate the contrast between two ways of life more eloquently than these two dinners: on the one hand the gracious hostess who even in the grim days of war knew how to turn a meal into an amusing surprise and gently twit the all-important guest from overseas; on the other, the pomp and pageantry with which the masters of the Kremlin sought to impress the emissaries from lands whose help and friendship they sought.

Anyone who has ever coped with a man's prejudice in the food line will admit that Harry Hopkins' delight in the camouflaged Brussels sprouts was a major triumph for his hostess. How did she do it? We inquired from friends of the Churchill family in England and we were told that she merely dressed up the traditional purée of Brussels sprouts with a little mace, a little grated nutmeg and ground cloves blended into the white sauce.

The basic recipe for:

PURÉE OF BRUSSELS SPROUTS

calls for:

2 pounds of Brussels sprouts
4 tablespoons of butter
1 tablespoon of flour
1 cup of meat broth
2 egg yolks beaten with
¼ cup of cream
¼ teaspoon of ground cloves
½ teaspoon of grated nutmeg
Pinch of mace
Salt and pepper
1 piece of stale white bread

Cook the sprouts quickly in salted water, in an uncovered pan with the piece of dry bread, for about 10 minutes. The bread serves to absorb some of the stronger flavor of the sprouts and is removed as the sprouts are drained. If the sprouts are exceptionally fresh, young and sweet-tasting, a little of the water in which they were cooked may be added to the meat broth. If the taste of the water is strong, it must be discarded even if it means losing some vitamins and minerals!

While the sprouts drain, melt the butter and blend in flour, adding the meat broth and possibly the sprout broth, before the flour begins to take on color. Cook a few minutes until the mixture is slightly creamy. Add the spices and the sprouts and cook over low heat until the sprouts are very soft, which takes between 12 and 15 minutes. Force the sprouts through a sieve.

Since the strength of the spices varies, the mixture must be tasted carefully at this point to make sure that no flavor predominates. Add salt and pepper and make whatever corrections your taste buds suggest: a pinch of turmeric, a mere hint of saffron or curry may prove enjoyable additions.

Beat the egg yolks into the cream. Slowly stir in the sprout purée. Taste once more. Heat thoroughly without allowing the mixture to boil.

DINNER AT THE KREMLIN

The twenty-three-course dinner of the Kremlin presents a wide choice for the seeker of new ideas. The menu does not list one of the really worth-while Russian treats though it was there: real black Russian bread. A shopper can find a bread that approximates true Russian variety in Russian and Jewish delicatessens in our big cities. It comes in huge round loaves from which the dealer cuts off chunks by the pound. To be right it should be pretty dry; covered with sweet butter it goes superbly with fish bites or cheese.

What could be more tempting than sturgeon in champagne as a hot appetizer? To some, champagne as a cooking medium may seem the height of extravagance, but in this combination, even the best champagne is a mere commoner. Its price is as nothing compared to that of the real sturgeon, which at times was worth nearly its weight in gold.

This was in the days before World War I, when Russian grand dukes, wealthy blue bloods from many lands vied with millionaires rising to world eminence in the display of supreme splendor and lavishness. In sturgeon season racing troikas would carry the live fish in tanks from the river to trains winding through the plains of Russia to Moscow. Gathered around the tanks of sturgeon, couriers, who had traveled four–five days and nights, would compete for the purchase of those sturgeons that were frisky enough to survive another long trip across borders to the fancy restaurants where the mighty feasted, be it in Paris, London, Vienna or some of the elegant spas scattered over Europe. The gourmets who'd ordered sturgeon to stagger their guests generally made it a point to choose their own out of the tanks in which the fish swam. No maître d'hôtel could cheat because the gourmet's aide would watch the removal of the *vesiga* from the sturgeon's back—the *vesiga* being a special kind of marrow and nerve in the spine of the fish, which ranks almost as high as the sturgeon itself since it is used in the preparation of the real *coulibiac*, and similar delicacies.

Today, air flights have simplified the transportation problem, but for the real gourmet, sturgeon still has as much romantic appeal as its companion, the champagne.

STURGEON IN CHAMPAGNE

To cook a 3-pound sturgeon in champagne the *poissonnier* —the chef who cooks nothing but fish—starts with a garniture à la Russe. For this he butters a thick earthenware baking dish. On it he places:

    2 young carrots, cut in thin slices
    2 leeks
    2 onions, sliced
    1 tablespoon of finely cut celery root
    1 teaspoon of peppercorns
    1 bay leaf
    1 twig of thyme
    1 piece of *beurre manié* (fresh, sweet butter mixed with a little more than its own weight of flour)

On top of this bed goes a buttered piece of paper and a tight-closing lid, and then the dish is baked in a 350° oven; the vegetables are stirred very gently from time to time and after about 45 minutes they should be soft but not mushy or watery.

In the next step they are placed at the bottom of a fish pan. The fish that has been salted and given a slight sprinkling of freshly ground pepper is placed on the vegetables, covered with a quart of fish broth and a half bottle of good, dry champagne. Chopped parsley and chervil, possibly a hint of fennel, go in next and the whole is covered by another piece of buttered paper and a tight-fitting lid. Simmer for 40 minutes; the fish should be done, though the cook will check carefully that it is cooked all through before he skins it and places it on the warm platter on which it will be served. It must be covered to prevent its cooling while the sauce is being finished.

Remove the bay leaf, peppercorns and twig of thyme; stir the broth in which the fish has simmered, blend in some more *beurre manié* and a cup of cream. Bring quickly close

to the boiling point. In the last minute add a tablespoonful
of Sauce Hollandaise (page 264) to thicken this mixture
and to give it the consistency that makes it possible to blanket the waiting fish with it. The balance of the sauce goes
along to the table in a well-heated sauceboat. This should
be enough for six to eight guests.

MAMALIGA

When sturgeon or a similar fish is not served as an in-
dependent hot hors d'oeuvre, French and Russian chefs
serve it with rice, though some hold that Rumanian *mamaliga* is the traditional accompaniment. Into a quart of salted
boiling water stir 2 handfuls of cornstarch which has been
blended with cold water, mixing with a wooden spoon.
Boil at high speed for about 15 minutes. By then the mixture should be smooth and firm enough to hold the shape
of the pan in which it has been cooked. Press a wet, wooden
spatula around the edges and turn onto a warm platter,
from which it is served.

Just because most of us cannot obtain sturgeon, there is
no reason to forego the delight of enjoying a good fish—be
it turbot or sole or blackfish—cooked in champagne à la
Russe. The basic procedure is the same as the one described above—though your famous chef will sprinkle
chopped parsley or chopped parsley and chervil over the
sole à la Russe in its blanket of sauce.

Who would cavil at sole or turbot or other fish cooked
in champagne, served with a glass of dry champagne?
Many of us would even be satisfied with a fish cooked in
white wine with the garniture à la Russe. But to come up
to gourmet standards

FISH IN WHITE WINE À LA RUSSE

calls for an addition of sliced mushrooms and some mushroom broth. If you do use sole, be sure to simmer it very

gently, and to be stingy with the broth, the wine and mushroom juice to obtain more of a poaching effect than out-
right simmering. Fish filets should be placed with skin side
up to benefit from the butter on the paper covering, while
the unprotected side absorbs the flavor of the vegetable
and wine base.

FISH BROTH

Some may ask about fish broth. Much of the cook's success depends on it. Marcel Boulestin, for instance, advocates cooking a simple, well-tasting fish for the family table
in a court bouillon as a starter. Take enough water and wine
or vinegar to cover the fish, using a tablespoon of vinegar
or a port-glassful of white wine to two pints of water. Add
onions and shallots, parsley, thyme and a bay leaf, peppercorns and salt, possibly some mustard seeds, or a little
fennel and cook for ½ hour. Put in your fish, turn down the
heat to make sure that it only simmers or, as the French
cooks say, "merely trembles."

In the next step use the court bouillon in which the
simple fish has cooked, put in its head and fins, the head
and fins of the fancy fish you are readying for the party,
and if possible some pieces of meat from fish that produce
a good broth, such as pike, turbot, sole, halibut.

Add some more finely cut onion, and leek, thyme, parsley, clove, a bay leaf, a little garlic. Simmer in a hermeti-
cally closed pan for 20 minutes, strain; then add white wine
or red wine, depending on the fish you plan to cook. If your
recipe calls for a mushroom taste, this is the point at which
mushrooms are cooked up in the broth for a few minutes
and fished out again to leave only their flavor.

The careful planner may keep some court bouillon in
readiness in the icebox for a day or two, but once court
bouillon has been raised to the level of fish broth, it should
be used quickly. Unlike meat and vegetable stocks which

don't resent a longer stay in the refrigerator and are always ready helpers, fish broth develops a slightly stale aftertaste, even under refrigeration.

The second hot hors d'oeuvre served at the Kremlin is one that received ample publicity during the state visit of Premier Khrushchev to the United States:

MUSHROOMS IN SOUR CREAM, OR SMETANA

I regret to say that most European cooks have an advantage over the American cook: they have a great assortment of mushrooms growing in forests or in the open countryside which are more flavorful than the very pretty varieties grown for us in caves.

One of the best cooks I know on this side of the Atlantic, who concocts excellent mushrooms Smetana, literally "ages" the mushrooms, i.e., she keeps them around for a few days before cooking them. She claims that they have more flavor after they have lost some of their pristine whiteness and just before they start to develop wrinkles. For mushrooms in sour cream, take:

1 pound of mushrooms
4 tablespoons of butter
¾ cup of sour cream
1 tablespoon of flour
2 medium onions, finely minced
1 garlic toe, crushed on wood with a wooden spoon
¼ teaspoon of cayenne pepper, salt
1 teaspoon of freshly chopped dill or dried dill
Pinch of thyme
1 teaspoon chopped chives
2 tablespoons of clear bouillon, or milk
4 teaspoons of lemon juice

Separate the stems and caps of the mushrooms, rubbing them with a dry cloth to remove all sand rather than washing them, which has a tendency to make them leathery. Slice the stems and caps separately.

Sauté the minced onions and crushed garlic in 2 tablespoons of butter until the onions are soft and transparent. Add the sliced stems, stirring and frying briskly. They need a little more time than the sliced caps, which go in next with salt, cayenne pepper, thyme and dill. Stir while they brown a little around the edges.

Simultaneously melt the remaining butter in a separate pan with the flour, add some of the juice that has formed in the mushroom pan and a squirting of lemon juice. Blend well, add the bouillon or milk, cooking until the flour no longer tastes raw when you mix in the sour cream. Pour this concoction over the mushrooms. Mix well, heat for a few minutes without ever reaching the boiling point. Sprinkle with chopped chives. Serve in ramekins that have been in the oven just long enough to acquire a little color on top, or on squares of bread that have been browned in olive oil flavored with a tiny piece of garlic.

TARTELETTES DE VOLAILLE

are aristocratic cousins of our ubiquitous chicken à la king, sporting truffles and cocks' combs and nary a trace of flour in the golden sauce, encased in patties made of the Russian many-purpose dough.

RUSSIAN DOUGH

To make this dough, take:

½ cup of cream cheese (an 8-ounce package)
½ cup of butter, lightly salted
1 generous cup of flour
Pinch of sugar

Place the cream cheese and butter in a bowl, blend them either by hand or with two knives until they form a thoroughly unified paste. Add the flour and the few grains of sugar, kneading until you have a smooth dough. Wrap in wax paper and chill in the refrigerator for 12 hours, but don't get it too cold. If you do, it gets crumbly and hard to roll.

When ready to bake, roll the dough to ¼-inch thickness and cut into one batch of rounds big enough to fit into your tartlet shapes and to rise a little over the rim and another smaller batch of rounds to serve as lids. On the bottom sprinkle a few bread crumbs mixed with a hint of salt and pepper. Put in your filling. Butter the inside of the lid you will place on it, bring the dough that stands over the rim of the tartlet back on the lid and pinch together firmly. Prick the top with a fork to give the steam a chance to escape, or make a chimney. Heat your oven to 400° and bake for about 15 to 25 minutes until golden brown. The baking time will depend on the size of your tartlets.

Your favorite creamed chicken may go into them. The genuine Russian version would call for the cooking of a very plump chicken in very little chicken broth that has been prepared with various cut-up roots in it—celery root, parsley root, carrots, bay leaf, peppercorns, celery seed, juniper berries. Salt after the chicken has begun to boil, turn down the heat and simmer slowly to make sure that the meat does not get stringy. An extra discreet beef bone smuggled in the pot will give more flavor to the chicken, and an extra veal bone, preferably a knuckle or a calf's foot, will make the broth more velvety.

The ambitious cook, bent on getting as strong a taste of chicken as possible in her concoction, uses the same trick as the Russians, the Chinese and the wise little Paris *bourgeois:* they'll first take all the chicken feet they can get hold of, burn off the outer skin and cook those chicken feet to a fare-thee-well with some cut-up roots. That broth would be delicious on its own, but for important occasions it will be brought to a boil with the above-mentioned additions and the chicken finally cooked in it.

But how many American cooks have the time to prepare chicken feet? They might use chicken necks and backs for the basic broth in which the chicken is to be cooked, but these are not in the same upper-gourmet bracket as the chicken feet.

When the chicken is done, cut into tiny slices, mixing white and dark meat. Strain the broth and taste to make sure that it has enough salt, pepper, possibly a trace of nutmeg if you like it, or a touch of turmeric. If you plan to use truffles, as the Russian chef did, heat the slivered truffles in as much broth as you plan to use. Add cocks' combs which can be bought ready cooked in little bottles.

If you had a veal knuckle or chicken feet in your sauce, it should need only the addition of a few egg yolks to acquire the desired thickness. If you find it too thin, mix 1 teaspoon of arrowroot with a little cold broth, counting 1 teaspoon of arrowroot per cup of broth. Bring this quickly to a boil with the truffles, cocks' combs—possibly a few mushrooms if no other dish on the menu contains mushrooms—and round off the sauce with egg yolks. Pour over the slivered chicken, warm this mixture and pack into the shapes filled with dough and press on the buttered lids.

Most European chefs use puff paste to make their *tartelettes de volaille* and similar dishes. But the Russian dough or the French *pâté* dough (described in the chapter about the *pâté veau et jambon*) are far less temperamental than the puff paste and have a certain heartiness that is enjoyable. The Russian dough has another advantage: it can be rich as in the above recipe, and it can be made a little drier by using cream cottage cheese instead of cream cheese in mixing it. The drier version lends itself well to the making of cocktail bites, in the shape of *piroshki*.

PIROSHKI

To make these bites, cut the well-chilled dough in squares, put your filling in the middle, fold together to form a triangle after moistening the sides, pinch them firmly together, stand the triangle on its longest side, turn the front corner slightly toward the back on one side, turn the back corner toward the front on the other. This gives your bite the shape of a little ship and reduces the danger of any filling escaping, which it often does when the bites are baked lying on their side.

What would you put into them? If you like fish, spicy Norwegian *gaffelbitter*, of various kinds that come in small cans, do well, or you can make a different Polish sauerkraut filling or a beef filling which serves equally well for small bites and for a bigger roll-like concoction to be sliced and served either hot or cold.

POLISH SAUERKRAUT FILLING

1 cup of well-cooked sauerkraut
2 tablespoons of onions, cooked in butter
½ cup of finely chopped cooked meat or ham
1 teaspoon of finely chopped dill pickle
Dill, thyme, marjoram, salt and pepper to taste
1 egg
1 teaspoon of sour cream

Heat the sauerkraut, onions, meat, spices, herbs, dill pickle. Mix in the egg and sour cream.

Roll the chilled dough, to ¼-inch thickness. Slide the dough onto a greased baking sheet. Put the filling on one half of the dough, fold over the other half, moisten the edges, press together on all sides to seal well. Turn so that the seam is at the bottom. Prick the top to allow the steam to escape.

Bake in an oven that has been heated to 450°. After

about 25 minutes, the loaf should be golden brown and ready to serve, sliced, as hot appetizer or as accompaniment to a soup.

While cabbage certainly does not rank in the higher echelons of gastronomy, many a traveler to Riga and Baltic lands will remember with pleasure hot little "pasties" enjoyed with a strong drink on a cold winter evening. Most of them are made with this same all-purpose dough dressed up with a coating of egg yolk mixed with water and filled with a real:

CABBAGE FILLING

often spiced with caraway seeds or tiny chunks of dill pickle or a generous sprinkling of ground nutmeg. Chop a small, fresh head of cabbage, very fine; steam it in 2 ounces of hot fat mixed with 1 teaspoon of sugar and ½ cup of browned onions, until it is a soft mush that goes into the tartlets—a far cry from the fancy *tartelettes de volaille* but popular enough to be served in famous restaurants run by refugees from East European lands.

If the idea of the sauerkraut mixture scares you, you can reduce the amount of sauerkraut used and increase the proportion of meat, or you can forget about the sauerkraut and make a regular:

RUSSIAN MEAT ROLL

1 pound of finely ground beef
½ cup of finely minced onions
1 teaspoon of capers
3 chopped, hard-cooked eggs or sliced eggs
½ teaspoon of salt
1 teaspoon of chopped parsley and chives,
    thyme, marjoram, freshly ground pepper to taste
1 teaspoon of sour cream or of Sauce Hollandaise

Brown the meat and onions together, add the capers, salt, spices, herbs; when done add the cream and the chopped eggs and proceed as for the roll with the sauerkraut filling. You may serve it as a whole course with a meat sauce, or mushroom sauce or tomato sauce. Sliced it goes well with cocktails.

If you are among the lucky cooks who have leftover venison, chop it and replace part or all of the chopped beef with it and you'll have a dish in the best of East European cooking tradition.

Cooks to whom cakes are important will find the Russian all-purpose dough a good ally. They need add only 2 tablespoons of sugar when mixing the basic dough. Some of the fancy-looking cakes we admire in the shop windows of Paris or Vienna or Prague are made of it. There is, for instance, the golden

APRICOT TART

Roll ⅔ of the dough, that has been properly aged in the refrigerator, on a floured cloth to ¼-inch thickness. Butter or oil a shallow pan and line it with the dough. Cover it with ¾ cup of apricot jam, sprinkle some slivered almonds or minced filberts over it. Spread a latticework of dough over the whole and bake in a hot oven (400°) for about 20 minutes, until it is golden brown. Cool a little and dust with confectioners' sugar—a lovely concoction that can be whipped up quickly to impress unexpected guests—provided you have a good hunk of the dough in reserve in the refrigerator for just such emergencies!

The Gourmet Beat

BURNET HERSHEY

ONE OF THE founders and past presidents of the Overseas Press
Club, who was also president of the Association of War Correspondents in the course of its existence, Burnet Hershey, reached
the shores of Europe in 1917, covered both world wars and has
reported to American papers and magazines from all over the
world in times of peace and near peace. And as a wise traveler
he checked carefully on gourmet dishes wherever he went. He
writes:

ONCE UPON A TIME there was a Foreign Correspondent
who had covered two world wars, three minor wars,
numberless riots and revolutions. He had occupied grandstand seats at the crucial happenings during the most agi-
tated half century in history—all of which added up to
hundreds of newspaper clippings. His wife had pasted up
his best work in a set of scrapbooks, but he had added
something else. Alongside many a clipping was a penciled
footnote giving the name of a restaurant, a menu, a recipe
or the name of a wine or liqueur. Long after the reporter's
return to home base, these notations continued to serve as
a guide to good living. There was enough material in those

scrapbooks for an ample cookbook with a wine list to excite the most discriminating *sommelier*.

Whether these gustatory recollections end up in a cookbook or as still another set of journalistic memoirs, there is one premise with which most correspondents will agree: overseas reporting and gastronomy are clearly affinities, marching hand in fork through a variety of assignments in variegated lands.

Big wars produced big generals and big groaning tables. Above the platoon level, there was no such thing as a poorly supplied officers' mess. K rations were for the birds. Only Ernie Pyle owned a mess kit.

Big peace conferences offered even better pickings. Diplomacy went hand in hand with good eating and *bons mots*. The touch of Lucullus often made the whole world kin. The first United Nations was really a Holy Alliance of the gourmets. This tradition was interrupted by the Hitler era. After it ended, good manners and friendly meetings around the victuals were revived, as at the 1959 Foreign Ministers' conference in Geneva and, of course, later during Nikita Khrushchev's tour of the American banquet circuit. (Did you get a load of those menus?) A newsman covering this coast-to-coast argosy remarked: "The occupational disease of the old-time diplomat—gout—is on its way back. Only now it's also getting us reporters."

Our reminiscing correspondent smiles a scornful smile at this. Gout, indeed! From creamed chicken and peas? Washed down with bourbon and water? Man, he thinks you haven't even got a heartburn worthy of Bisodol. The palate, as one professor once stated, has a remarkable memory and our correspondent, reaching into the deepest recesses of that memory, comes up with this:

"Why, in those Versailles Conference days the American newsman was international table-hopping on a grandiose scale. The French Government staged its banquets in the palatial dining hall of the Quai d'Orsay and trotted out the

Napoleonic gold plate. The score was six gala *Affaires Etrangères* dinners and twelve luncheons during the first ten months of the Paris Conference. Here is a dinner menu right from the scrapbook, too:

Consommé Royal*
Croustades Dieppoises*
Filet de Boeuf Renaissance*
Timbales de Suprêmes de Volaille
Cuissot de Chevreuil Sauce Poivrade
Salmis de Faisans et Perdrix
Dinde à la Périgueux
Foie Gras à la Française*
Salade de Saison
Pointes d'Asperges Sauce Veloutée
Glace Maltaise
Gâteaux Lucquais
Susinets au fromage
Dessert

VINS:

Château d'Yquem
Chambertin
Champagne

The guests at some of these dinners extended by the French Foreign Minister, M. Pichon, included President Woodrow Wilson; Colonel House; Herbert Hoover; a young State Department hand, John Foster Dulles; Barney Baruch —and sign of the new times—ten to fifteen correspondents! They also turned up at dinners to honor General Pershing, or chiefs of states that had rewon their independence such as Thomas Masaryk and Eduard Benes of Czechoslovakia. For the first time in history statesmen of the world paid tribute to a labor leader when a sumptuous dinner was thrown in honor of Samuel Gompers! Those who were lucky enough to cover any of the dozen

* Recipes follow.

or more international meetings that followed Versailles will recall the rivalry among the different delegations, each vying with the other for the best chefs, the most lavish menus and—for the favors of a handful of correspondents who worked for powerful publishers.

Perhaps the most fantastic host of the time immediately after Versailles was the Swiss Government. It invited twenty American newsmen on a three-week de luxe tour of Switzerland. A complete train with *wagons-lits* and diner took the reporters from Paris to every important city and resort, in every canton of the republic. Gala lunches, luxury hotels, costly souvenirs and prepaid cable tolls were all part of the largesse. Lincoln Steffens, William G. Shepherd, Herbert Bayard Swope, Lucian Kirtland and all the others were accorded the honors of visiting potentates. After three weeks and forty-two *déjeuners* and *dîners*, many had to stop over in Vichy to "take the cure."

Not to be outdone in this bid for the first American tourist patronage after the war, the French Minister of Tourism invited some two dozen American correspondents to make a "gastronomic tour" of France. This group, including the two lone survivors of the Swiss junket, traveled to some twenty departments of France to sample famous regional specialties. *Naturellement* the local wines and the cognacs and the liqueurs—poured into the appropriate glasses—accompanied the repasts. This was truly a contest for the survival of the fittest.

Certainly all of us have eaten strange and exotic foods in widely diverse surroundings. But nothing ever approached the generous kitchens of France.

When the first "restaurant" opened in Paris about 1765, the restaurateur hung over its door this legendary sign: COME UNTO ME THOSE WHO HAVE HUNGER AND I WILL RESTORE THEE. The chefs and the restaurateurs of Paris are once again contemplating the display of this sign over Parisian eating establishments. They want it revived as a symbol and a notice that the gourmet and the culinary art of France were neither Nazified during the war nor pushed aside by the Americanization process of the postwar years. They want it known that those reports of a deteriorated cuisine, a "canned goods mentality" with ersatz overtones, are false and libelous.

Old Paris restaurants sometimes fade away, but new ones arrive every season. Little bistros, owned by Bretons, Angevins, Périgourdins and Provençals, change their checkered tablecloths for white ones, the *maître d'hôtel* puts on a tuxedo and the prices take a vigorous leap—*Voilà!* a new Paris restaurant for the guidebooks. In these eating places the cook's hand has not lost its cunning, the sauces are as subtle and brilliant as they ever were and the proprietors display their games and roasts and cheese and wines with the same ferocious pride of a Jean Casenave or a M. Bracquessac.

To those accredited World War II correspondents who worked out of the Hotel Scribe, one of the saddest sidelights of Paris's bitter ordeal was the manner in which some of the old restaurants were corrupted and debauched during the German occupation. Not that the food had deteriorated, nor was it even the loss of a few culinary masterpieces for want of butter or truffles, or the unobtainable spices from the Indies. It was that in a number of them the Germans and the high French traitors gathered during the occupation to carouse, while everybody around them—the old and the children—went hungry. Parisians have long memories for aromas—political as well as culinary, and the meeting places of *collaborateurs* were doomed after "Liberation day."

Going further back: Veteran reporters of the Battle of Paris (World War I) remember how many wondered whether Paris would ever again enjoy the reputation for good eating that it had acquired in the nineteenth century. Pessimists moaned that the decadence of *bon vivantism* had been under way for some time. Thackeray, in the *Roundabout Papers* in 1860, lamented the passing of those Paris restaurants he had loved in 1828: "My spirit goes and dines there." In *Les Misérables* (Chapter VI, Book V) Victor Hugo had his character Papa Gillenormand deplore, under Louis Philippe if you please, the fact that the nineteenth-century France does not know how to eat well or enjoy itself. They say that between 1875 and 1885 Guy de Maupassant and Émile Zola were the most conspicuous prophets of gloom. For them, Paris was doomed. It would never glitter again!

But it did!

The Boulevard historian who told me, "Don't worry, Paris comes up after every war, every disaster," had been right.

In the early thirties Lincoln Steffens, who knew his Paris at the turn of the century, took me on a "gastronomic tour" of the capital. Our hope and expectation was to recapture the atmosphere and quality of some old eating places.

The famed Paillards on the Boulevard des Italiens, where fine chefs and *maîtres* were trained, had closed its doors. Marguery of the fabled filet of sole was in a state of decline. Voisin, still an enchanting eating place, was a little tired. Steffens was sure that there were no longer any really good restaurants in Paris, certainly none like those "before the war." Yet Larue was still maintaining its mundanity and price. Foyot's, full of senators and old ladies, was holding fast to its traditions. There were at least a dozen more in that galaxy of famous restaurants and of those we sampled, Montagne, that rare inn kept by Prosper Montagne, in the Rue l'Echelle, Lucas, near *Larue's*, on the Place de la Madeleine, Viels, the Grand Vatel, Henri's in the Rue Saint-Augustin, Lapérouse and a sprinkling of smaller but better than good Parisian restaurants were all upholding prewar standards.

The mouth waters and the palate tingles and the spirit soars at the recollection of the food, the wines and the brilliant guests at the Caneton, Petit Coin, Maillabuau, Emil and Gênét—all near the Bourse and the A.P.; the Quatre Sergents de la Rochelle, near the Bastille; L'Avenue and Trianons in Montparnasse.

If that is what was left after a cruel and devastating war, what do you suppose it was like in Lincoln Steffens's youth? "Man may not live by bread alone, but he has to have bread—and a good sauce to dip it in," said Steffens the day before we ate our last meal together.

That final luncheon was at a little sidewalk café near the old New York *Sun* office. It was—and still is—located on the Place Gaillon, off the Opéra. Like most "little sidewalk cafés," it had long since gone high-hat with a head waiter in a tuxedo, a butler in blue tunic and white instead of checkered tablecloths. It looked like an inn in a comic opera. Because the owner had a small truck and relatives in the provinces, we found the menu heavy with tributes from many corners of France; chickens from Le Mans, *pâtés* from Amiens, pigs' feet from Sainte-Menehould, snails from Bourgogne, oysters from Marennes, minced pork from Tours. Since it was June, mushrooms and strawberries were making their seasonal debut, also asparagus from the Parisian suburb of Argenteuil with the fabled *vin rosé* from the same suburb. Finally, some old Boulestin cognac— thousands of bottles were buried in its subcellars, hidden from the Germans. Oh, yes. "*Garçon,* the addition!" Three thousand francs per head! About eight bucks. Tip—900 francs. Hat check—200 francs. Dear, dear Paris. Very dear.

"How did you like this little place?" I asked Steffens.

"Not bad—but there's a difference," he replied.

"A difference?" I asked.

"A vast difference—before the war, when I finished my dinner here I used to lick my fingers. Now—I bite them."

While journalism and gastronomy coexisted comfortably for many years (or as long as the expense account went unchallenged), the black market and inflation drove many Paris newsmen into their own kitchens. As a consequence, a new breed of reporter appeared on the Gourmet Beat.

The *Correspondent en Chef* became the chef-correspondent. Escoffier was more important than the Prime Minister, and Brillat-Savarin—because he could write as well as cook —was the new prophet. A Cordon Bleu was a more coveted decoration than the little red ribbon of the Legion. Some remarkable cooks emerged from this press gang, among them the late Henry Noble Hall (an early O.P.C. officer), who won many culinary certificates; C. F. Bertelli, of the Hearst organization; Percy Phillips of the New York *Times;* and dozens of others. Our own Larry Blochman achieved no mean status as an epicure-chef, helping to glamorize artistic eating even in mysteries. Another O.P.C. past vice-president, Waverley Root not only knew what's cooking in France but wrote a best-seller cookbook about it and became the outstanding contemporary authority in the field. Charlie Ferlin, a founder of the O.P.C., turned his European knowledge of cooking into a profitable channel by taking kitchen jobs when the editorial ax fell, as it frequently did even on the best of us. Victor Hugo may well have been right when he wrote: "Everything changes, and the only thing which remains immovable across the centuries and fixes the character of an individual or a people, is its cooking." And we, the foreign correspondents can sally forth to taste the delicacies from many lands while hunting for the scoop of the day.

Notes from the Editor and from Cooking Experts

There can't have been much dust on those scrapbooks, and the notes on memorable dishes mentioned in them must have been copious to judge by the zest with which Burnet

Hershey shared in the task of selecting some of the dishes from the historical menu or super-bistro menus that can be of use to home cooks.

Take, for instance, the:

CONSOMMÉ ROYAL

which figured on the menu of the banquet that was served to the chiefs of state in 1919, on gold plate in a Paris palace. It is really a clear chicken broth with fancy embellishments. Queen Victoria's chefs would send it to the table with "gratinated crusts" and "some shapes of chicken custard" known as *desclignac*.

To have your soup for six deserve the title of Royal, take:

6 cups of your best, clear chicken broth
6 gratinated crusts
1 portion of chicken custard, cut in diamond shapes

Heat the broth and just before serving add the above-mentioned embellishments that you have prepared beforehand.

GRATINATED CRUSTS

may sound simple, but have no illusion on this score: to be right, they call for a good deal of work. Take small, white rolls that you rasp down to the shape and size of an egg. Remove the inside without disturbing their shape. Put them on a baking sheet in the oven, at 325°, to crisp them and give them an appetizing brown color.

Then put them in a shallow dish and pour enough of your chicken consommé over them to cover; place the dish on a low fire until the crusts nearly stick to the pan and are gratinated. Then slip them back into the oven for a final crisping.

CHICKEN CUSTARD À LA DESCLIGNAC

can be prepared beforehand. It calls for:

2 egg yolks, beaten in a dish with a little grated nutmeg
¼ cup of chicken broth, salt to taste

Strain this through a fine sieve into a buttered flat pan that is placed in a slightly bigger pan containing hot water. Steam this as you would any other custard. Since this is a small quantity most chefs carry out this operation on top of the stove on a low flame, which gives them a chance to end the cooking as soon as the custard is firm. Let it cool well before cutting it into diamonds or fancy shapes.

When ready to serve, heat your consommé, put in your custard pieces, heat just a little more, then top each plate with one gratinated crust that has been kept hot in the oven.

If a mere "royal" soup does not sound high-class enough for you, you may serve:

CONSOMMÉ IMPÉRIAL

which calls for a strong beef broth, that earns its title by sporting custards à la Desclignac made with beef broth instead of chicken broth.

Studying the historic menu, we came to the conclusion that the *croustades Dieppoises* are well worth copying. They start with a base of mussels à la Marinière, which in itself is a delightful dish.

MOULES À LA MARINIÈRE

For four persons take 4 quarts of mussels. The best way to clean them is to place them in a sieve above a big pan of cold water. While you scrub them dip the sieve into the water from time to time, but not long enough for the mussels to feel at home and to open. If they do, they lose the salt water that gives them their extra flavor.

Into a big pan put:

3 tablespoons of chopped parsley
2 chopped shallots or onions
1 sprig of thyme
1 cup of white wine
Black pepper
No salt! Optional: 2 tablespoons of butter

Place the mussels on this bed, cover, turn on the heat as high as you can. Lift up the pan and shake it up and down to switch the mussels around. Remove as soon as they open. Fish out the parsley, thyme and onions. Bring the remaining juice to a quick boil with a big piece of butter and finely minced parsley. Reduce to about one half. If the mussels are to be eaten immediately without an extra fancy sauce or setting, remove one of their shells, distribute them and divide the sauce fairly.

If you want to serve them with:

SAUCE DIEPPOISE

take the mussels out of the shells, soak them in their sauce. You will need:

3 cups of the cooked mussels
1½ cups of small, cooked, shelled shrimps
4 egg yolks
4 ounces of melted butter
1 teaspoon of lemon juice
Optional: slivers of truffles soaked in excellent sherry

Mix the mussels and shrimp, pour off the mussel sauce, cool it and blend in 4 egg yolks. Put 4 ounces of butter into the top of a double boiler, over water that is nearly boiling. Add your egg yolk mixture, whip as for a Sauce Hollandaise. When the sauce has the proper consistency, reheat the mussels and shrimp in it and give the whole a final squirt of lemon juice. If you are set on putting on airs, cut in a few slivers of truffles that have been soaked in a very good sherry.

You now near the final operation for achieving eight

CROUSTADES DIEPPOISES

The real *croustades* are crunchy, providing an interesting contrast to the rather soft mussels and shrimp. Cut slices of a fine textured bread, to 1½-inch thickness. Remove some of the inside, leaving a bottom and a circle, or boat-shaped sides. Fry them in deep fat until they are crisp and brown. Dry them carefully on paper and fill them with your mixture. Slip the *croustades* into the hot oven just before serving to give them an extra little burst of heat, but not enough for the sauce to soak into the *croustade*.

No home cook need cling to the orthodox method pre-scribed by famous chefs: the traditional Dieppe *croustade* can be replaced by cases made of puff paste, homemade or store-bought, by little cases of *pâté brisée* (see page 255) baked on the backs of muffin pans or in tiny ovenproof dishes, or by cases baked from the Russian all-purpose dough or your favorite piecrust.

Belonging to the school that believes guests should be given something to do besides just eating, drinking and talking, I find American popovers pleasant bases for mix-tures similar to the *dieppoise*. The guests get them red-hot; they are then supposed to cut the popovers in two, drop a dab of butter in each crusty half and fill it up with the well-heated, creamy concoction.

If you belong to the school that feels starches should be avoided whenever possible, put your *dieppoise* that blan-kets mussels and shrimp, or scallops or shrimp into sea shells. Sprinkle a little fine bread, finely minced parsley and a hint of grated Parmesan over the whole, topping off with a few dabs of butter. Pass quickly under the broiler.

The main dish at the banquet which Burnet Hershey remembers with extra fondness was

FILET DE BOEUF RENAISSANCE

For the secrets of this dish I went to the chef of the Overseas Press Club, M. George Ovide, whose mastery is known on both sides of the Atlantic.

Take a whole, real *filet mignon,* which your butcher will get for you if he is a friend of yours. Wipe it well, braise it very slowly and when its heart has reached the degree of pinkness you prefer, cut even slices with a very sharp knife and place each of them on a *croustade.* The latter can be fried in deep fat, but in this case it does more justice to the aristocratic meat topping if it has been fried in butter.

Over the whole pour a sauce made with the reduced liquid from the braising, finely cut truffles and a carefully made brown sauce, known as Sauce Espagnole. To decorate, take artichoke bottoms sautéed in butter.

Most cooks have their own version of braising meats, which experts agree is one of the most delicate kitchen operations if perfect results are to be achieved.

BRAISING MEATS

Best results are achieved if you marinate your meat for a few hours in a little of the wine that you intend to use for the braising.

The bed on which you plan to cook the meat should contain for each pound of meat 1 ounce of sliced carrots, 1 ounce of thickly sliced onions slightly cooked in butter, a toe of garlic and less than 1 ounce of blanched pork or lard rind. Roll this all together with salt, pepper, bay leaf, thyme, peppercorns, and marinate with wine. After the meat has marinated sufficiently place it in a sieve, let the wine drip off and rub it dry.

In a heavy pan that fits your roast, heat clarified fat. Sear the meat in it on all sides.

Remove it to a warm platter, pack your vegetable mixture in the bottom of the pan. Pour over the wine in which the meat has marinated and reduce very quickly until the vegetables form a softish mass. Take the best beef broth you have, mix it with a little *glace de viande*, or beef jelly, bring to a boil. Place your roast on the vegetable bed. Pour the hot beef broth over it. Cover the pan and slip it into an oven that has been preheated to 350°. The meat will be done if no blood escapes when you try it with a tester. It takes about 12 to 15 minutes per pound of meat, depending on the degree of pinkness you want.

To make sure that the meat does not dry out toward the end of the operation, keep on turning it from time to time, and if need be, add a little wine.

What is left in the pan when the meat is done must be passed through a sieve very quickly. Blend a little arrowroot in the liquid thus obtained. Cook and mix with your brown sauce and the truffles that may have been marinating in Madeira or sherry for several hours.

As M. Ovide, our chef, said, the sauce on the filet Renaissance should include Sauce Espagnole. To achieve a perfect one is relatively simple provided you have mastered the art of making a good French *coulis*, a reserve of which, kept in the refrigerator, will do wonders for many a dish. It is one of the secrets of the real French cook.

A TRADITIONAL COULIS

¼ cup of bacon or salt pork cut into tiny squares
12 ounces of rolled veal
2 sliced carrots
4 cups of bouillon
4 ounces of butter
4 tablespoons of flour
Salt

Start melting the bacon in a heavy pan. Before it is really hot put in the meat and carrots, cover and cook very slowly on a low fire to draw the juice out of the meat. Then increase the heat until the meat almost sticks to the pan. Cut down the heat so that the meat gratinates gently but thoroughly. When this has been accomplished remove the meat and vegetables to a warm plate. Drop your butter into the pan, blend in the flour, cook until the mixture is really brown. Then pour in your hot bouillon. Return the meat and vegetables to the pan and cook for 2 hours on the lowest possible fire, skimming off the fat from time to time. Pass your *coulis* through a fine sieve.

This will give you 4 cups of *coulis*. Use as much as you need for your Sauce Espagnole and store the balance in your refrigerator for future use.

The *coulis* should not be too thick and it should have the color of a fine stick of cinnamon.

You may ask, for what could one use the *coulis* besides Sauce Espagnole? There is the:

SAUCE MARINIÈRE

that will turn a humdrum steak or roast into a Lucullan dish. Reduce your *coulis* by one quarter after adding one squirt of garlic juice and a tablespoon of finely minced parsley. Mix in the drippings from your meat, add about 5 cooked mussels per portion and when this mixture is really

hot, salt and pepper it and, removing it from the fire, blend
in the yolk of an egg to give it its final roundness. Pour
over your steak so that its juices blend with the sauce
when you cut it.

To turn the *coulis* into the famed:

SAUCE ESPAGNOLE

take:

2 cups of *coulis*
½ cup of white wine
½ cup of bouillon
Bouquet of parsley and chives
1 toe of garlic
2 cloves
1 bay leaf
2 tablespoons of olive oil
1 onion, sliced paper-thin
Pinch of ground coriander

Cook this all together in a heavy pan on the lowest possible flame for 2 hours; skim off the fat, pass through a fine
sieve and add salt and white pepper. This should net you
two cups of Sauce Espagnole.

Luckily there is one dish on the historic menu that does
not call for that much labor. It is

FOIE GRAS À LA FRANÇAISE

Chef Ovide describes it as a composition of "a generous
slice of goose liver *pâté*, served with scallion, a radish rose,
thin slices of cucumber and young carrots in olive oil, vinegar and salt—as enjoyable an appetizer or reviver of a
lagging appetite as one could wish for."

In writing about Happy Gourmet and news-hunting days
in Paris between and after the wars, Burnet Hershey mentioned restaurants for which correspondents used to make
a beeline as soon as they had attended to their most press-

ing duties after reaching Paris. They'd be brought up to date quickly by their friends about the places that had remained true to their "specialties." The closer they came to old-fashioned French home cooking, the more they delighted travelers tired of hotel and dining-car meals.

There was Casenave, for instance. The *spécialité* that seemed—and was—beyond compare, were his

POTATOES ANNA

To make them you need a pan that closes well and can be turned upside down. Lucky French cooks still have special brass and copper pans to turn out this dish, but with a little imagination, the home cook can arrange for a substitute. My solution is to take two 9-inch cake pans with straight sides that are less than an inch high, using one as receptacle for the sliced potatoes, and buttering the bottom of the second one to press it down on the potatoes like a tight-fitting lid.

    2 pounds of potatoes of even, cylindrical shape
    2 tablespoons of butter
    1 teaspoon of salt ½ teaspoon of white pepper

Butter the inside of pan number 1 and the bottom of pan number 2 most generously. Slice the peeled potatoes very thin, striving for even silver-dollar-size slices. Rub them with a clean cloth to remove some of the potatoes' moisture—not all. Then pack them evenly, layer by layer into the buttered pan. Between each layer dust with the salt and pepper and scatter in a few dabs of butter. Then press the buttered bottom of pan number 2 on top of the potatoes. Weigh it down, if need be, with a flat, well-washed stone or whatever you have that won't mind the heat.

Slip this contraption into an oven, giving it bottom heat of 400° for 40 minutes. By then the bottom layer should be crisp and golden. To achieve an equally crisp and golden top, turn on the top heat for an additional 10 minutes. You then have a flat cakelike round that can be slipped onto a serving tray and the pieces cut just the way you cut a pie.

If whatever you are baking in your oven at the same time requires less heat, just give your potatoes a little more time. Casenave's potatoes were baked in wheel-sized copper pans with a low rim, with the result that you enjoyed two nicely crisped layers with just a slight filling of soft but tasty potatoes, which lent extra glamour to any meat with which they were served.

But Casenave and the other restaurateurs whom we remember as masters of their craft would be hurt if we failed to pay attention to one *spécialité* that plays an important role in all French menus:

SWEETBREADS

Thrifty souls may feel that they are too expensive, but they have no bones and they will go a long way because they like the company of freshly cooked peas, carrots, carved young turnips, olives, mushrooms, slices of ham, rice or potatoes in all shapes and forms.

Whether you plan to serve them roasted on a spit, in a cream sauce, fried or braised, sweetbreads must be prepared beforehand—at least 6 hours before they are cooked. Plunge them in ice-cold water and if there are traces of blood on them keep on changing this water. Let them soak for about 45 minutes. Then two courses are open to you.

You can either drop them into boiling water and simmer slowly for 20 minutes; the boiling water should contain:

1 teaspoon of salt	1 bay leaf
2 tablespoons of lemon juice	2 slices of onion
1 stalk of celery	

for two pairs of sweetbreads.

Or, if you like your sweetbreads firmer, blanch them in cold water that you bring to the boil quickly and keep boiling for about 2 minutes—for medium-sized sweetbreads.

After one of these two operations, give them another cold bath, remove the fatty or tough parts in the folds, but make sure that you don't damage the membrane covering the sweetbreads proper. Roll in a towel, put them in the refrigerator until ready to cook. French chefs like to put a small board topped with a heavy weight over them in this phase of the preparations. The resulting shape is more attractive and the sweetbreads cook more evenly.

This kind of corseting is specially important if the proud owner of a spit wants to show off his or her cooking prowess. Stick the spit through the length of the sweetbreads, which fare better in this case if you have larded them with bits of bacon. Then roll them into well-buttered paper and cook for about 25 minutes. Remove from paper but keep them near the fire for 12 more minutes to give them a chance to brown. Baste them with a little good veal broth, sprinkle with salt and very little mignonette. Serve with the sauce that has accumulated at the bottom of the pan, minus the fat.

What is mignonette? It sounds like a fancy herb, but it is your favorite mixture of black, white, and gray peppercorns, broken, chopped or coarsely ground to look like seeds. The best way to find the

MIGNONETTE

you prefer is to have a tasting bee some quiet evening when you plan to cook nothing but hamburgers and try out various proportions of pepper on them. Put the mixture you prefer in a small well-closing container, ready for use. In time you will discover which of the various peppers does most for your favorite dishes.

BRAISED SWEETBREADS

Prepare your braising bed carefully. For each pair of sweetbreads use about:

1 tablespoon of butter
½ onion, sliced
½ young carrot, sliced
2 chopped sprigs of parsley
1 sprig of thyme or ½ teaspoon of dried thyme
¼ bay leaf
1 finely sliced small celery stalk
1 tablespoon of sherry
½ generous cup of chicken or veal broth
Optional: ¼ pound slices of mushrooms

Put the butter in an ovenproof skillet, add the first seven ingredients and cook them for a few minutes, then moisten with some of the chicken broth and cook a little more. When the vegetables look slightly shiny, place the sweetbreads on them. Cook over low heat until the vegetables begin to turn golden. Add the sherry and the remaining chicken broth, and place the dish in the oven that has been heated to 375°. Bake for about 45 minutes, basting from time to time. The sweetbreads should be brown and shiny.

If the sauce that has formed in the pan seems too thin, dissolve some arrowroot in cool chicken or veal broth or sherry and simmer for a few minutes, then pour over sweetbreads.

Sliced mushrooms, sautéed separately, or whatever delicate vegetable tempts you, are served with them, as is rice or young potatoes browned in butter or mashed potatoes.

If you have guests who crave more solid meat, give them

RIS DE VEAU NIQUETTE

This calls for a crown made of sweetbread halves alternating with slices of ham. In the center place creamed carrots.

If you want to be swanky, serve

SWEETBREADS À LA TOULOUSAINE

which are stuck with pieces of truffles before they are cooked and garnished with little chicken dumplings, mushrooms, olives and truffles. Or if the title

FINANCIÈRE

tempts you, cover your sweetbreads with the sauce of that name, as do most of the restaurants near the Paris Exchange. This is merely made of the drippings from the sweetbreads, stretched with a little *coulis* or Sauce Espagnole that boasts of half a cup of good Madeira for each quart and is perfumed with essence of truffles.

From Paris to Rabat

BARRETT MCGURN

THOUGH some of us like to belittle the importance of formal social occasions in our professional lives, the fact is that the correspondent who reaches the point where cabinet ministers, tribal
chiefs, monarchs and tycoons proffer invitations to big or small
dinners is the one who gets the vitally important information,
which is, after all, our main purpose.

No correspondent would underestimate the importance of the
astute little or big man behind the scene, who'll tip him off on
occasion and provide background information, but at a state banquet there is always a chance to get a clearer understanding of
the aims of the men who really shape policies. And regardless
of the continent on which they live, on these gala occasions big
and small powerholders put their major-domos, their chefs, their
favorite restaurateurs to work to devise the kind of meals that
will impress or please the palates of high-ranking guests and
respected enquiring reporters.

Barrett McGurn, correspondent of the New York *Herald Tribune,* who was stationed in Rome in 1959, had a chance to compare propaganda methods along the political and gastronomical
line both in France and in Morocco, as may be gleaned from the
following:

ROME is one long happy encounter with the forty-plus varieties of spaghetti but Paris, where I passed three years of my current Latin assignment, produced, of course, the most spectacular tableside experiences.

Two are especially memorable. The food as usual was fine but the circumstances were what fascinated me.

The first was a private dinner for a selected few correspondents organized by a cabinet minister. He laid on the feast at his ministry itself. It was on the banks of the Seine in a two-century-old palace which had played a gay role in the fall of the monarchy and the rise of the Napoleonic dictatorship. Footmen in long tail coats received us in the glass-walled entrance, showed us with deep bows to the broad staircase to the upper-floor salons and signaled for other footmen to receive us above.

The minister welcomed us in the second room. A tall handsome man, a veteran of a dozen years of top French politics, he entertained us with parliamentary gossip and related small talk until another servant—brilliant in a ruffed white blouse, tight gold jacket and skin-tight yellow knee breeches, pushed open the doors to the dining hall. There at an imposing table beneath a great crystal chandelier our places were set.

In this brilliant setting, as waiters brought on waves of courses and three of the most celebrated French wines, the minister came to the point. France, he said frankly, faced new grave difficulties. He had a few news tips he was willing to give us exclusively. Publication of them would be in the French public relations interest abroad and, at least a little bit, might help.

The spectacle of the rueful amid such riches still had me mildly dizzy a few weeks later when another assignment as my paper's Paris man sent me to North Africa. Algeria was just brewing but Morocco was getting the headlines then. In Rabat the French were quite open and cordial, the Moroccan underground was much more cautious. It was the never-never moment of a change-over: officially the underground was beyond the pale; in fact the French were letting it rise to the surface so that a hand-over of some grace could be accomplished and the salvageable could be saved.

Contact with the underground was established and I was asked to dinner. My hosts met me at my hotel, spirited me through the alleys of the forbidden native quarter, a zone Westerners hesitated to penetrate unescorted, and brought me at last to an apartment house which would have looked at home in Jamaica, Queens, except for the wide air well where the half-imprisoned Moslem women get their share of the outdoors.

Dinner soon was served. The main course was *couscous*, the North African Moslem mélange of grain, vegetables, sauces and mutton, all of it eaten from a common platter and plucked up with the three fingers of the right hand as desert-edge protocol prescribes. The experts were able to shake the loose grains together with a dice-tossing sort of gesture, packing them into a small ball ready to be tossed into the mouth, but press as I would I could not get the loose material to adhere. Ingloriously I used a proffered spoon. Olives, chicken, almonds and dates in delightful combinations rounded out the feast. A servant with two brass receptacles, soap, warm water and a towel passed occasionally so that we could clean up.

But again it was the scene and the conversation which most impressed my story-conscious mind. For our Arabian Nights banquet we had been arranged on the floor of a room like any other back home in Long Island. My host was an Atlas tribal chief who had been banished to the Moroccan capital to keep him and his men out of mountain trouble. Try as he might he could not quite succeed in turning a modern apartment house into a tent.

His conversation, like the French minister's, was appallingly far removed from the delights of our table. He had only one refrain: "The United States should give us guns, even rifles." Against whom he meant to use them he did not say but the alarmed French cabinet member could have guessed. Both meals were a delight and, to the extent that they could, each meal had been organized to cancel the other out.

In footnote it may be added that the white-bearded chieftain on the middle-class floor was an advisor of the Sultan of newly free Morocco when I got back there next. The minister went on to serve in many another government as the quick sad political changes in Paris continued.

The cabinet minister in the palace on the banks of the Seine and the tribal chief camping in the heart of Rabat had seen to it that while their guest listened to their political arguments, he also enjoyed a meal that was up to the highest tradition of their national cuisine.

The Cooking Experts Speak Up

Though Barrett McGurn had trouble coping with the slippery *couscous*, this dish has so many fine possibilities that the chef of General de Gaulle even served it to visiting generals during the Italian campaign. We shall describe this French version in connection with the story of Richard de Rochemont.

The Arab course that obviously delighted Barrett McGurn was the dessert, and there is no doubt that the Arab cook can give us fine pointers in the art of blending precious flavors and fruits with a true artist's touch.

When cooking quince jelly, for instance, for his master, he won't be satisfied with its ruby-colored sweetness; he will seek to heighten its flavor by crushing cardamon seeds and sprinkling the powder into the boiling jelly. He'll serve it, not on plain bread and butter, which would delight most mortals, but on a bed of carefully browned almonds chopped and mixed with a softish semolina pudding, which is one of the simpler versions of the famous Arab dessert:

EL MISTOUF

For a real *El mistouf* cooked to impress a guest, the process is more complicated. For a party of 10 to 12 this dish calls for:

1 pound of medium semolina
1 pound of stoned, chopped dates
½ cup of seeded muscat raisins
¼ cup of candied orange peel and lemon peel
1 teaspoon of cinnamon, all blended with a little orange water
Candied cherries, candied angelica for decoration purposes
½ cup of sugar
½ cup of almonds
Pistachios

The semolina is soaked in water overnight; then it is cooked in steam, resting on a piece of cheesecloth that is tied over a pot of fiercely boiling water.

After this initial step, boiling water is poured over the semolina, three times in succession to give it the gooey consistency required by tradition. Then the chopped, stoned dates and the fruit mixed in a mortar are worked into the semolina pudding, which is finally decorated with red cherries, slices of candied angelica, almond halves and whatever colorful bits of candied fruits are on the kitchen shelf.

For those who are not bound by the anti-alcoholic rules of the Koran, the orange flower water may well be replaced by rum or a favorite orange liqueur. A sauce of thinned quince jelly often completes this exotic but delightful dish.

Dinner of the Three Emperors

CURT L. HEYMANN

LIKE the Arab chief who cooked for the banquet Barrett Mc-Gurn attended, the chef of the French cabinet minister who had invited the American correspondents studied famous menus of the past for inspiration. There is a great similarity in the pattern of state dinners. There is, for instance, the famous "Dinner of the Three Emperors." It ranks so high in gastronomic history that when the committee of the Fêtes de Paris prepared for the festive season in 1959 it decided to give a repeat performance of the once-famous banquet.

Curt L. Heymann, former correspondent of the *Berliner Tageblatt* and the New York *Times,* who now makes his headquarters in Paris, writes about it.

THIS title is not absolutely correct. When the dinner was first given at the Café Anglais on June 7, 1867, it was attended by two crowned heads and one future sovereign. They were Czar Alexander II of Russia; his son, the Czarevitch, who became Alexander III; and the King of Prussia, who four years later became Emperor Wilhelm I of Germany.

At the repeat performance given for a hundred un-crowned tycoons of the world of finance, there was only one guest of imperial lineage, Prince Napoléon. The Romanoffs, like the Hohenzollerns, had lost their empires and the once glittering names of the *Almanach de Gotha* had lost much of their glamour.

The dinner was given on the exact anniversary of the banquet of the Three Emperors, but this time on the first platform of the Eiffel Tower. Strange to say, the basic price was the same on both occasions. It cost the old-timers 460 gold francs to enjoy this opulent meal, washed down with fabulous vintages. The epicures of 1959 paid 50,000 francs, which approximates the $100 bill of 1867.

A study of the menu reveals that what sent the price up was the cost of precious wines served with dishes that are similar to those which appear on menus of state banquets in the Presidential Palace in Paris, or at the Quai d'Orsay or in state functions of big embassies.

This is the menu:

POTAGES:
>   *Impératrice*
>   *Fontanges*

RELEVÉS:
>   *Soufflé à la Reine*
>   *Filets of sole à la Vénitienne*
>   *Escalopes de turbot au gratin*
>   *Homards à la Parisienne*
>   *Sorbets au vin de Champagne*

ROTIS:
>   *Canetons à la Rouennaise*
>   *Ortolans sur canapé*

ENTREMETS:
>   *Aubergines à l'Espagnole*
>   *Asperges en branches*
>   *Pâté chaud de cailles*
>   *Cassolette, Princesse*

DESSERT:
>   *Bombe Glacée*

VINS:
  Madère, "Retour des Indes 1848"
  Xérès 1821
  Château d'Yquem 1847
  Château-Margaux 1847
  Chambertin 1846
  Château-Latour 1847
  Château-Lafitte 1848

Notes from the Editor and Cooking Experts

Few hosts in our country will be able to serve their guests hundred-year-old French wines or Madeira that traveled all the way to the Indies in 1848, acquiring that dreamed-of extra velvety quality as it was buffeted in the holds of some romantic-looking three-master, but an ambitious home cook could concoct some of the dishes of the $100-a-plate dinner.

POTAGE FONTANGES

for instance, appears on many a family menu in France. In its everyday version all it calls for is a well-made, slightly thin pea soup, mixed with melted and puréed sorrel and decorated with some light plumes of chervil.

The epicure version uses a pea soup made of fresh garden peas. Take:

  2 pounds of peas and shell
  1 finely minced small onion or shallot
  1 teaspoon of salt
  1 teaspoon of sugar
  1 lettuce, medium size
  6 parsley stalks tied together
  4 tablespoons of butter
  3 cups of veal or beef broth or vegetable broth
  A few feathery chervil tops
  Pinch of thyme
  Salt, pepper
  2 ounces of sorrel stripped of their ribs
  Optional: 1 tablespoon of finely cut bacon

Shred the lettuce and place in a pan with the onion and 4 cups of water. Cook until the lettuce is half done, then add the peas, salt, sugar; while this starts to cook put 2 tablespoons of butter in a pan, let it foam and add the sorrel. Keep shaking the pan until the sorrel melts, i.e., turns into a soft purée, if your sorrel is really young; if it is not, you had better pass the sorrel through a sieve.

Add this purée to the cooking peas, with your pinch of thyme and one cup of broth. When the peas are soft remove the parsley stalks, the lettuce and the onion. Retain a small cup of the peas and pass the rest through a blender or a sieve. Beat in the remaining butter, add the broth, salt and pepper. Boil for another 10 minutes, then add the peas and the chervil plumes. If you have no fresh chervil, put a tiny bit of dry chervil in to cook with this *potage* right from the beginning.

Taste carefully before the final heating to check on the salt and pepper and to make sure that the sorrel taste does not predominate. If it asserts itself with too much energy, a little extra broth will help give the peas their rightful predominance.

This will give you six cups of soup—or enough for six to eight guests depending on the size of your plates.

If you leave out the sorrel, you will have an aristocratic

POTAGE SAINT-GERMAIN

that likes to be decorated with tiny squares of white bread fried in butter to which a pinch of thyme has been added.

Some cooks hold that the flavor of these soups comes out more clearly if you cook a little bacon with the lettuce, onions and peas.

While we think of sorrel, we might just as well take a look at a proletarian cousin of the *potage Fontanges:*

SORREL SOUP, OR SOUPE À L'OSEILLE

The sorrel is treated as above. After it is melted, add 3 pints of water and 3 very mealy potatoes—big ones—cut into small squares. Cook for 30 minutes, pass through a sieve or crush with a fork. If the soup seems too thick, add some water or milk, or a little broth.

As a final touch, after adding salt and pepper, break an egg into a pan, beat it with ½ cup of milk, pour the hot soup on it, add a few squares of crisp fried bread and chopped chervil. If you have no fresh chervil, sprinkle some dried chervil into the soup while it is cooking.

The second course included a soufflé à la Reine, which is made with chicken. One of the tricks for a good soufflé is to use a proportion of four egg whites to three egg yolks in your basic mixture and to stay right with the soufflé until it is done, while those who are to enjoy it sit ready with fork in hand to sample it before its bloom is gone. That makes it rather a temperamental dish for households without much help, whereas the Venetian Sauce, which the plutocratic guests had with their sole is a much more reliable helper of the home cook.

VENETIAN SAUCE FOR FISH

1 cup of white sauce made with fish stock (see p. 12)
½ cup of wine vinegar
1 finely cut shallot
Sprig of tarragon or ¼ teaspoon of dried tarragon
1½ cups of fish stock
1 cup of heavy cream
3 ounces of green butter

Reduce the vinegar on the shallot and tarragon. Add the fish stock and reduce this by half. Then work in the white sauce, cooking very gently. Reduce again by half, then work the cream in gradually. Finish with 3 ounces of green butter to provide the light green sheen that distinguishes Venetian Sauce.

GREEN BUTTER

To obtain "green butter" without the help of synthetics, wash and chop a pound of spinach and a good handful of chives. If you have a vegetable juicer, run the greens through it. If you don't, use your blender and put just enough water into a pan to cover the bottom and cook the greens in it very quickly. Press the juice out of them and reduce it by about one half in the top of a double boiler. When it is cool, mix this dark emerald-colored potion with double its weight of butter. Use a fork or a mortar for this operation. Your butter should look as bright and gay as a harlequin at a masked ball in Venice.

Conservative souls will be satisfied with spinach and chives as their dye, specially since it gives a pleasant, slightly meatlike flavor with a hint from the onion family. But experimenters may find an addition of cress, or a hint of finochio, or a little lovage, tarragon, chervil, good purveyors of surprising flavor provided they are used with discretion.

After filet of sole with its rich Venetian Sauce, after slices of turbot under a cover of crisp cheese gratin, after lobster, diners might feel a little weary. To revive their appetites, the chefs provided ice-cold:

SORBETS AU VIN DE CHAMPAGNE

a tangy sherbet, with a slight lemon taste in which champagne replaces the fruit juice. This refreshing semi-dessert is to ready the guest for the main "roast," which in the dinner of the Three Emperors was

ROUEN DUCKLING

This specialty from Normandy is a relatively small bird, which is so tender that it is done in about 30 minutes. Rouen duckling should never be stuffed, merely wiped dry inside, salted, peppered and given just a tiny pinch of ground cloves.

The sauce to go with it is made of the duck's liver that is pressed through a sieve while 2 chopped shallots are cooking slowly in 2 tablespoons of butter. When they are soft and almost dry, add ½ cup of bouillon mixed with a hint of tomato paste. Blend in 2 tablespoons of "worked butter," i.e., half butter and flour, and cook for a few minutes. Pour over 4 tablespoons of warm brandy and light it. Continue to boil slowly, with salt, pepper, cayenne. When all taste of flour has disappeared, add a little hot bouillon and pour over the liver. Heat well, without allowing the mixture to come to a boil. Scrape some of the drippings out of the pan in which you roasted the duckling and add them to the sauce—possibly with some Madeira—before sending bird and sauce to the table.

Incidentally, the family carver must remember that duck is never to be cut on the bias. It's slivers must be cut straight in a line parallel with its backbone, or the duck, if it is small, can be cut in four with shears.

Most of our ducks are heavier and a little tougher than those from Normandy. For a 3-pound duck, preheat the oven to 400°. After trussing the bird, sprinkle its inside with salt, pepper and the hint of ground cloves. If it looks as if it might be pretty fat, stuff an apple into its insides, but be sure to remove it before serving the duck. Give the bird a slight covering of sweet butter before placing it in its pan and start basting it after 15 minutes. Since it is a slightly squarish animal it has to be roasted on all four sides unless you own a spit that will brown it all over for you. In theory, the duck should be done in an hour, but to avoid disagreeable surprises, keep checking on its doneness in the final cooking phase: two ducks that look like identical twins when placed into the oven may react quite differently to the cooking process; the one may be tender very quickly, the other may insist on an extra 15 minutes to reach perfection.

If some duck is left after the party, save it and its bones for a superlative *cassoulet* (page 224).

AUBERGINES À L'ESPAGNOLE,

or eggplants Spanish style, which figure on the menu, are rather thick slices of eggplant cut lengthwise and fried in olive oil after being rolled in flour. When they are nearly done, cover them with peeled, quartered tomatoes that have been cooked in olive oil, with salt, pepper, basil, garlic, chopped parsley. Sprinkle each eggplant-tomato island generously with bread crumbs, douse with some more olive oil and bake in a medium oven for ½ hour. Serve with a light tomato sauce, and decorate, if you feel the urge, with thinly cut, stoned green olives.

There is really no limit to the list of delectable *bombes glacées*, in which ice cream is packed firmly along the sides of a mold and a softer, different mixture of fruit and ice is placed in the middle. To mention only a few: There is *bombe Aïda*, with an outside of strawberry ice cream and a heart of kirsch sherbet. *Bombe Alhambra* is made with vanilla ice cream on the outside and strawberry ice cream inside and topped with berries that have been soaked in kirsch—since kirsch brings out fruit flavors better than any other liquid.

What Paris chefs call *bombe Américaine* has a base of strawberry ice cream and a filling of tangerine sherbet and the whole is decorated with pistachio ice cream.

Bombe Fauvette is a delicious concoction of pistachio ice

cream, with a filling of a banana ice cream flavored with
kirsch.

If you have a weakness for oranges, *bombe Maltaise* will
serve well: orange sherbet, mixed with tiny slivers of
candied orange forms the outside, with curaçao-flavored
whipped cream inside, the whole topped with candied
orange slices, or fresh orange slices that have had a bath
of good white wine.

Incidentally, if you plan to serve an orange or a lemon
sherbet, a nice trick is to pass around little dishes of
candied orange and lemon peel just before serving the ice.
This will heighten the flavor of the dessert for those who
nibble the sweet beforehand.

Another variety of ice cream that always wins applause
is made with chestnuts. For it you need:

½ cup of cooked, chopped chestnuts that have been soaked in
1 tablespoon of kirsch and a little dark rum
8 egg yolks
1 cup of sugar
1 quart of light cream flavored with vanilla

Beat the egg yolks with the sugar. Stir into the cream
and heat slowly in a double boiler. Be sure to stir with a
wooden spoon. When this mixture is nearly thick, stir in the
chestnuts. Freeze and when the ice cream has reached
the proper consistency, decorate with extra pieces of
candied chestnuts and cream into which you have mixed
some more kirsch. A slight dusting of grated chocolate adds
a needed color touch and brings out a little more of the
chestnut flavor.

If you prefer the flavor and texture of the old-fashioned
fruit ice-cream dessert made with cream, take:

1 cup of fruit pulp
1 cup of milk
1 cup of heavy cream
About 1 cup of sugar

The amount of sugar depends on your taste, but be sure that the mixture tastes a little sweeter than you like it after you have mixed in the sugar and milk. Whip the cream and beat in the fruit juice mixture, and freeze.

Lest the editor be accused of failing to be explicit enough about homemade ice cream, here is a recipe of one of Chicago's famous authors and hostesses, the late Janet Ayer Fairbank, which she used for smaller parties that did not call for the big freezer:

1 quart of ripe strawberries
¾ cup of sugar
⅛ teaspoon of salt
1 cup of heavy cream, whipped

Crush the strawberries and mash in the salt and sugar. Stir into the whipped cream and pack into a refrigerator tray. Freeze until about 1-inch rim has been frozen. Turn into a chilled bowl and mix until the whole is of an even texture. Return to the refrigerator tray and freeze until firm. Some cooks like to add a dash of vanilla, which seems as insulting to a good strawberry as it is to knowledgeable taste buds. If you feel that the strawberries may not be as flavorful as they should, a dash of really good burgundy or a trace of excellent kirsch will be of great help—and will make "store-bought" ice cream pale in comparison.

Part II

TRUST OPERA AND THEATER FOLKS
WHEN IT COMES TO FOOD!

The Men Who Came to Dinner

JAMES P. HOWE

WHEN it comes to fun and fancy eating, the opera and theater folks and their friends have it all over high-echelon hosts, even if the latter have a corner on the gold plate and famous chefs. The leading lady and the leading men, the tenor and the basso, not to forget the baritone, the soprano, the mezzo and the contralto—they know their kitchen secrets and how to turn a meal into a good show.

None loved this sport more dearly than the star of "The Man Who Came to Dinner," Alexander Woollcott, who also starred in a "gastro-pastoral adventure" in one act, staged by his California friends and admirers in 1940. To make it seem like a real show the hosts, instead of providing menus, had regular theater programs, patterned on the *Playgoer* of San Francisco, emblazoned with "The Man Who Came to Dinner." The menu was nicely divided into "Prologue," "Main Act" and "Epilogue." James P. Howe, former Associated Press correspondent who reported from London, Berlin, Warsaw, Moscow, Peking and many other points, still has the menu-theater program, and the recipes for the Lucullan dishes amateur chefs concocted for their version of the "men who came to dinner." He writes:

OUR PRODUCTION was staged on Gopher Ranch, in Walnut Creek, California, at the foot of Mount Diablo, with hills as a backdrop and musical pigeons from Peking providing the musical accompaniment as they circled overhead with the light whistles I had brought from China hidden under their feathers.

The "Prologue" consisted of:

Les escargots à la Provençale (snails with Sauce Provençale)
Les rissoles de cervelle (fritters of brain)
Boules de Gruyère (cheese balls)

washed down with champagne.

The "Main Act" was rich with:

Le potage Bisque aux clams du Pacifique
Le Calmar sauté à la Génoise
La Selle d'agneau au carré et les légumes Jardinière
Une fondue aux truffes de Franche Comté
Salade de cresson aux pommes

The "Epilogue" boasted of *fraises flambées*, Grande fine champagne 1848, the traditional *café noir* and liqueurs.

The list of wines that went with the dinner was as fabulous as the dishes that were cooked—not by professionals, but by Dr. Raoul H. Blanquis and Dr. George A. Selleck, famed doctors in their everyday life. Where others play poker or golf as a pastime, they go in for cooking, and some of the dishes they served should inspire other amateur chefs.

Take the snails, for instance. Your true food lovers in France, in Alsace, across the border in Germany, in Baden and Württemberg or in Switzerland will go out to the vineyards and choose the best-looking snails they can find and put them in an enclosure in the back yard for a few weeks, feeding them on grape leaves, salad leaves and some spicy herbs until they are extra fat. And if they have no back yard, they'll do the fattening up right on their porch.

Thanks to the canning industry of France and Switzerland we can serve snails as a hot hors d'oeuvre provided we know how to make a good garlic butter—or a Sauce Provençale. One of the tricks is to drop the skinned garlic toes into hot water and let them stand for a minute before you start chopping them very, very fine.

GARLIC BUTTER

For 50 snails—out of a can—take:

10 ounces of butter
Several toes of garlic, finely mashed
2 finely chopped shallots
1 tablespoon of finely chopped parsley
Salt and pepper to taste

Mix this all into a smooth paste. Put a tiny bit of it into the bottom of the shell of the snail (the shells are sold with the canned snails), put in the snail and fill the shell to the brim with the garlic butter. Top with a thin layer of bread crumbs.

Most American homes don't have the special pans for baking snails and one does not really need them. Cut 1-inch squares of white bread and toast them on one side. Place them on your baking dish, putting the toasted side directly on the pan. Then maneuver your snails into position on the untoasted upper side so that the opening stands straight. The oven must be hot—about 450°, when you slip in your pan with the snails. They should be done in about 8 minutes. Some of the butter will bubble over, but it will be caught on the little pieces of toast that are served with the hot snail on top of them. But the "men who came to dinner" had their snails in:

SAUCE PROVENÇALE

instead of garlic butter. The cooks made a sauce of:

1 tablespoon of chopped parsley
1 tablespoon of chopped green pepper
3 finely chopped cloves of garlic
2 tablespoons of olive oil
1 glass of white wine
½ tablespoon of flour
2 egg yolks
Bread crumbs, salt, pepper, butter

Heat the oil and fry the parsley, pepper, garlic in it. Stir in the flour and wine; cook for 3 minutes. Add the snails and cook for another five minutes. Mix in the egg yolks. Fill the shells, close off the top with bread crumbs and butter. Bake for 15 minutes. Serve on toast squares. If you do not have forks that are small enough to fish out the snails, toothpicks will get them onto the toast with which an ordinary fork can cope.

RISSOLES DE CERVELLE, OR BRAIN FRITTERS

No canning industry can help the cook with the fried slices of brain, but the budget-conscious cook who is not afraid of work will appreciate them as do most diners. Soak as many calves' brains as you expect to need in cold water for 2 hours. Keep dipping them in water while you remove the thin membrane and the little veins until the brains are an even creamy white. Place in a pan with enough cold water to cover well, add some vinegar, salt, pepper, a pinch of thyme, a few tiny onions, a bay leaf, a few leaves of lettuce, a little carrot, parsley and garlic. Cook on medium heat until tender, but not soft, which takes about 20 minutes, depending on the size of the brain.

BLACK BUTTER

For a plain meal, serve this cooked brain with "black butter," i.e., butter melted in a pan until it is dark brown. Remove the pan from the fire, incorporate slowly a driblet of vinegar, some capers, minced parsley, salt and pepper and reheat before pouring it over the brains.

For the *rissoles,* or fritters, cut the brain in slices, about 1 inch thick, dip the slices into frying batter, roll in fine bread crumbs, fry in deep fat with a few sprigs of parsley to serve as garnish with a few slices of lemon.

FRYING BATTER

The simplest frying batter is made of:

4 ounces of flour
1 egg yolk
½ cup of lukewarm water
1 tablespoon of olive oil
1½ tablespoons of brandy or wine
2 stiffly beaten egg whites
1 teaspoon of salt
Optional: 1¼ teaspoons of "Four Spices"

Mix the flour, egg yolk and water until it forms a smooth paste; beat in the olive oil and beat some more; finally add the brandy or wine; beat some more and let this dough rest for at least an hour. Just before using it, incorporate the beaten egg whites. The wine or brandy helps the dough puff up while it is being fried and thus enhances whatever dish you are preparing.

One old French recipe calls for the inclusion of ¼ cup of beer in this mixture to further increase the lightness of the batter. If frying batter is to be used for a dessert, such as deep-fat fried apple slices, for instance, then add some sugar to the mixture before it is given its resting period. But whatever you do, be sure to stir the flour mixture with utmost energy. Since the quality of flour varies, the cook may find it necessary to add a little more water, after the batter has rested, to secure a batter that is thin enough to cover the slices of brain or whatever is to be deep-fried, completely and evenly. Yet the batter must be thick enough to cling firmly to whatever it is to protect from the sudden drop into very hot oil, or fat.

French cooks like to spice many of their dishes with *Quatre Épices,* or "Four Spices," which can be bought ready mixed in small bottles. For those who like to blend their own spices, here is the recipe.

Pound together in a mortar:

4 ounces of white pepper
¼ ounce of cloves (one quarter)
½ ounce of nutmeg
1 ounce of ginger

Keep in a well-closing small bottle.

CHEESE BALLS

The *boules de Gruyère* belong on the blacklist of anybody who fears calories, but they go well with cocktails or as the final course to take the place of a platter of cheese.

½ cup of flour
4 tablespoons of grated cheese, preferably Gruyère
3 tablespoons of water
3 tablespoons of butter
¼ teaspoon of salt
Pinch of pepper and a bit of paprika
½ teaspoon of baking powder
2 eggs
1 beaten egg white

Melt the butter and water on your stove, put all the flour into this mixture at once, stir and cook until it separates from the sides of the pan. Remove from fire. Add one egg at a time, beat, add the baking powder and the cheese. Take out spoonfuls and fry in deep fat, until the balls rise to the surface. Take out and roll quickly on absorbent paper. Serve very hot.

BISQUE OF SHRIMPS AND CLAMS

The *potage bisque aux clams du Pacifique* was inspired by none other than the famous chef Escoffier. When he was interviewed by Thomas R. Ybarra of the New York *Times* some thirty years ago, Escoffier confided that America had one delicacy for which he envied her chefs: clams.

To prepare eight servings of *bisque of shrimps and clams* take:

1 pound of shrimp, raw, thoroughly brushed
12 well-brushed big clams
3 tablespoons of butter
Parsley, onions, carrots cut fine in ample amounts
2 bay leaves, dill, pinch of red pepper, thyme
¼ cup of cream
1 teaspoon of caraway seed, salt, peppercorns
3 tablespoons of tomato paste
9 cups of water

Cook parsley, onion, carrot, caraway seed, salt, peppercorns, dill, in 4 cups of water for 6 to 8 minutes, add the shrimp and cook until they are soft, which depends on the size you have chosen.

Shell the shrimp, set aside the meat, put the shells in a blender, covering with some of the strained broth thinned with a little water. Run at high speed, repeating this operation several times. Cook this thickish mixture very slowly with the strained broth and one cup of water. Pass through a sieve and add a pinch of red pepper.

To prepare the clams put butter, chopped parsley, water

(4 cups), onions, pepper, into pan with the clams. Turn up the heat and shake the pan. As soon as they open, remove the meat from the shells, pass through a sieve the broth in which they were cooked and add it to the bisque from the shrimp. If the bisque seems too thin soak a tablespoon of bread crumbs in it, then cook on the lowest possible fire for 10 minutes. Add a pinch of red pepper and the cream.

Cut up some of the shrimps and clams and drop into the soup, which should be a bright pink; if it is too pale for your color effect, a little extra shrimp butter will prove helpful.

Nora Hodges will tell you how to make it.

Some cooks like to enrich this sauce with egg yolks, which make it seem more festive but reduce the oceanic flavor.

Though in most banquets the fish is supposed to introduce a lighter touch, the "men who came to dinner" continued to enjoy rich fare. The *calmar*, being squids, were fried in deep fat and the sauce that went with it was the *Génoise*, prized by epicures like Alexander Dumas.

The chef of Queen Victoria, Francatelli, also thought highly of this sauce. This is his prescription:

"Cut some ham, carrot, celery, onion, parsley roots and mushrooms into very thin slices; place these in a stew pan with a little butter, some thyme and a bay-leaf, a blade of mace, 2 toes of garlic, two cloves, and fry them for a few minutes; moisten with half a bottle of red wine (claret suits best). Boil the whole for five minutes; add a small ladleful of brown sauce and a little consommé; stir the sauce until it boils, and then set it to clarify by the side of the stove-fire; skim it and pass it through a tammy into a *bain-marie* for use. Just before dinnertime, add a piece of anchovy butter, a spoonful of chopped and blanched parsley, a little grated nutmeg, and lemon juice."

Anyone reading this book will have his own recipe for lambsaddle with spring vegetables. The latter, to rate the title of *Jardinière,* in the eyes of chefs of the old school should be tossed in a Sauce Allemande, which is a white cream sauce, but to our generation that has learned all about vitamins, this seems a gastronomic crime; what could be better than young carrots, young onions, young peas, string beans, cooked up separately and quickly, and each served in its own reduced juices with a bit of butter and a sprinkling of freshly chopped chives, or parsley, or chervil, or winter savory?

Let your own taste buds experiment until you find the herb that does most to dramatize the flavor of the vegetable you plan to serve. Chervil does a lot for carrots and peas, while there is the school that holds no peas or string beans can be at their best without summer savory, just as no tomato moves into the upper bracket without a bit of basil and a mere hint of garlic, and most cucumbers like the company of dill. And, for some mysterious reason, the taste of most of these herbs becomes more pronounced if you smuggle a tiny bit of finely minced parsley among them, provided you can scare up healthy parsley that has not lost most of its pep while waiting to be used. Being a sturdy plant, parsley usually perks up if its stems are placed in a glass of cold water, like a bouquet.

For the "men who came to dinner," and for those who plotted the meal, its artistry would not have been perfect if they had not had at least one dish celebrated by one of the all-time "great masters," Brillat-Savarin. This was the *fondue aux truffes de Franche Comté.*

There was nothing "bourgeois" about his version of the "fondue" first perfected in the shiny kitchens of Swiss peasants and dairymen in little houses high on the mountainside or nestling in lovely valleys. Brillat-Savarin counted two eggs per guest. He had them weighed in their shells, cracked into a pan that had been rubbed with garlic. Then he added:

Grated Swiss cheese weighing ⅛ of the weight of the eggs
Butter weighing ⅛ of the eggs
With each egg went 1 tablespoon of milk or white wine
Very little salt
Lots of freshly ground black pepper

The whole mixture was stirred on a "lively heat," until it began to bubble. Then it was poured into a very hot dish, into which truffles had been sliced, and the dish was put on the table, above a flame that kept the whole bubbling.

The Italians go Brillat-Savarin one better. They have a version that is baked in little paper boxes, or ramekins. They take:

4 ounces of grated Swiss cheese
4 ounces of grated Parmesan
4½ ounces of melted, sweet butter
Good pinch of powdered white pepper
Small pinch of salt
1 teaspoon of sugar
10 egg yolks
10 well-beaten egg whites

Mix well the first seven ingredients, then fold in the egg whites, drop into buttered ramekins, bake in a hot oven, (425°) until they are golden brown, and rush to the table on well-warmed platters.

What with 10 eggs, this fondue is about as temperamental as a soufflé. Don't try it unless the spirits that inspire the vagaries of soufflés have given you their blessing.

CAUTIOUS FONDUE

For the cautious there is a fondue that is bolstered with bread cubes. It calls for:

2 cups, i.e., ½ pound of grated cheese
2 cups of milk, scalded
2 cups of dry bread cubes
1 teaspoon of salt
½ teaspoon of pepper
4 egg yolks
4 beaten egg whites

Mix the bread cubes, cheese, salt, pepper, into the scalded milk. Cook slowly, stirring until the cheese is melted. Beat the egg yolks slightly, pour the cheese mixture over them. Fold the egg whites into the cheese batter. Pour into small ramekins or into a big 1½-quart fireproof dish. Bake at 375°. The length of the baking will depend on the size of the dishes. The big one needs about 50 minutes.

The Swiss mountaineers sneer at these concoctions, claiming that the eggs, sugar or even the truffles spoil the character and flavor of their national dish. You'll find the authentic Swiss recipe in another chapter.

It seems hard to believe that "the men who came to dinner" could have done more than just sit back and admire the flaming strawberries after this wealth of rich dishes. In fact, to make sure that he'd be able to cope with all the courses the star of the evening, Alexander Woollcott, had been careful to arrive early to take a long nap before the festivities began, gleefully shocking some by saying that his doctor had ordered him to take regular naps because he had reached "the change of life."

FLAMING STRAWBERRIES

The strawberries had been soaked overnight in excellent French red wine—just enough of it for the berries to absorb some wine without giving it a chance to impose its flavor on them. Then they were sprinkled with sugar and kept very cold. Just before serving, the cook poured a thin blanket of warm brandy over them. A little sugar was placed at the bottom of a warm ladle that was filled with more, carefully warmed brandy, to be ignited and poured over the strawberries, setting aflame the thin layer of brandy that was poured in earlier. Thus the heart of the fruit remained cool and refreshing. Less experienced cooks will find it safer to cheat a little by adding a touch of rum to the brandy when it is being warmed, since rum ignites more easily than other liqueurs.

It had taken our amateur chefs and a retinue of helpers two full days to prepare the feast. Had it been worth the effort? It had, to judge by the beaming, reminiscent smiles of the survivors, some twenty years later, as they relished the memory of dazzling conversation and the warm companionship that spreads among people who know how to enjoy a Lucullan meal, accompanied by carefully chosen wines, that turn it into a work of art.

The Diva Suffered for Her Art!

MYER AGEN

NOT ALL stars can indulge their love of food as happily as Alexander Woollcott and "the men who came to dinner." But even
when they must go through the ordeal of dieting, the world
travelers among them are quick to ferret out local specialties that
rank as sin on the dieter's list and for the sake of which they'll
do some fancy juggling.

None did this more charmingly than Edith Mason, the diva
whose sad plight Myer Agen remembers when she had to pass
up most of a luncheon at the Ritz in Paris and with whom I
shared a good number of forbidden calories. He writes:

IN THE EARLY 1920s I was with the Paris edition of the
New York *Herald,* and later was in charge of the American
column in the Continental edition of the London *Daily
Mail.* During my stay in France between World War I
and World War II, I had numerous occasions to dine with
interesting visitors to Paris.

I particularly recall a luncheon I had at the Hotel Ritz
with Giorgio Polacco, who conducted at the Chicago Opera,

and his then wife, Miss Edith Mason, who had several engagements at the time at the Paris Opéra.

The luncheon was delicious and prepared in the usual Ritz style, supervised by Maître d'Hôtel Olivier. I don't exactly recall what was served, but I remember that I thoroughly enjoyed the food.

Miss Mason would have liked to eat everything as we did, but her husband watched over her like a hawk, and she was merely permitted to nibble here and there. "Remember, dear," Giorgio admonished, "you are singing tonight. You must watch what you eat."

As I had no singing to do, I did full justice to the meal, but I certainly felt sorry for Miss Mason.

Editor's Note

There must have been a twinkle in the eyes of the diva as she watched the gentlemen enjoy their lunch and as she was supposed to be suffering for her art! On a good number of occasions when she found the lunch too skimpy she would slip out with lovely, slim, gay Eleanor Painter, who was also singing in Europe in those days, to their favorite *pâtisserie* in one of the side streets near the Ritz. I was along on some of these sinning expeditions. The divas knew exactly when the French *petites brioches* would be coming out of the oven and Edith Mason would always insist they could not interfere with her singing, because they were such "simple little cakes made mostly of eggs."

These were the old-fashioned brioches, which have a much finer texture than their modern successors. You need for real

PETITES BRIOCHES

1 yeast cake
½ cup of flour
½ scant cup of lukewarm water
Pinch of sugar
3½ cups of flour
10 ounces of butter, or 2½ bars
2 scant teaspoons of salt
1 teaspoon of sugar
6 eggs
1 extra egg yolk mixed with a little water

Dissolve yeast cake in lukewarm water to which a bit of sugar has been added. Mix it into ½ cup of flour to form a soft dough which you put into a buttered bowl, cover well and keep out of the draft which our French friends distrust so profoundly.

While the yeast goes to work, sift the flour, salt, sugar into a bowl, cut the softened butter into it and knead quickly. Break in the eggs, one at a time, mixing energetically with a wooden spoon after each addition. When this mixture is smooth, work in the yeast, stirring vigorously. Cover the bowl and keep in a protected corner until the dough has doubled in size.

Butter brioche or muffin pans that have been warmed a little. Punch down the dough which is so light that it is hard to handle. Reserve one quarter of the dough for the little tops of the brioche. Put flour on your board, roll a round soup spoon in the flour, dip it into the dough and drop this ball into the little pans. When your first set of pans is filled, roll out small balls for the top of the brioche out of the reserved dough. Moisten a spoon or your finger and make a depression right in the middle of the dough in the pans, moisten the base of the little ball and insert it in the depression. Some prefer to make a cut with a knife in the middle of the dough in the pan to squeeze the little ball into it. Paint with the egg yolk that has been beaten with a little milk. Set aside to rise for another hour or until double in size.

Have the oven heated to 425° when you slip in the pans. Bake on a lower rack, until the brioches are shiny and golden brown. Reduce the heat to 400° after a few minutes. The length of baking time, depending on the size of your pans, is from 20 to 30 minutes.

This yields between eighteen and twenty-four brioches. If you want fewer, put part of the dough in a slightly bigger pan to make one bigger brioche to serve as cake, letting it rise and bake a little longer than the brioches.

Your practical friend will say that this is too much work, when you can go down to the nearest French bakery and get ready-made brioches. This simply means that this practical soul has never eaten real brioches, fresh from the oven, with a dab of butter on them and possibly a little Bar-le-Duc jelly. What is more, the homemade brioche, with its full quota of eggs and butter, will let you heat it up the next day, and be almost as good as if it had just come out of the oven.

Have no illusions about it: brioche dough is temperamental. It likes to be mixed in a pan that is just a little warmer than room temperature; it wants its eggs, yeast and flour at room temperature. Don't think that you are doing it a favor by putting it in a really warm corner to rise: the extra warmth will make it taste yeasty. It does want its time.

Some famous chefs like to use brioche dough to make the Russian *coulibiac* of salmon, or *coulibiac* of beef, or various other *coulibiacs*. You'll also find it in the realm of Princess Grace of Monaco and in all the swank eating places on the Riviera. There it appears as *pissaladière*. The brioche dough is wrapped around a mixture of onions cooked in olive oil, chopped hard-boiled eggs, anchovies, cut-up black olives, capers, thyme, garlic, white sauce. It is shaped into a long loaf, baked in an oiled dish. Slices of the loaf are served either hot or cold with cocktails or *apéritifs*.

If you feel that friends and family will be satisfied with a less aristocratic brioche, there are short cuts, for a more "bourgeois" concoction. Here is the recipe:

TIME AND EGG-SAVING BRIOCHE

½ cup of milk
½ cup of butter
⅓ cup of sugar
1 teaspoon of salt
1 package of yeast
¼ cup of warm water
3 eggs, beaten
1 egg yolk
3¼ cups of flour
1 egg yolk beaten with a little water

Scald the milk and cool it to lukewarm. Cream the butter with the sugar. Soften the yeast in the water. Mix butter, yeast and milk.

Sift flour and salt and blend with above mixture. Add the egg yolk and the beaten eggs and stir vigorously for at least 2 minutes.

Cover and let rise until double in bulk, which takes about 2 hours. Punch down and beat hard. Form a ball that you put into a greased bowl, cover with foil and refrigerate overnight.

When ready to use, preheat oven to 425°.

Punch down the dough and place on a floured board. Reserve one quarter of the dough for the topknots. Divide the main part into 16 little balls that go into well-greased brioche or muffin pans. Shape the topknots and place them on the dough in the pans. Cover and allow to rise until double in bulk. This will take about 1 hour.

Just before slipping into the oven, brush on beaten egg yolk mixed with water. Bake for about 20 minutes until golden brown.

Since this variety of brioche dough will tolerate a stay in the refrigerator, it fits better into modern schedules, when the home cook may want to serve them for a holiday breakfast or brunch—but the texture is not as rewarding as that of the old-fashioned variety for the sake of which our famous singing friends played hookey from their mentors!

After Edith Mason had enjoyed her secret brioche, she'd say contentedly: "Now, I can take my mimosa soup with equanimity for a few more meals!" Her "mimosa soup" was clear beef broth into which the hard-cooked yolk of an egg had been grated (on a coarse grater) and in which a few very thin slivers of string beans had been cut, to give the effect of mimosa flowers and leaves. Pretty indeed—and a good counterbalance to calory-laden brioches!

Part III

PAGING FAMOUS AUTHORS

Luncheon with Selma Lagerlöf

FLORENCE BROBECK

As a correspondent Florence Brobeck reported from Sweden, Czechoslovakia, Germany, France and England for the old New York *World*, for the NEA Syndicate and for many American magazines. With a deep interest in the arts, applied arts and the warm human elements in the story of the day, she spent seven years as woman's editor of the New York *Herald Tribune*. Thanks to that background she was able to break through the ring of self-appointed protectors who were trying to shield Selma Lagerlöf from visitors after fame and success came her way. Florence Brobeck writes:

SHE IS TIRED of interviewers," my kind Swedish friends told me at Stockholm, when I told them that I was eager to meet their great writer, Selma Lagerlöf. "She lives far away from Stockholm. She is seventy years old. She will not receive you." Nevertheless, I set out for her faraway home not merely as a pilgrim to the shrine of a writer whose accomplishments I admired, but primarily because her personal history made all "country girl makes good" stories

pale in comparison. How many country girls are there in
this and the nineteenth century who, despite illness and
poverty in their youth, have created works that have been
translated into thirty languages?

Mårbacka was my goal, the farm home which her parents
had lost but which she had regained for herself and her
family. In the days of her childhood the trip must have
been much longer than the overnight ride which I took. It
lay in Värmland, the country she brought to the literary map
of the world—with its crystal-clear lakes, dark rocky hills,
rich fields and abundant orchards. The winters were long
and snowy. Contact with cities was rare; the occasional
visit between relatives was so noteworthy that family and
friends prepared for it with excitement for weeks and talked
of nothing else for months later. Contact with the world, until Selma Lagerlöf was a young woman, had been through
visiting musicians, her father's army friends and other
travelers.

As a visitor to that same country district, I found myself
let off the train at five in the morning at Kil. From there,
in the rainy dawn I rode in a modern, streamlined bus
thirty miles over streams, through pine and birch woods,
ferried across one lake in a creaky, hand-pulled ferry, up
hills and down dale, past spring-filled orchards and so
to Sunne. There we stopped at a working men's lunch
counter for a coffee-and-buns breakfast, and then on by a
private car for a few more miles to Mårbacka. I had expected a typical farm house, such as the red and white
frame structures which I had seen everywhere in the Swedish countryside. But before me stood, in great dignity and
beauty, a stucco and tile-roofed dwelling that looked somewhat like the châteaux of southern France. Preconceived
pictures of homely cottages tumbled before this house, especially before the little figure that stepped onto the front
terrace to receive me. Snowy hair, clear, sparkling, keen
blue eyes, a simple black dress, a warm smile—these were

the first impressions of Mårbacka and its mistress. But I remember most the smile and her greeting: "You have come so far. You must come in and have coffee." Coffee, the inevitable symbol of Swedish hospitality.

We lingered only a little while downstairs in the great drawing room, the lovely yellow-and-white dining room, and the entrance hall. She was eager to be again at her desk, in the long green-and-gold study on the second floor. There, sitting behind the table piled with correspondence, with new books in French, German, English and the Scandinavian languages, she talked to me. She told me how her father and his father before him had lived in this house and how she had grown up here. It was in this room and the front drawing room on the first floor that she had listened long hours to her grandmother's talks of the countryside, and to the stories the musicians and the farmers who came to call would tell around the fireside. When still a child she tried to write these stories, simply putting them down, then trying them in verse and in plays. But lamps were scarce in those days, paper and pencils were found only at the school.

When Selma's school days were finished, the family having lost the homestead, she went away to the south of Sweden to teach school and there was little time for writing anything but marks on her pupils' examination papers. Then she heard of a prize offered for stories about her own country and she remembered her early efforts. She got them out, put them together as *Gösta Berlings Saga*. It became her most famous novel. The young school teacher won the prize which made her name known throughout her own country. This was in 1891. From that time on she kept slowly and persistently at the writing down of tales about Sweden, especially about Värmland. She knew no other world; she had an unending urge to write stories, and a necessity to earn money as well.

For eighteen years more the writing and teaching continued and then world-wide recognition came to her through the winning of the Nobel Prize for literature. This meant a large sum of money at once . . . about forty thousand dollars. Fame and fortune came hand and hand in her case. Soon after this, she was elected a member of the Swedish Academy, the first woman member. Now indeed her long years of struggling and writing—the only medium in which she saw opportunity for growth and success—were rewarded. Out of the country she had loved and extolled in her books, financial security had finally come.

Her first act after the overwhelming Nobel award was to buy back Mårbacka. She began to restore it, building around the old house a new one which includes and preserves the old one. One of her countrymen, an architect of rare skill and taste, helped her to achieve a place of distinguished beauty in both the exterior and interior. Her gardens and orchards, the dairy and farm buildings were much the same as in the days of her childhood except that she could at last hire gardeners and farm hands to keep them in excellent and prosperous condition.

In her kitchen, when I was at Mårbacka, were Alma and Anna, who kept the blue and white tiles shining, polished the row of copper tea kettles until they looked like mirrors, made apple strudel, and arranged the *smörgåsbord* for the luncheon table and much else.

There were good portraits of Lagerlöf in her home, a bust in the entrance hall: there were fine porcelains, handsomely bound books, a generous display of fine furniture mostly made of native birch, the same gleaming, yellow wood making the doors of the house. Lagerlöf in passing one of these doors, rubbed it gently, pointing to the beauties of the wood. She was proud of this house. It was a dream come true for her, for she remembered, and her face saddened as she told of the days when her father struggled to keep the home, of how her mother helped him, of the difficulties of a large family, a sick grandmother, of back-country living shutting them off from ideas and avenues that could have helped them. Ill health was a constant shadow at her side. She limped a little from some childhood ailment never quite banished by the inefficient doctoring of the time.

But she began to write. She kept on writing when there was no visible market. Recognition finally came and it could not have been more spectacular. A new novel was in the making when I visited her. It began on yellow tablet paper in pencil, the loose sheets piled neatly on a little table beside a comfortable chaise in her study.

But she rested long between her working periods. She loved the outdoors, her windows stood open to the garden and to the pleasant views over her orchards and fields. She went down to the front porch to receive callers or to the kitchen door to settle an argument about the distribution of the dairy products. Or (rarely) she went in her comfortable limousine into Stockholm. There were occasions at which her presence was required officially as one of the foremost citizens of Sweden, as one of her country's outstanding, world-famous women.

Here are the recipes for three of the delicious dishes served the day of my visit at Mårbacka.

SWEDISH FISH SOUFFLÉ

⅓ cup of butter
½ cup of all-purpose flour, sifted
2 cups of milk
2 cups of flaked or ground cooked fish
4 eggs
Salt and white pepper
½ teaspoon of sugar
Butter and bread crumbs for baking dish

Start oven at Moderate (375°F.). Butter a 1½-quart soufflé dish, scatter crumbs generously over buttered surface. Melt butter in a saucepan, stir in flour smoothly, stir and cook 2 minutes over moderate heat. Add milk gradually, stirring well. Stir and cook 5 minutes. Remove from heat and let cool. To the cooled thick white sauce add the fish and beaten egg yolks, and mix well. Add salt, pepper and sugar. Whip egg whites until stiff, fold into yolk mixture. Pour into prepared baking dish. Set dish in shallow pan of hot water and bake in a moderate oven 30 to 40 minutes, until soufflé is risen and golden on top. Serve at once with melted butter or a lobster sauce. Makes six to eight servings.

Editor's Note

My Norwegian grandmother made the same dish, using raw cod instead of the cooked fish, which she found much too soft. She got my aunts and all the females in the family to help pound it. They hated her, the "slave driver," but still they were proud that they had learned to make a real "fiske pudding" they deemed much better than the Swedish version. They gladly taught me, the newcomer from America, how to make it and many a time my guests have enjoyed *fiske boller* with a Sauce Aurore made with the coral of lobster, or a Lobster Sauce Cardinal, or a dill sauce. My grandmother would shudder, but I confess that on many an occasion I used canned fish balls or fish pudding but only after I had found a variety that honestly tasted of fish and not of some overpowering spices.

But let us return to Mårbacka and its:

SWEDISH BEEFSTEAK

2 pounds of good steak, sliced in ¾-inch wide strips
2 teaspoons of salt
½ teaspoon of white pepper
4 tablespoons of butter
⅓ cup of bouillon
1 large sweet onion, peeled and sliced or 3 or 4 small onions

Pound meat slices until very thin, sprinkle with salt and pepper. Heat half of the butter in skillet, sauté onions until golden. Place in the center of a warmed serving platter. Drain fat from skillet, rinse skillet in boiling hot water, and place over high heat. Add remaining 2 tablespoons of butter and cook the meat. Cook about 2 minutes on each side. When browned, arrange on the platter around the onions. Pour browned butter from the skillet over the meat and onions. Serve with au gratin potatoes, or pan-fried sliced potatoes. Makes six servings.

As dessert the cooks of successful Selma Lagerlöf served:

APPLE PUDDING

6 medium-sized apples
1 tablespoon of sugar
1 cup of butter
1 cup of brown sugar (packed)
2 cups of all-purpose flour, sifted

Start oven at Moderate (375° F.). Wash, pare and core apples. Slice thinly into a buttered deep pie dish. Sprinkle with sugar. Combine butter, brown sugar and flour, stirring with fork until crumbly. Sprinkle these crumbs thickly over the apples. Bake in moderate oven until apples are cooked, 30 to 45 minutes; the crust should be golden brown. Serve warm with very cold cream or whipped cream. Makes six servings.

Peacetime Lunch with Tristan Bernard and Wartime "Tea" with Paul Reboux

JULIETTE ELKON

JULIETTE ELKON, correspondent, world traveler and author of the *Belgian Cookbook*, was one of the reporters who enjoyed the privilege of knowing Europe's literary lights in the days before and during World War II. She remembers when:

TRISTAN BERNARD, the famous playwright with the flowing beard who had provided entertainment for theater-goers for close to half a century, was one of the guests of honor at the opening of a new and long-forgotten restaurant in Paris in 1938. I was at his right and on his other side was a poetess known for her deep voice and the violence of her feminist views.

From the time the *barquettes de langouste* were served, on to the *potage Crécy*, the *poularde Louise d'Orléans* and the *Montrachet* which had us all in the mellowest of moods, the lady ranted on about the equality of the sexes. Whenever she stopped to catch her breath, Tristan Bernard would shake his head and beard and mutter: *"Oui, oui."*

We were somewhat disappointed by his patience: we had looked forward to some of his famous witticisms, to bits of conversation that would get repeated from salon to salon. We began to fear that he was handicapped by the traditions of the old school, or that he was a cavalier who lets the little woman have her say. We were mistaken.

After the *crêpes Bourdaloue* and the coffee, the poetess rose. He also rose, gave her a comradely slap on the back and said loudly, for everyone to hear: *"Alors,* you come along with us?" and headed straight for the men's room.

The gossips had a field day. So did the recipe collectors, as may be seen from the following:

POULARDE LOUISE D'ORLÉANS

1 large roasting chicken
1 whole goose liver either canned or fresh
Pepper and salt to taste
1 cup of Madeira wine
1 small can of truffles
Enough dough to envelop the bird in it (either piecrust dough, which Juliette Elkon suggests, or the French dough, described under *pâté veau et jambon.* French chefs hold this should be the version made with lard and warm water that lends itself better to this dish than the kind made with butter).

Preheat the oven to 450°: if the goose liver is fresh, poach it for 15 minutes in veal broth laced with ½ cup of cooled Madeira. Insert a few slivers of truffles in the liver, salt and pepper it and place it inside the chicken. Rub the chicken with the fat from the liver, and roast it for 20 minutes in the hot oven. Cool the chicken and turn down the temperature to 325°.

While the chicken is roasting you roll out the dough,

that was prepared the day before, to a big enough sheet to cover it. Slice the truffles, place them on the chicken after salting it. Wrap it in the dough so firmly that no liquid can escape. After establishing it in the pan in which it is to be finished, make a small round opening on the top, surround it with a ring of dough and pour in the Madeira. Bake for 1¼ hours, or more, if the chicken is oversized. This can be served hot or cold.

FOR 16 CREPES

(Allow batter to stand for 2 hours, at least, for best results.)

⅔ cup of flour
¼ teaspoon of salt
4 eggs
1¾ cups of milk
2 tablespoons of melted butter
1 tablespoon of rum, cognac or a little less vanilla extract

Sift flour and salt together. Beat eggs and add to dry ingredients. Add milk and beat with an electric mixer until smooth. Add melted butter and flavoring.

Heat a 9-inch frying pan (cast aluminum always rubbed with oil and never washed and kept exclusively for pancakes is best) over high heat until butter sizzles at the touch. Drop into it ½ tablespoon of butter. Shake pan to spread it. Ladle about 2 tablespoons of batter into it. Grasp pan while doing this and rotate to spread batter. Fry until dry on top. Turn quickly with a spatula. To get an even golden color on reverse side, hold pan about 1 inch above heat. Shake pan so that *crêpe* slides a little back and forth and does not stick. Lift side gently with spatula, and when golden slide onto hot platter. Pile *crêpes* on top of each other, keeping them in warm (225° F.) open oven.

Serve according to recipe. For hors d'oeuvres *crêpes*, omit flavoring.

CREPES BOURDALOUE

6 ripe pears
4 tablespoons of butter
½ cup of apricot jam
1 cup of kirsch

Peel, core, and dice pears. Melt butter in a skillet and simmer pears until soft. Add apricot jam. Place pear and jam mixture in the middle of the pancake and reserve a little sauce in the bottom of the pan. Fold pancake like a napkin in three. Turn over the edges and place the edge side down in a baking dish. Cover with remaining sauce. Heat kirsch and pour flaming over the pancakes. Serve 2 pancakes per person.

But the days of plenty were soon to be mere happy memories for many in Europe.

In November 1940 I was having tea in sight of the sunny blue Mediterranean, on the terrace of the Ruhl in Nice with Paul Reboux, the author of the *Art of Cooking,* the *Art of Dieting* and *Diet for Epicures* and other books. Because of war shortages there was, of course, no tea. The toast we munched on was black and unbuttered and made with potato flour, the jam in the minute container was a German ersatz and furthermore it happened to be a Tuesday, the day, according to one of the latest German edicts, when no wine or liquor could be served. As all hungry people do, we talked of nothing but food: pheasant under glass, racks of venison, fat chicken stuffed with oysters, filet of beef strasbourgeoise, the wines we enjoyed most, etc. We were fully aware of the fascination our conversation held for an unmistakable gumshoe who was practically drooling in his lemonade two tables away from us. Our joviality, however, was mounting at a rate seldom connected with concoctions such as tisane from linden tree blossoms.

Old, frail Paul Reboux got up quite jauntily and announced loudly that the tisane was excellent, and that he was going home to start a new book called *L'art de cuisiner avec rien du tout*. When he said it, he looked threateningly at the German stooge, whereupon the *garçon* snatched away the remains of our *tea*. On his tray were the two largest teapots in the house: they had been filled with Heidsieck Dry Monopole which we had been sipping out of porcelain cups, as a tribute of the management to the famous gastronome.

Editor's Note

If there ever was a man who shocked French gastronomic circles in the happy days of pre-World War II, it was Paul Reboux. After his *Plats Nouveaux* appeared, chefs angrily referred to him as a "parasite," a "writer who should stick to his writing and keep his hands off the handles of cooking pans." They held his historical novels about the love life of Madame Du Barry and others in higher esteem than his cooking suggestions. Their loudly voiced disapproval did not prevent his many charmingly written and entertaining books from becoming best-sellers, despite what he himself described as "weird" recipes.

Soup made of radishes, or of frogs, or of nettles, potatoes cooked with honey, were among his hair-raisers as were his sandwiches of "beer and ham," his mixture of eel and rabbit, of veal and salmon, to mention only a few—but in between there were many amusing, worth-while suggestions.

One of the vegetables M. Reboux felt had been given an unfair deal by gastronomic experts was the Jerusalem artichoke or, as the French call it, *topinambour*. Since he first wrote about it, doctors have established that it has excellent dietetic qualities, being specially helpful to people who suffer from diabetes. But quite apart from this, the Jerusalem artichoke is a delightful "gay deceiver," since slices of it quickly cooked replace the expensive artichoke bottoms in fancy dishes. Raw little sticks of it mixed into a salad provide crunchy bits of a pleasant, surprising flavor. They are most impressive in a

SALADE DEMI-DEUIL

which is made of little strips of artichoke mixed with thinly cut sticks of truffles marinated in a regular French dressing. The artichoke may be raw or cooked, depending on your taste.

FAKE ARTICHOKE SOUP

is another delicacy that ranks high in gourmet circles. Use your favorite recipe for creamed soup and mash in peeled Jerusalem artichokes cooked in very little water, or sliced and baked in a gentle oven until they are soft enough to crush with a fork. Add a little pepper and sprinkle with minced parsley—and none but your enemies will fail to believe that this is a regular artichoke soup.

A Memento from G.B.S. Instead of a Meal

ELLISEVA SAYERS

IN A WAY Elliseva Sayers, was frustrated just like Joseph Peters on his trip to Saloníki—she got no lunch—but as a good Fleet Street reporter and an enterprising young woman she knew how to make the most of the George Bernard Shaw memento without sharing any of the vegetables that were his favorite fare. Since her meeting with the famed Irishman, she has spent years in Japan to become an expert on the Far East and public relations. This is her story:

A BOUT ONE WEEK before Bernard Shaw's seventieth birthday I first met him.

My good friends, the Yeats sisters, had given me a letter of introduction to him. They had known Shaw in the Dublin days when he was a hot chocolate faddist. He never ate meat, fish or fowl. Nevertheless he paid some attention to his food—his wife made him.

I was a columnist on the Dublin *Evening Mail*, just out

of college. Meeting the great Shaw seemed a wildly impossible dream; he was one of my teen-age idols.

Arriving in London, I telephoned him, somewhat diffidently. Shaw had a formidable reputation as a man of many and telling words. "Who are you and what do you want?" he bellowed when he came to the phone. I told him meekly about the letter. "Oh," he said, "you want to look at me." "Yes, but I'd also like you to look at me," I blurted out marveling at my boldness. But he laughed and said, "Come over tomorrow morning at half-past eleven and you can look at me." I could hardly believe my ears; it was so easy! Needless to say, I arrived promptly, carefully dressed, in black, with a new hat that showed my red hair to advantage.

An immaculately groomed man, tall and straight, with a snowy white beard and twinkling eyes stood in the hallway as the maid let me in. He shook hands, ushered me inside to a comfortably furnished and slightly cluttered drawing room, where he sat me down, directly facing him as he sat, straight as a poker, in a great, throne-like chair. I at once felt completely at ease with a kind, friendly and sympathetic human being to whom I could talk without constraint.

He asked me questions, interviewing me. My age, my plans, my school, where I lived, and so forth. I remember we laughed a great deal.

He paid me many compliments, which I am old enough now to remember with pleasure and without undue modesty. When his wife came in she stood behind him putting her arms on his shoulders, saying after the introductions, "What would you like for lunch, GBS?" He only replied, "Don't you think she has a pretty face?" She smiled and nodded and instead of talking about the menu, they discussed me. I was too flustered by all this attention to note what menu was eventually decided upon. I do remember that he asked me to stay, but I forewent the opportunity of a vegetarian lunch with GBS, his wife and Sir Barry Jackson of the Birmingham Repertory Theatre who had just arrived and to whom GBS referred me in case I should ever have a play worth producing.

Before I left, GBS gave me a memento—in the place of the meal perhaps—which I still have and which proved over the years considerably more useful: a galley proof of one of his essays giving advice to aspiring playwrights. Though I was not an aspiring playwright, the common-sense, down-to-earth professional counsel it contained helped me again and again to overcome a certain squeamishness in regard to money matters.

"If you should ever need help," said GBS as he saw me out, "call me." I took his kindness literally and was not disappointed. I called him many times for interviews, which he frequently gave me. I would just announce: "I need some money to go to Europe; can you give me an interview?" And he would laugh and say: "Send a questionnaire along and if it doesn't take me three years to answer, I'll do it!" He usually answered.

I didn't have a chance to eat lunch with GBS, but his interviews paid for many a meal of mine!

Cooking Ghosts Fare Best

"AS TOLD TO . . ."

I AM A GHOST and proud of it. To be exact I am a "ghost writer," and some day you'll see my name on the flyleaf of a book, behind the words "as told to . . . ," but for the moment I can't be more definite, for reasons you'll understand after I let you in on my secret.

It all started when my boss, a publisher, was on a grand tour of England, on the lookout for new authors. At a shoot in Scotland he shared the laird's hospitality with a shy, old gentleman and his beautiful, regal-looking wife who reminisced most enchantingly about their past adventures. Before the shoot was over they had signed a contract to write a book with the help of a ghost the publisher had in readiness. I was that ghost.

The future authors were charming when I called on them in the cold villa that was their home on the southern coast. We had meals together in the little resort hotel; we drove to colorful old inns to enjoy British specialties, and they were expert guides. They knew what was good. Time and again I had tea and delicious dainties in their salons that were filled with interesting antiques and mementos. But when it came to unpacking their memories of the past, they'd ramble on, dodging vital points. Even when I turned up with the extra rare bottle of sherry her ladyship loved, or the Armagnac of which his lordship approved, their inhibitions kept the upper hand. My publisher began to lose patience and threatened to replace me with a more subtle soul searcher.

When the future of this ghost looked dim indeed, love came to the rescue in the shape of a dashing traveling salesman. He carried off the family's cook with the fire of a passionate Italian. The wedding was a storybook affair. What followed was a grim search for a new cook. My charges kept getting thinner and thinner. Our conversation began to center around nothing but food. I regaled them—at least I thought I was regaling them—with stories about the wonderful meals my Scotch grandmother and my Czech grandmother would cook in competition with each other to turn this hamburger-devouring boy scout into a gourmet who knew how to prepare the good dishes of their homelands.

His lordship's mouth watered. Getting tired of my boasts, he dared me to show what I had learned. He refused to believe that my Scotch forebears' beefsteak and kidney pudding could have been as good as the ones he remembered from his boyhood. I took up the dare. After they sampled a few of my specialties, the barriers came tumbling down: I'd finally become a trustworthy character. Diaries were opened for me, boxes full of letters were put at my disposal. While watching me flip scones on the griddle, my charges would be reminded of this or that colorful event of the past. Copy reached my happy publisher regularly, but since he believes in the power of mind and scorns anything that could produce cholesterol, I can't let him know that my cooking did the trick!

Our Christmas party had a real Dickensian atmosphere with jolly, well-fed guests trying to scintillate around the festive board while snow was blanketing the countryside.

After they tasted my beefsteak and kidney pudding, I had a whole line of prospective memoir writers anxious to tell me their stories.

I feel I deserve the acclaim that came my way because I've made a study of:

BEEFSTEAK AND KIDNEY PUDDING

which is ideal fare for a cold winter night. As my British friends put it, "It sticks to the ribs even better than ham and eggs."

There are many versions of it. Queen Victoria and her Prince Consort, for instance, preferred the Cumberland version in which oysters usurp the space of some of the kidney. The Queen's chef, Charles Elmé Francatelli, preferred it to the plain version. A pupil of the famous Carême, as he proudly boasts on the cover of his cookbook, he was the inspiration of many a famous chef or cook of the mauve decade on both sides of the Atlantic. After twenty-six editions of his *Modern Cook Book, a practical guide to the Culinary Art in all its branches,* had been published in London, T. B. Peterson and Brothers of Philadelphia published an American reprint in 1889; many a bride of the nineties received this six-hundred-page tome as a wedding present and guide for her future entertaining.

The following is a modern adaptation of the pudding for a party of about eight:

¾ pound of suet, freed of all membranes
4 cups of flour
1 teaspoon of salt
Cold water (just enough to mix the dough)
2½ pounds of good beef—steak, roast beef, round steak—cut into inch cubes
3 lamb kidneys, or a small veal kidney, or part of a good-looking beef kidney, cut in pieces
1 tablespoon of chopped onion
1 teaspoon of chopped parsley

Salt, pepper, paprika, thyme, marjoram, bay leaf, 1 tiny dried sharp
pepper broken up, turmeric, grated nutmeg, a few juniper berries and a few allspice
Boiling hot bouillon or hot water
Optional: mushrooms, or oysters, or a dash of red wine or a dash of
ale

Scald and wring dry a big piece of muslin. Butter an
earthen bowl of about 15-cup size.

Use the bones from which the meat has been cut as base
for a good broth, together with some soup meat, if you
prefer to use bouillon instead of hot water.

To make the suet paste, chill the suet, mince it and mix
into 3 cups of flour with salt, a very little thyme and marjoram. Add enough cold water to make a dough that can
be kneaded and rolled to ½-inch thickness. Line the dish
with part of the dough, allowing about ½ an inch to hang
over the rim. Hold back enough dough for a lid and for
some tiny dumplings.

Roll the meat cubes and pieces of kidney in the remaining
flour that has been mixed with salt, fresh ground pepper
and paprika. Pack them lightly into the dish lined with
dough, sprinkling as you go along with the chopped onion
and parsley, a pinch of turmeric, the dried sharp pepper,
thyme, marjoram, grated nutmeg, a few crushed black juniper berries and a bit of allspice. Be stingy with the spices
and herbs: no single taste except that of the meat should
predominate. Cover with hot broth or hot water.

Roll out the remaining paste and cut a lid that is big
enough to cover the dish. Mix some minced parsley or chives
into the leftover paste and shape it into tiny dumplings that
you scatter near the top. Put on the lid, folding back the
edge that hangs over the rim; moisten the edges and make
sure that the pudding is firmly sealed.

Flour the muslin and put it over the top of the bowl,
tying it under the rim. Bring back the four corners and

tie over the top. Set the dish on a trivet in a big pot. Fill the pot with boiling water to the rim of the dish. Cover and boil, gently, steadily for 4 hours. As some of the water evaporates, add more boiling water, making sure that it is always up to the rim.

When ready to serve, two courses are open to you: if you are daring, plunge the dish in cold water, invert the pudding on a platter that is carried into the dining room in triumph if it holds its shape. That is the way M. Francatelli would have had his chefs do it. But the pudding remains hotter and just as impressive if you put a gleaming napkin around the dish in which it has been cooked, place it on a tray and serve!

Some cooks hold that it is smart to have extra sauce in readiness to go with the pudding, but if you have been careful to pack in the meat loosely so that the bouillon or water surrounded it well, there should be enough sauce to cover the pieces of dough, the dumplings, the meat and kidneys on your plate: no emergency gravy can compete with the one cooked in the pudding.

To counterbalance such solid fare, I'd whip up an occasional light dish, such as my Czech grandmother's:

SPINACH SOUFFLÉ

1 medium-sized onion, chopped fine
1½ tablespoons of butter
1 cup of milk
1½ tablespoons of cream of wheat or semolina
2 tablespoons of cooked, chopped spinach, passed through a sieve
Salt
1 teaspoon Parmesan, grated nutmeg
5 eggs

Butter a soufflé dish and sprinkle with fine bread crumbs. Sauté—or as my grandmother used to say "sweat" the onion in butter until it begins to turn pink. Pour on the milk and sprinkle in the cream of wheat. Cook until it is a thick paste. Add the strained spinach, salt, nutmeg, Parmesan. Mix well and break in one egg at a time, beating after each addition. Pour into the soufflé dish, filling it only half full. Place in pan filled with warm water and bake for ½ hour.

Serve with a cheese sauce or a mushroom sauce. If your guests are the kind who are unhappy without meat, put a little fine-cut ham into the soufflé, or into your cheese sauce that should be quite creamy and thick. If you serve with a mushroom sauce, cut a few sautéed mushrooms into the spinach mixture before baking.

NORWEGIAN FISH PUDDING, OR FISH BALLS

Pudding and fish balls come in cans, with ample recipes printed on the labels. I like to heat fish balls in the juice that is in the can. Then I melt butter and flour as for a white sauce, add chopped dill, a little milk, cooking until the flour is done. I thin with the broth in which the hot balls have been heated, pour the sauce over the balls and serve.

The British neighbors of my memoir-providers got into the spirit of the adventure and they prepared the fishballs with sauce they prefer to see on sole, on big occasions, which is:

SAUCE À L'AURORE

Put the jewel-like red coral of a lobster into a mortar with 3 ounces of butter and pound with energy. Ready 2 cups of Béchamel Sauce in a pan, adding the juice of half a lemon, salt, cayenne pepper and the pounded lobster roe. Heat slowly, stir carefully and don't let this boil. If the sauce gets too hot, the fine "aurore" color will fade away.

If one is short of time, a good canned lobster bisque, can prove equally decorative, though nothing can compare with a carefully made:

LOBSTER SAUCE CARDINAL

that turns a canned fish pudding into a work of art. For this you need:

1 small lobster, cut in two
3 tablespoons of butter
Chopped carrot, shallot, onion, garlic, thyme, bay leaf, parsley
2 tablespoons of olive oil
1 tablespoon of beef extract
Salt, pepper, saffron, curry
2 cups of dry white wine
1 teaspoon of cognac
3 tablespoons of heavy cream

Sauté the lobster pieces in butter until they are red. Add the chopped carrot, shallot, onion, garlic, parsley, the thyme and the bay leaf. Pour in the olive oil, stir and brown a little; add salt, pepper, a pinch of saffron and of curry, the wine and brandy. Cook for 10 minutes. Take out the lobster pieces; let them cool and dice the meat. Continue cooking the sauce until it thickens. Take out the bay leaf and thyme; pass through a sieve or the electric blender. Stir in the warmed cream and diced lobster.

Butter an ovenproof dish. Put in the fish balls. Mix the juice from the can with the lobster sauce, pour it on the fish balls and bake until the dish is hot. Don't cook too long; otherwise the little pieces of lobsters get tough.

Since teatime was important, I baked Scotch oat cakes in the oven or on the soapstone griddle.

SCOTCH OAT CAKES

1 cup of sifted flour
1 tablespoon of sugar
1 teaspoon of baking powder
½ teaspoon of salt
½ cup of butter
About ½ cup of milk
2 cups of rolled oats

Sift together the flour, baking powder and salt. Blend in the oats. Cut in the butter. Stir in the milk slowly until you have a soft dough. Divide into six equal rounds, that you flatten and roll on a floured board to form a 4-inch circle. Cut into four pieces; place on a well-buttered baking sheet. Heat the oven to 375° and bake for 12 to 15 minutes until the cakes are lightly browned.

BUTTERMILK SCONES

proved equally successful and did well on the griddle.

2 cups of sifted flour
½ teaspoon of soda
½ teaspoon of salt
¼ cup of shortening
¾ cup of buttermilk

Sift the flour, salt, soda together. Cut in shortening and stir in the buttermilk. Knead and divide in two. Roll each half to form a round of ½ inch thickness and cut in four. Bake slowly on well-heated, well-greased griddle for about 20 minutes.

For little tarts, I used the crust recipe which the Quaker Oats Company advertised in magazines some time ago because it is crunchy and because the shells keep well, in readiness for emergencies.

OATMEAL CRUST

1½ cups of sifted flour
½ teaspoon of salt
⅔ cup of shortening
½ cup of oats, uncooked
4–6 tablespoons of cold water

Sift flour and salt together. Cut in shortening until mixture resembles coarse crumbs; stir in oats. Slowly add water, stirring until pastry forms a ball. Let rest 5 minutes. Divide into 8 parts for bigger shells, or 16 for small ones. Bake in hot oven (425°) for 15 to 20 minutes, depending on the size of the shells. Fill with fruit or jelly—or store for future use.

For fancy occasions, *Muerbe Teig*, provides an excellent base for fruit or jellies if it is made with a shot of cognac instead of water.

MUERBE TEIG

1 cup of flour, a pinch of salt
½ cup of soft, sweet butter
1 tablespoon of sugar
1 egg yolk
Shot of cognac or rum

Sift the flour and salt onto a board and make a well in the center. Put the butter, sugar, egg yolk into it and mix until smooth. To facilitate this operation add just enough cognac to have a firm dough that comes easily off the board. Put the dough in a small container, covering well, and chill for at least 1 hour or overnight.

This is enough dough to line one 9-inch pie plate. The final cake looks more like the delicacies served in Karlsbad in the old days, if you roll out a longish strip about 2 inches wide, build up the sides carefully, to have a rim for the future filling. Or if you have a longish aluminum ice-cube tray, butter the base of it thoroughly and shape your dough on it. Prick it at regular intervals and bake for 10 minutes at 400°, reduce to 350° and bake for about 15 more minutes.

If you want to bake the fruit in the shell, be sure to chill the dough thoroughly before filling and dust it with sugar, with bread or cake crumbs, grated lemon rind, or a sprinkling of slivered almonds or other nuts.

Around Christmastime nothing tastes better than thin slices of *pain d'épice* covered with a layer of sweet butter. The Borglums, the famous artists and their heirs, have the best recipe I ever found for:

PAIN D'ÉPICE

Butter a 6-cup bread tin, then take:

1½ cups of boiling water
1 cup of sugar
¼ teaspoon of salt
4 cups of flour
2½ teaspoons of soda
2 teaspoons cinnamon
¾ cup of honey
2 teaspoons of liquid anise flavor or a few drops of essence
3 tablespoons of rum

Sift together the flour, soda, salt, cinnamon and sugar. Pour the boiling water over the honey; put in the anise essence or liquid. Pour onto the flour mixture, mix well and stir in the rum.

Instead of using anise essence, I take 2 teaspoons of aniseed, boil it up in a little water; after the seed has cooked a few minutes, I pass it through a strainer and use this anise tea as part of the required 1½ cups of hot water. I also sprinkle four or five aniseeds into the dough just before baking.

Bake in oven that has been heated to 450°. After 10 minutes reduce heat to 350° and bake for another 50 min-

utes. Since honeys differ widely, it is better to check on the
progress of the baking by inserting a toothpick or a thin
skewer a little before the 50 minutes are up.

When the *pain d'épice* is done, wrap it firmly in wax paper
and don't cut until the next day. Repack it every time after
you have cut off a few slices.

May I add a tip for other bachelors: no Beau Brummel
ever had as fine a bevy of sweet young things, with that
famous peach-and-cream complexion, vying for the honor
of helping him than I did when I acted as chef. And their
fathers, in their fine mansions, gave me as warm a welcome
as any man could enjoy, taking me along on hunts or on
personally conducted tours of cellars that still boast of fine
old vintages.

In conclusion, I assure one and all that cooking ghosts
have fun, and I hope that some of my specialties will prove
equally enjoyable to you!

Part IV

ON THE NEWSBEAT IN PEACETIME

I Shared a Secret with the Aga Khan

JED KILEY

IF YOU want to hear more about the gay twenties and the stars that brightened night life in Paris, Berlin, Monte Carlo, New York in those days, page Jed Kiley. As a reporter, night club owner, organizer of parties, public relations specialist, little in the world that likes to be entertained escaped him, including a secret of the Aga Khan, about which he writes:

MAYBE it was because of his fabulous wealth, or because of his incredible girth, that editors on the home front kept sending queries about Aga Khan III to their Paris correspondents, all through the happy twenties and thirties. And this wise gentleman, grandfather of the present Aga Khan IV, and father of Aly, famed for his romances and horses, had developed pretty sound ways of avoiding enquiring reporters. But I always knew where to find him on Tuesdays and Thursdays whenever he was in Paris. I shared the secret of his whereabouts with him on those two days. To tell the truth, it was a delicious secret.

Everybody knew of his pride in his stables of racing horses, but even they ran second in importance when it came to keeping his Tuesday and Thursday appointments.

I discovered the Aga Khan's secret in the early twenties and benefited from it for many a year. I was walking along the Avenue de Neuilly, a few blocks from the Paris gate of the same name, when I saw the Rolls Royce of the Aga Khan standing in front of a sidewalk café. The place was one of the bistro type one sees in the poorer districts, with a zinc bar in the back and working people taking their afternoon *apéritifs*. It was about 4 P.M. I asked the chauffeur what he was doing there.

"His Highness has just finished his lunch," he answered, "and he is now ordering his lunch for the day after tomorrow."

That was intriguing. Being on the staff of the Chicago *Tribune* at the time, I thought that I knew all places worth knowing. I had never heard of this one before. It was called Le Café du Progrès. I walked in. It looked as ordinary inside as it did out. Then I noticed a closed door marked "Restaurant." I tried it. It was locked. A waiter looked supercilious and said the place was closed. I said I had a message for the Aga Khan. The name was an Open sesame!

So I walked in and got the surprise of my life. For a minute I thought I had stepped into one of the rooms in the Château Henry IV, at Saint-Germain. Its classical simplicity was delightful. There were about thirty tables in the place and only two people. As I stood there gaping, the Aga Khan got up, and introduced me to Monsieur le Patron. Plunking back on his seat, he invited me to try a certain dessert that was the specialty of the *maison*, while he finished his talk with the patron. "I can recommend it very highly," he added. "I have just finished three orders myself."

Then he went on planning his next meal. I learned that

he ate here alone, every Tuesday and Thursday, always planning and ordering the next meal *after eating*. When he saw that I was astounded by his appetite, he laughed: "I am one of the few who can mix business and pleasure profitably," gleefully referring to the fact that every year his followers gave him an offering of gold, corresponding to his exact weight. The more he ate, the more gold would be his! In the Café du Progrès he saw to it that this should be a pleasant task.

How pleasant it could be, I discovered when my dessert came. I'll never forget the taste. It was a chocolate pudding—no cornstarch though—served in a soup plate. The pudding was unsweetened and warm, but you poured a sweet ice-cold custard sauce over it. Maybe it tasted so wonderful because it reminded me of the days when I was a kid and used to bite off a chunk of unsweetened cooking chocolate in our kitchen, and follow it up real quick with a spoonful of sugar.

As I smacked my lips over the dish, I listened to the two epicures seriously comparing the advisability of picking fresh mountain trout cooked with grapes rather than a plain *merlan* (whiting to you) with maître d'hôtel sauce, or possibly a *matelotte d'anguilles*. I knew this to be a fancy stew with eels in it, the mere thought of which made me shudder. Would roast game birds be better at this time of the year than a veal chop *en papillote*, or would a veal chop *printanière* be preferable? The Aga Khan had a yen for chestnut purée, with his entrée, but the patron thought he should try his eggplant salad, Rumanian style. He thought he could give the Aga Khan the chestnut taste in his dessert. Its name, Bibesco, struck my fancy because of the elegant princess of that name who dazzled Paris society in those days.

I listened eagerly, bent on gleaning names of dishes with which I could impress our gang that included Floyd Gibbons, Maurice Chevalier, beautiful Princess Pignatelli, the opera singer Mary McCormic, the Gershwins and others.

As I pocketed a menu, both the Aga Khan and the patron made me promise not to divulge the former's secret: the secret of his eating twice a week in the unassuming little restaurant, which he called "the best in the world." The owner was not anxious for American customers. "Americans," said he, "smoke while they eat. They drink whisky and hard liquor before their meals, which makes it impossible for them to appreciate good cooking."

His waiters saw to it that no such errors in taste occurred under their watchful eyes. I once took a batch of very snooty visiting firemen, who considered themselves epicures, to the Aga Khan's haunt. We had started the evening with many a drink at the Ritz Bar. Once installed in the restaurant, I was relieved to see that no one seemed to mind the scotches we were imbibing with the appetizers. But when the real food began to arrive, the *sommelier* calmly took away our glasses. We could see him drain the half-empty ones in a nearby corner. Indignantly, my oldest guest pointed this out to the patron. He shrugged, explaining that it would be quite a while before the *sommelier* would sit down to his meal; therefore the drinks could not impair his taste buds. But since we obviously cared more for the whisky than the food, we had better try another place. He would not charge us for what had been consumed so far. Luckily I had been careful not to mention that this was the Aga Khan's favorite restaurant; otherwise my guests would have insisted on staying.

But the day came when I gave his secret away. Henry Wales of the Chicago *Tribune* called me one afternoon, saying that he could not find the Aga Khan. The home office had cabled that the Feast of the Ramadan, at which the Aga Khan received his weight in gold, was coming up in a few weeks and it wanted to know how much he weighed. "What day is it?" I asked Hank. "Tuesday," he said.

So I drove him out to Neuilly and there was our man, just finishing his third plate of *chocolat à la Maison*. His baggage was already at the boat train, he explained in an interview in which he revealed his weight—a neat 278 pounds.

Hank had his story and I got a real meal at the Café du Progrès for my part. The bill for the four of us, as I recall it, was some sixty dollars. Vive le expense account!

Notes from the Editor and the Team of Cooks

The picture of grown men, including the 278-pound potentate, spooning their dessert out of a soup plate is rather an enticing one. But anyone who samples the chocolate dessert and some of the traditional dishes of French home cooks in which the café specialized will agree that they deserve to be adopted in our country.

THE AGA KHAN'S FAVORITE CHOCOLATE DESSERT

The cooking experimenters of the O.P.C. thought that a chocolate soufflé done in the old-fashioned French manner might have been the base of this dessert. To make it for six to eight people we took:

½ cup of butter
¼ cup of sifted flour, mixed with ¼ teaspoon of salt
¾ cup of milk
2 ounces of chocolate, unsweetened, cut in small pieces
3 egg yolks
3 egg whites, well beaten
½ teaspoon of cream of tartar
½ cup of sugar

Cook the butter, milk, flour, chocolate over low heat, stirring constantly until the mixture is thick and smooth. Remove from heat. Next beat 3 egg yolks until they are thick, adding gradually ½ cup of sugar. Blend the milk mixture into the yolk mixture. Fold in the egg whites that have been stiffly beaten with the cream of tartar; pour into a buttered 2-quart baking dish. Set in pan of water 1 inch deep. Steam-bake, until puffed and delicately browned in a 350° oven for about 45 minutes to 1 hour.

We tried this out on a homesick Paris gourmet; he smacked his lips all right after the ice-cold custard sauce was poured over it, but then he said firmly, "This is a perfect example of American extravagance. No chef in the Café du Progrès would waste eggs, even if he were cooking for the Aga Khan, if he could achieve the effect he was after without them. The big trick of this dessert is to have it as 'chocolatey' as possible. By adding eggs, you cut down the chocolate flavor." Then he proceeded to tell how his thrifty French mother cooked the chocolate pudding, of which he thought as highly as the Aga Khan and Jed Kiley. One of the points she insisted on was to find an exceptionally good chocolate before she cooked this dessert. For her small family of three she took:

½ cup of milk, scalded and blended with
4 ounces of cut-up chocolate
1 cup of rich milk
1 tablespoon of unbleached flour
1 tablespoon of butter
¼ teaspoon of salt

While the chocolate was melting in the scalded milk, she mixed a little of the rich milk with the flour and salt; she creamed the butter into this, then added the remaining milk. This was cooked carefully to prevent scorching or lumps until it was a smooth paste and no one could suspect the presence of flour. Then the milk-chocolate mixture was added and the whole was cooked for another 6 to 8 minutes until it was of the right consistency to be poured into soup plates or deep little dishes, ready to be rushed to the table, followed by a container filled with custard sauce that had been thoroughly iced. Each guest must pour his own portion of sauce on the hot chocolate to get the full impact of the conflicting temperatures.

To some it may seem foolish to cook up one's own chocolate pudding when there are so many packaged varieties that can be dressed up with shaved curlicues of some extra good chocolate. But most of them are sweet and somewhat cornstarchy, which precludes the contrast that makes this a simple yet sophisticated dessert.

CUSTARD SAUCE

For the custard sauce, which should spend at least a night in the refrigerator, take:

1½ cups of light cream or canned milk
1 teaspoon of vanilla
4 tablespoons of sugar
3 egg yolks
3 egg whites
1 tablespoon of cognac or sherry
Pinch of salt

If you prefer vanilla bean to vanilla essence, put a small piece of it in the cream to be scalded. Otherwise, add the vanilla essence to the scalded milk. While the milk cools, beat the egg yolks and sugar together. Put them in a double boiler, pour the milk over them and beat with a rotary beater while the mixture nears the boiling point. Beat until it has reached the desired consistency, add the cognac or sherry—beat some more, then fold in the beaten egg whites to which the pinch of salt has been added.

Jed Kiley and his friends made it a point of sampling the dishes picked by the Aga Khan. The mountain trout stuffed with grapes seemed a kind of effete dish, despite the delicious wine sauce in which it was cooked. But its proletarian counterpart, the whiting maître d'hôtel, the *matelotte,* the veal chops and other dishes deserve closer study since they would be good additions to American menus.

WHITING À LA MAITRE D'HÔTEL

With a sharp knife slice open the back of a whiting to remove the central bone and the little fins. Roll the washed and well-dried fish in a well-beaten egg that has been slightly salted. Surround it with a coat of fine bread crumbs. Fry in a pan or in deep fat, together with parsley tops.

The incision which you made in your initial operation will show. Fill the gap with:

MAITRE D'HÔTEL SAUCE

For 4 whitings take:

½ pound of butter
2 tablespoons of chopped parsley
1 teaspoon of salt
Pinch of pepper
Juice of 1 medium-sized lemon
Optional: 1 teaspoon of mustard

Cream the butter, work in the other ingredients; stuff into the opening of the hot fish. Decorate with the fried parsley and thin lemon slices.

MATELOTTE OF EEL (OR OTHER FIRM-FLESHED FISH)

Whoever is squeamish about eels is really missing a treat. When they are small they can be rolled in sage and broiled. When slightly bigger they are excellent in a green sauce with dill, and still better in a *matelotte* made according to recipes from Burgundy. Naturally, eels do have their peculiarities. They are so full of electricity that they keep wriggling even after their heads have been chopped off. I know because I once asked a friend to pick up a parcel of eels readied for me in Berlin. As she carried it across a wide avenue, she felt violent movement in the package under her arm. She dropped it in horror, the paper burst and eels seemed to be slithering all over the place, stopping the traffic, with delighted Berliners picking them up for her and reassembling them while she, a big husky girl, gave them an entertaining performance about how a scared American reacts. Berlin fishmongers don't skin the fish for you, which meant that the eels had an extra dose of electricity left in them. For safety's sake be sure that your dealer skins them for you and, as an extra precaution, have him cut them in the right size lengths for you.

For the *matelotte*, you need a fair-sized eel of 2 pounds and the chunks should be about 3 inches long—a little longer where the fish grows thinner. You may substitute another firm-fleshed fish, or a mixture of various kinds.

For 4 pounds of fish which should feed eight, you'll need approximately:

½ cup of finely chopped onions
2 toes of finely chopped garlic, or a little more
1 teaspoon of peppercorns
A *bouquet garni* of thyme, parsley, bay leaf
1 big finely cut carrot
2 tablespoons of butter mixed with 2 teaspoons of flour
2 cups of very small, round onions
1 bottle of good red wine
Salt, pepper

A few hours before cooking the fish, rub it with coarse salt and let it rest in the salt. This will prove helpful in case the fish has spent some time in muddy waters. Wash the salt off well when cooking time comes. Make a bed of the onions, garlic, peppercorns, carrot, the *bouquet* in the bottom of your pan, salt it, then place the fish on it. Pour over enough wine to amply cover the fish. Cook for about 20 minutes over medium heat. Before the fish is done, remove to another pan, covering it to keep it warm. Bring the contents of the pan to a quick boil, and cook until it is reduced by about one-third. Add the butter and the flour, cooking until the sauce seems almost creamy. Pass it through a fine sieve onto the fish.

In the meantime you will have cooked the tiny onions in butter. When they are done, add them to the fish and sauce. The little onions should remain recognizable.

Some chefs also add finely cut mushrooms at the same time as the onions, as well as a big spoonful of tiny shrimp. This is optional, but croutons—slices of bread fried in oil with a touch of garlic—*must* always be served with the *matelotte*. Since it is a specialty of Burgundy, burgundy wine is best with it.

After a dark-colored *matelotte,* the Aga Khan often picked a veal chop for color contrast. The choice between the various kinds would depend on the season. For a really good veal *à la printanière* you need fresh, young greens.

VEAL CHOPS PRINTANIÈRE

Even if you think pretty highly of your butcher's willingness to sell you high-grade veal, make sure that he gives you a chop that is of even thickness. The run-of-the-mill chops with the thickly cut bone and the thinly cut meat are a handicap for the careful cook, and I often wonder whether our grandmothers would have been as patient about careless cutters as we are. Or do we fail to criticize because we don't want to appear bossy? Yet, in the long run, the careful shopper who dares to speak up is the one who helps raise standards.

To make sure that your veal is tasty and tender soak it in lemon juice for a while before cooking. These admonitions count for all varieties of veal.

For the *côte de veau printanière,* take:

1 chop per person, and for each chop:
1 tablespoon of butter
1 tablespoon of sorrel, without ribs
1 teaspoon of chervil, chives, parsley, shallots (each)
¼ teaspoon of thyme
Salt, pepper
Wine or milk

Chop the shallots finely and start them in butter together with the sorrel that you have deprived of its ribs. The sorrel almost melts into the butter. Add the minced parsley, the chervil and thyme. Cook this all together until it is well blended and almost soft. Then taste carefully. If the taste of the sorrel comes out too strongly, tone it down with a few chopped leaves of lettuce or spinach, possibly a pinch of flour and some extra butter; if it does not come through, add a few ribless pieces of sorrel.

Dust the chops with flour, fry them in butter. When the bottom side is barely brown, turn the chop and coat the top side with the green mixture. When the new underside is done, turn again so that the green mixture gets on the bottom of the pan. Add salt and pepper, then cover the whole with milk or wine and finish cooking in the oven at 350° until the chops are really tender, about 20 minutes. There should be enough sauce around the chops to make the serving of extra sauce unnecessary. A last-minute squirt of lemon freshens the taste.

CÔTELETTES DE VEAU EN PAPILLOTES

Cut the parchment paper or foil in heart shapes, making them big enough to completely wrap the chops and their filling. You will need for each chop:

1 tablespoon of olive oil
2 slices of ham
Enough *duxelles* mixture to cover both sides of the chop
Salt, pepper

Spread olive oil over the parchment or foil heart. In its middle put a slice of ham, cover it with your *duxelles;* place the chop on this bed after salting and peppering it, coat it with *duxelles* and top with the second slice of ham. Then fold your foil firmly around the package so that no juice can escape and place the package on a baking sheet. Bake at 400°, with the time required depending on the thickness of your chops. Serve wrapped in foil and let each guest do his own unwrapping to make sure that he gets the full enjoyment of the aroma.

The simplest *duxelles* is made of equal parts of fried, minced onions and finely cut fried mushrooms, a smaller portion of minced parsley, salt and pepper. The frying medium should be, French chefs hold, half oil and half butter. They generally prepare a big batch of it, frying the mixture until it is quite dry; then they put it in a covered dish in the refrigerator ready to use whenever they need it.

When the time to use it comes, they will take:

4 tablespoons of dry *duxelles*
1 cup of wine
½ cup of good stock
½ cup of fine bread crumbs
A bit of pressed garlic
Salt and pepper to taste

Cook the mushroom mixture in the wine until it forms a soft paste. Add the stock, garlic, bread crumbs—or if you prefer, flour, and cook until the mixture has reached the consistency you need for the special dish you are cooking. This is the point where the venturesome chef can do some fancy experimenting, adding some tomato sauce, for instance, or an egg yolk, or a bit of cream, some sliced truffle or some sliced ham. In fact, cream added to the *duxelles* of the veal *en papillotes* makes for a smoother, juicier dish.

What to serve with the veal? The Rumanian eggplant salad suggested by the patron of the Café du Progrès is a rich dish that calls for tricky treatment.

RUMANIAN EGGPLANT SALAD

Bake a big, healthy eggplant in the oven until it is nearly black. Cool it enough to be able to pull off the black skin. Have a wooden board in readiness on which you drop the inside pieces of the eggplant. As you go along, while they are still warm, pour olive oil on them and start chopping them, not with a knife of metal, but with a wooden knife because the metal makes the eggplant turn black. Place in a china bowl, add salt and stir with a wooden spoon while adding olive oil, drop by drop as if you were making mayonnaise. Finish off with lemon juice and decorate with finely slivered onions and sliced tomatoes.

The real Bibesco which the patron promised to the Aga Khan is a meringue made with hazelnuts, baked in layers, shaped like a crown, and put together with a chestnut purée. The whole is topped with whipped cream, mixed with chestnut purée.

BIBESCO

For a big Bibesco you will need:

15 egg whites, and ¼ teaspoon of salt, stiffly beaten
½ teaspoon of cream of tartar
½ pound of sugar
A little over ½ pound of browned, ground hazelnuts
Pinch of salt

Whip the sugar and cream of tartar into the egg whites, which have been slightly salted; add the hazelnuts. Shape this into four round crowns of equal size and bake at 250° for an hour. When the crowns have cooled off, paste them together with chestnut purée. This concoction will look like a tower, with an opening in the middle. Fill this opening with whipped cream into which a chestnut purée has been mixed and decorate with a few pieces of candied chestnuts.

If you are a hardy soul, bent on making your own chestnut spread, take a sharp knife and make a clean cut into the round side, the "bay window" of the chestnuts. Put them in a pan in which you have heated some olive oil, heat it for a few minutes. As soon as the brown skin of the chestnuts begins to crack, remove from the fire, quickly tear off the shells, remove the second skin with your sharp knife. Wash well and cook the peeled chestnuts in a mixture of cold water and milk. When they are tender, pass through a sieve. Put a piece of butter, some milk, a piece of vanilla bean and sugar into a pan, add your chestnut purée and cook for a few minutes, stirring to prevent burning.

Should you want to serve chestnut purée with your meat course, then you would naturally omit the sugar and vanilla.

This same chestnut purée can be used for another delicious dessert, known as the Mont-Blanc. In this case you rice the purée into a pudding mold. Turn the mold out on a platter and coat the whole with a thick layer of Crème à la Chantilly, which is merely whipped cream mixed with sugar and vanilla.

Many up-to-date groceries through our lands carry an excellent and generally reasonably priced French "candied chestnut spread," that greatly eases the task of the lover of Bibesco. And a good imitation of this delicacy may be achieved with plain layer cakes.

BIBESCO ERSATZ

Take two well-made layer cakes, or an angel food cake. Cut the angel food cake in four layers. If you use plain layer cake cut each layer in two and remove a round from the middle. Put the layers together with chestnut spread mixed with a little whipped cream, fill the center with the cream and dot either with small pieces of *marrons glacés* or chopped hazelnuts. This won't be as featherlight as the meringue concoction, but even the Aga Khan and the patron of the Café du Progrès would not spurn this cake.

A Favorite Dish Opened the Gates of Buckingham Palace

JAMES P. HOWE

"BUCKINGHAM PALACE has been successfully invaded by an American newspaperman," was the lead of the story which appeared in the London *Daily News* of May 8, 1928, under the headline: INTRUDER AT THE PALACE.

The "invader" who slipped by the military guards and the Secret Service men was James P. Howe of the Associated Press, whose long career took him to London, Berlin, Warsaw, Moscow, Peking, Tokyo and many other posts.

He can now reveal the secret of how he carried out his "invasion" that upset the chamberlains of the Royal Household. He writes:

S OME MAY cherish the memory of watching the thrilling pageantry of one of the glittering receptions given to kings and queens by the King and Queen of England, in a jostling crowd somewhere along the roads through which the royal coaches rumbled, surrounded by guards of honor mounted on beautiful, spirited horses. But I can boast that

I witnessed such a gala display right from inside Buckingham Palace, taking in every colorful detail.

I saw two kings and a pair of queens alight from their carriages quite close to me, and I listened to the polite exchange of welcoming words between the monarchs of the British Empire and the King and Queen of Afghanistan. And when I sent my cable home to the Associated Press, describing my day in the palace, a hue and cry went up. English correspondents in Washington and New York cabled parts of my story back to London and the British capital had a new mystery: How had this American correspondent managed to get inside Buckingham Palace?

Some doubted my reportorial veracity. A Buckingham Palace press release published in the London *Daily News* asserted: "No one could enter the Palace like that, let alone prowl about."

But the truth is that I had prowled about that historic residence, which dates back to the days of George III. My host of the day saw to it that I caught a glimpse of many parts of the palace. It seemed like a vast picture gallery to me with all its hallways and salons hung with paintings by Rembrandt, Hobbema, Teniers and many others. The King's Postmaster joined me as I looked at the paintings. I tried to question him about them, but he wanted to talk about horse racing: What might be the best bet of the morrow at Newmarket? Another attendant, whom I asked where Their Majesties took their breakfast, guided me to the Chinese Room. He led me to a small rickety elevator with a hand pull and up we went two flights. I enjoyed the gorgeous oriental coloring and the rich lacquers in the room. On the wall, opposite French windows overlooking the garden where summer parties are given, was an old-fashioned mantel surmounted by an ancient clock, one of the King's large collection of old timepieces.

Later, as I went further behind the scene, we met three

tall, bright-coated men in knee britches, brass buttons and gold braid. Each carried a tray. "Teatime," my guide remarked. "That's tea for Their Majesties." Then he took me to the Ball Room, where that evening a banquet would be given in honor of the royal guests. It was a dazzling sight. The horseshoe table was set for 140 guests, with four gold plates at each place and gold side dishes. This was the famous gold-plate service which had served royalty on gala occasions ever since the feast days of the Georges. Legend described this service as pure gold, worth, as the English saying goes, "nearly as much as the Bank of England."

But the "keeper of the Service," on whom I called next, frankly remarked: "It's not solid gold by any means, but I suppose the people prefer this fairy tale to the truth." The service is gold plated on silver, as I saw when he turned some dishes sideways to display a spot where the gold had worn off.

But there were beautiful treasures in his storeroom and he knew the history of every piece, including a vast array of ornamental pieces which had not been used since the days of Queen Victoria. There were a lot of old-type mugs, once the pride of George III. There was the mug that had belonged to Prince Albert, Queen Victoria's Consort, and a fancy one that had been used by King Edward VII.

Attracted by appetizing odors, I drifted toward the kitchen. The floor space was somewhat like that of a four- or five-room house. The walls glittered with copper and brass pots and pans. And the neatly aligned knives of all sizes and shapes were a joy to behold for any amateur chef!

Numerous white-capped and aproned assistant cooks were hard at work at the stoves. One of them explained that they used gas in the big city, but that at Windsor Castle old-style wood fires were still popular with both the Royal family and the cook. Better flavor for the meat!

On the chef's bulletin board I was shown a copy of the

menu of the day. Two courses had been scratched. "By Her Majesty herself," volunteered a functionary.

In a corridor off the kitchen was a tank about 40 feet long and 3 feet wide. Fresh water was gushing in at one end. It was stocked with sprightly trout for which the King had a particular liking. Further on, on a lower level, I came up against a regular bar. There were the shelves behind it, with all the bottles and trimmings of glassware, with beer and ale on tap, just as in any little London pub. This was for the exclusive use of the palace staff, some two hundred strong. Several men and women were enjoying their favorite drinks. The bar was run exactly according to municipal regulations, just nine hours a day. By royal prerogative the King could have had the bar kept open all night, but he insisted that city rules be respected.

No one to date had reported such intimate glimpses from inside Buckingham Palace. But I could have told more. I could have told of sipping champagne and munching thin little French *gaufres* in the living room of the apartment of one of the King's staff when I reached the palace, or of having tea at the end of my day in that same room and enjoying some of the little cakes that had been baked for Their Majesties.

And I owed all this to nothing but my love of good stewed tripe and my curiosity about food in general! At the Savoy I'd struck up a friendship with its famous chef, M. François Latry. We both loved tripe, that dish made famous by Antoine Carême, who gave it its social standing by serving it to King Louis XVIII. From time to time M. Latry would cook a mess for himself and invite me over to his private dining room, off the Savoy kitchens. I did my best to help establish tripe's social standing in our times!

After M. Latry gave me his recipe for the tripe, I mailed it to New York to be held for release. Then came the evening when the Prince of Wales brought an after-theater party to the Savoy. One of his young guests, who was shy, whispered that she would like trout. The waiter claimed to have heard "tripe." He somehow had M. Latry's cache of tripe on his mind. He said that he would be delighted to serve this delicacy to the group.

The Prince of Wales gaily joined in the adventure. The whole party had tripe including the Prince and the shy young girl. They relished it. I sent a cable releasing my tripe recipe and the next morning many an American paper carried a story to the effect that the Prince of Wales had enjoyed tripe, the kind of tripe cooked in the Savoy. Nobody worried about calories in those days.

With my rating as "food lover" high in M. Latry's estimate he took me along to a banquet given in honor of a delegation of French chefs who had come to London to act as judges in a gastronomic fête at Albert Hall. His co-host was M. André Cédard, *chef de cuisine* to King George V. Being the only outsider at this most sumptuous of feasts I have ever enjoyed, I naturally met him—and we found a subject that interested us both: tripe. With twinkling eyes M. Cédard remembered that Dickens had written about it and that "Monsieur" Pickwick had appreciated it. By the end of the evening I had an invitation to call on M. Cédard: he would let me know of an opportune moment.

He kept his word. When he telephoned me he gave me the password that would allow me to enter the palace. "Monsieur," he cautioned, *"n'oubliez pas les tripes."* A London bobby stood at the entrance to which I went; I mentioned the password. It worked like magic!

And this is how the famous chef made his tripe à la mode de Caen. Take a big earthenware *terrine* that has a lid and closes tightly. Cut tripe into small pieces. Make a bed of sliced onions, a sliced lemon, leeks, carrots, tomatoes, bay leaves, parsley, thyme, celery, garlic, cloves. Add a boned calf's heel, a knuckle of ham. Put in the tripe and cover with a mixture of cider and brandy. (Some cooks use white wine instead of the cider.) Cover tightly and start the cooking on your stove. When the liquid begins to boil, put on the lid, preferably with flour paste. Then slide it into an oven where the tripe must simmer steadily for 10 hours.

Don't try to make this dish without the calf's foot, which gives the special gelatinous quality to the sauce. Most French chefs insist that you must secure as many varieties of tripe as possible, including honeycomb tripe and pieces of the stomach, cut extra fine since they are generally thicker than honeycomb. The proportions are:

5 pounds of tripe
2 calves' feet, 1 ham knuckle
2 good-sized leeks
1 pound of carrots cut in round slices
½ pound of white turnips
3 stalks of celery
20 tiny onions
2 big onions stuck with a clove each
A little garlic, thyme, bay leaf, salt, pepper, nutmeg and enough cider, mixed with cognac or calvados to cover the meat and vegetables completely.

Rather reluctantly some of my French friends admit that one *can* cook tripe with water or with white wine, but the believers in traditional French cooking prefer to have ½ a cup of cognac or calvados added to every quart of cider that goes into this dish.

The Normans are not the only ones who know how to turn tripe into a delicacy. It enjoyed such high repute in our country in the last half of the nineteenth century that the publishers of the *White House Cook Book,* which appeared first in 1887, lists several ways of preparing it, including New England's prized fried tripe and Philadelphia's

famous pepper pot. Obviously the chefs of the White
House frowned on cooking with alcoholic beverages—at
least when writing about their recipes, since they cook
their tripe in half water and half milk.

FRIED TRIPE

For the fried tripe cook the tripe the day before using
and let it stand overnight. When getting ready for the final
operation, cut the tripe into longish strips, dip each piece
into beaten egg yolk and roll it in fine bread crumbs.
Then fry the pieces of tripe in "good beef drippings" that
are boiling hot, until they are crisp and brown, which takes
about 10 minutes.

The Parker House in Boston, which lists this delicacy
on its menu, does not fry its cooked tripe, it broils the tripe,
thus securing perfect dry and crackling morsels.

The White House chef suggests onion sauce to go with
tripe, which will make any good Frenchman or New Eng-
lander wince, because it should be accompanied by a
Devil's Sauce—the hottest possible sauce you can devise.
Escoffier used to bottle his Devilled Sauce and it can still
be bought. All you need do to it is add butter to round it
off. But if Escoffier's product escapes you, you can make
your own:

DEVIL'S SAUCE

 2 yolks of hard-boiled eggs
 1 teaspoon of sharp French mustard
 Pepper, salt
 2 tablespoons of olive oil
 3 tablespoons of wine vinegar
 1 tablespoon of walnut ketchup or mushroom ketchup
 ¼ teaspoon of turmeric and/or ¼ teaspoon curry
 1 teaspoon onion or shallot pulp

Pound the egg yolks with the mustard, then blend in the other ingredients. Rub through a fine sieve. If you find that the sauce does not seem as smooth as you would like it, an extra shot of oil, or of good stock or one more teaspoonful of sour cream may be stirred in. On the other hand, if the sauce does not seem sharp enough a little cayenne, or a trace of freshly, finely ground horse-radish will make it sting a little more. Since the strength of mustards, vinegars, condiments varies, the host's taste buds must be the final arbiter, even for a Devil's Sauce.

When well done it is excellent company for all kinds of fish and meat as well as *the* sauce for fried tripe.

The other American tripe specialty enjoyed such fame in the past that many a traveler made an extra stop at the Philadelphia railroad station's restaurant to enjoy:

PHILADELPHIA PEPPER POT

2 pounds of honeycomb tripe
2 pounds of plain tripe
2 calves' feet or 1 veal knuckle
4 quarts of cold water
3 young carrots
2 stalks of celery
1 sweet pepper, diced
4 medium-sized potatoes
1 large onion
1 bag of potherbs and spices composed of bay leaf, marjoram, peppercorns, thyme, basil, a pinch of chervil, 1 clove
Salt, pepper

Simmer the tripe, the veal, the onion, salt, pepper, and the bag of potherbs for 8 hours. Fish out the potherbs, skim off the fat, add the carrots, sweet pepper, celery, potatoes, all neatly diced, and cook for another hour. At this point two roads are open to you. You can thicken the soup with a tablespoon of flour mixed with a tablespoon of butter, or you may drop small suet dumplings into it.

Whatever you decide, cook for 10 to 12 more minutes, taste quickly to decide whether a tiny shot of sherry or one more turn of the peppermill is needed and finish up with a sprinkling of finely chopped parsley.

Philadelphia pepper pot plays the social game well: if your guests include squeamish souls who go into an act at the mere mention of tripe, just refer to it as a famous Pennsylvania specialty known since Revolutionary days. Only the connoisseur and gourmet will recognize the tripe flavor and gourmets, being wise and kind, will relish the soup and not mention the word that might spoil the enjoyment of other guests!

Note from the Editor

Since Jim Howe started this story in the royal Buckingham Palace, we should watch our language. But there is a dish that must be included in a chapter dealing with tripe, even if its name will shock some purists.

I first heard of it from H. R. Knickerbocker, one of the star correspondents and lecturer extraordinary in the days before and during World War II. He hailed from deep in Texas. Whenever he passed through Berlin, he insisted on getting a Philadelphia pepper pot at the Schultzes' because it reminded him of his favorite Texas stew. Before it was served he would disappear into my kitchen to add this and that to the soup to make it taste more nearly like the dish of his youth. The amount of chili and other peppers that went into it was appalling. But then Knick would emerge, preceding the maid with the soup tureen, and announce loudly, with a real boy's delight at shocking people:

"SON-OF-A-BITCH STEW"

Only when the guests included an ambassador or a foreign diplomat who might have been shocked, he toned down the announcement to "Son-of-a-gun stew."

Today Knick's name is on the honor roll in the Memorial Room of the Overseas Press Club among those of our friends and colleagues killed while on duty. Now I could cook a real "son-of-a-gun stew" for him since I received the recipe for it from Harold von Schmidt, the painter and illustrator who was born and raised in the West and whose works glow with the spirit of adventure of the old days. Knick and I never got his stew quite right, because the homesick amateur chef did not know that the camp cooks made it from the "innards" of a well-fatted calf, not from those of an ox.

To be absolutely right, this stew should contain marrow gut, which is the tube connecting the two stomachs of a cud-chewing animal, preferably a calf that is still living on milk. But the womenfolk in small towns when asked by their sons and husbands to copy the stew they had enjoyed on the range could rarely get marrow guts, and substituted plain tripe. The camp cooks who could get the "innards" right after the slaughtering, would cut some pieces of fat into a big pot. While it was rendering they would take the:

Heart, cut up into pieces
Skinned tongue (fresh)
Marrow gut, cut in pieces
Knuckles
Water to cover—cook until the marrow gut begins to soften. Then add:
Pieces of tenderloin
Sweetbreads
A little cut-up liver
Some onions and warm water to cover generously

They put a lid on and stirred occasionally while the stew cooked another hour. The brains would be cooked separately and mixed with flour to be added in the last phase of cooking, as a thickening agent. After a final addition of salt and pepper, the call "Come and get it!" would ring out for everyone to enjoy the son-of-a-gun stew together with the traditional sour dough biscuits.

From Hradcany Castle

FLORENCE BROBECK

ONE OF the happy experiences for authors and correspondents
after World War I was to sally forth to Czechoslovakia, the little
country that had fully understood the message of President Wilson that "the world must be made safe for democracy" and had
turned the struggle into its very own.

In lovely Prague, with its Middle-Age towers and turrets and
its historic bridges, they would seek out Thomas Masaryk, the
Father of this reborn country. Among the travelers was Florence
Brobeck, author of many a book and magazine story. She remembers the days of hope and happy achievement in Czechoslovakia
and, while omitting the discussion of weighty problems confronting the country's first President, she tells of the leisurely
grace of those times:

As I WRITE I can glance at my favorite photograph of that
great old man, Thomas Masaryk, which he gave me on
a long-ago summer afternoon, when I had gone to Hradcany Castle in Prague—in Masaryk's free Czechoslovakia
—to have tea with him and his daughter. The photograph shows this dedicated fighter for independence for

his people, relaxed and happy, among the books in the handsome library of Hradcany. He spent a great deal of time in that room, and in the spare, very small bedroom which he had chosen from the dozens of castle rooms to be his refuge.

He was not greatly concerned with social occasions but he had promised his Foreign Minister and diplomats stationed in England and the United States that he would welcome a few people at a garden party. From the library in the castle on the hilltop, where I had interviewed Mr. Masaryk, I went down to the gardens on the lower terraces with him and his daughter. Ladies from London and assorted friends and visitors from all over the world had begun to assemble. The tea table held all sorts of sweets and Bohemian cakes, tea, coffee, beer, and sweet cocktails. Here are the best of the cakes and sweets, and they are well worth adding to any American brunch or tea table.

BÁBA KALÁCS: COFFEE CAKE

½ cake of compressed yeast
¼ cup of lukewarm water
¼ cup of granulated sugar
4 tablespoons of butter
½ teaspoon of salt
⅔ cup of lukewarm milk
6 egg yolks
2 cups of all-purpose flour, sifted
½ cup of coarsely chopped almonds
½ cup of brown sugar (packed)
1 teaspoon of vanilla extract

Soften yeast in the ¼ cup of warm water 15 minutes, in a large mixing bowl. Stir white sugar in, the butter, salt, milk, and egg yolks. Beat well, add half the sifted flour and beat until smooth. Cover bowl with folded towel, leave in warm, but not hot, place half an hour. Combine nuts, brown sugar and vanilla. Stir remainder of flour into the batter, making a soft, spongy dough to be dropped from a spoon. Stir until it becomes elastic and blisters. Grease an 8-cup ring mold, spoon half the dough into the mold. Sprinkle with half of the nut mixture. Add rest of dough. Top with remaining nut mixture. Cover with towel, and let rise in warm, but not hot, place until doubled in bulk. Start oven at Moderate (350° F.). Bake ring 45 minutes or until golden brown. Let cool a few minutes in pan, then turn out on cake rack. Serve frosted or plain. Makes eight or more servings.

KOLÁCE: ASSORTED SWEET TARTS

Yeast dough for rolls or puff paste
Plum preserve
Sweetened cottage cheese with poppy seeds
Prune butter or apple butter
¼ cup of melted butter
2 beaten egg yolks mixed with
3 tablespoons of milk
Powdered sugar

Prepare dough, let rise in greased mixing bowl in warm, but not hot, place until doubled in bulk. Punch down well. Then take about 1 tablespoon of dough at a time, roll into a ball, flatten on a lightly floured board with a rolling pin into a round about ½-inch thick. If using puff paste, roll it out about ½-inch thick and cut in rounds.

Press center of each round of dough or puff paste with the fingers making a good indention. Fill with preserve, or sweetened cottage cheese with poppy seeds, or with prune or apple butter. Place not too close together on greased baking sheets. Brush with melted butter, and let rise about ½ hour in a warm, but not hot, place. Start oven at Moderate (350° F.). Brush rounds with egg-yolk mixture, sprinkle with powdered sugar and bake 30 to 35 minutes. Let cool. Makes 16 or more *koláce* using average dough recipe.

RUM FOAM

1 pint of heavy cream chilled
½ cup of rum, chilled
½ cup of vanilla sugar*

Combine cream, rum, and sugar in a bowl and beat until thick and foamy. Heap into dessert glasses, chill. Serve very cold. Makes 6 to 8 servings.

ANIS KRÄPFCHEN: ANIS COOKIES

4 eggs
1½ cups of sugar
3 cups of all-purpose flour, sifted
1 teaspoon of baking powder
3½ teaspoons of aniseed

Beat eggs in mixing bowl until light and foamy. Add sugar gradually, beating continually until mixture is lemon colored. Sift flour, baking powder, and aniseeds together, and add gradually to the egg mixture, beating well after each addition.

Start oven at Moderate (350° F.). Grease baking sheet and dust it with flour. Drop cookie dough from a teaspoon onto the prepared sheet. Bake in moderate oven 10 to 15 minutes. Makes about 5 dozen drop cookies.

CRISP TWISTS, OR BAKELSE

Under various names these delicacies appear in Czechoslovak, Polish, Yugoslav, Hungarian and German homes, are served with coffee and at the end of dinner with fruit or frozen desserts. They also figure prominently in Scandinavia, where cardamom seeds give them extra glamour. Bakelse is their Scandinavian name.

* Vanilla sugar: Bury a vanilla bean in a jar of sugar. Discard bean after one month, and replace with fresh vanilla bean. Add sugar and stir well each time any of the vanilla-sugar is removed.

4½ cups of all-purpose flour, sifted
1 teaspoon of baking powder
3 eggs
½ cup of sugar
1½ teaspoons of rum
¼ pound of butter, chilled
Fat for deep frying
Confectioners' sugar

Sift flour and baking powder together two or three times. Beat eggs, sugar, and rum together well. Mix into flour smoothly. Flake the cold butter into the mixture, kneading the butter well into the dough. Roll dough out on lightly floured board into a thin sheet. Cut in strips about 4 inches long and 1 inch wide. Slit one end of each strip, twist once and thread through the slit, or tie each strip loosely in knot. Fry in deep hot fat (375° F.) 2 to 4 minutes or until golden brown. Drain on thick paper towels. Sprinkle with confectioners' sugar. Makes enough for four to six people.

Notes from the Editor

These are only a few of the specialties that used to fill trays upon trays of temptation in the pastry shops of Prague, and of all places, Karlsbad and Marienbad, the enchanting spas where the wise and the wealthy of this world used to "take the cure." Internationally famous medical luminaries would check on their insides, prescribe regimes to control their ills and, if necessary, reduce their *embonpoint*.

Between the two wars you could still enjoy the hospitality of the hotel made famous by King Edward VII. In his gayest days at the beginning of this century Europe's most beautiful women and most successful artists would fill the spa. The King and his retinue would compete for their favors with Russian grand dukes, artists, princes and millionaires from all over the world.

In theory they obeyed their doctors' orders. And the

doctors must have felt an unholy glee when prescribing tough reducing diets, several kinds of mineral water that had to be sipped hot while taking a walk before breakfast and at teatime, thermal and mud baths, climaxed by poundings from the strongest masseurs to be found on the continent.

Though King Edward was only a memory in the twenties and thirties, some of the glamour of the past still clung to Marienbad. Chicago millionaires would compete for the honor of occupying the late King's suite. But on occasion they would rebel at the smallness of the portions served on doctors' orders. Nothing was funnier than to watch their reaction when the headwaiter would assure them that King Edward had gone through the same regime without complaining. They'd brace themselves as if they remembered what they owed to their exalted station and then they'd remember that once a week, they, like their illustrious predecessors, were allowed one day of gastronomic sinning. The choice confronting them was fabulous indeed: from delicate fish caught in mountain streams and lakes to pheasants and rare venison from the deep forests of Bohemia to tender Prague hams and desserts rivaling those of Vienna, Budapest or Paris.

The well-earned fame of Bohemian pastry cooks was such that even the man who hated Czechoslovakia and plotted that brave country's doom, Adolph Hitler, would allow none but a Bohemian cook to prepare the pastries that were the only food he appreciated. Those of us who sampled them at the annual tea which Hitler gave for correspondents at the Nürnberg Party Rally can attest that his choice of pastry cook was wise indeed. It was all the more striking in 1938 when throughout Germany potatoes and all kinds of ersatz were smuggled into bread and pastries to stretch the supplies.

In that same period Prague deserved to be called the

"most appetizing smelling capital of Europe." Correspondents from Germany, Poland, Hungary and Russia would descend on the hospitable capital to file copy to their home papers that they could not risk sending from lands where censors worked overtime. For short spells we would bask in the blessed atmosphere of a free country that was not turning its butter into guns.

When you passed the pastry shops near the Hotel Alcron billows of fragrant air would envelop you with the perfume of roasting or brewing real coffee, of warm baking bread, of browning almonds, of vanilla beans and chocolate, of peaches and strawberries.

At the corners of the main avenue you'd be greeted by whiffs of luscious-smelling little sausages steaming in big containers, which like those of Poland, Hungary and Rumania were spicy, juicy titbits to delight a gourmet's heart. In the windows of some of the big restaurants you'd see whole batteries of freshly roasted geese with shiny skins that seemed to crackle when you just looked at them.

If you entered Sroubek's, the headquarters for lovers of solid food where, on occasion, you'd meet the son of Czechoslovakia's grand old man, gay, optimistic young Masaryk, the perfume of Prague hams baking in their crusts, of sauces enriched with dill, Madeira or wild mushrooms, would sweep over you.

"And it did not take you long to learn to appreciate that Czech national dish, *knedlíky*," says Professor Charles Hodges, who crisscrossed Eastern Europe in the years when, to prepare their war, Nazis were organizing the German minority groups into fifth columns of traitors to the countries in which they lived.

Before he and his wife Nora left Czechoslovakia, as the clouds of war were threatening, the wife of a Czech diplomat gave them her own family recipe for *knedlíky* as a final souvenir of her country.

KNEDLÍKY

come in many shapes. There is the light one, made of cottage cheese, eggs and sugar packed around an apricot or a prune, which is enjoyed as a dessert and is really a cousin of the Viennese *knödel*.

But the bread *knedlíky* is the real thing. It is an over-sized dumpling that has earned its place in Czech cooking because it is the ideal accompaniment to fat pork roasts and meats cooked with rich creamy sauces that used to be middle-class fare. Its blotterlike quality makes it possible to sop up sauces that deserve to be relished to the last drop.

1 cup of flour
1 teaspoon of salt
2 egg yolks
1 cup of water
2 egg whites, beaten stiff
5 slices of white bread
Bread crumbs browned in butter

Sift the flour and salt. Mix in the egg yolks. Stir in the water and when you have a smooth sauce, pour it over the slices of bread that you have torn into small pieces, making sure that they are well soaked. Fold in the beaten egg whites.

Drape a napkin or linen kitchen towel into a sieve and pour your mixture into it. Tie firmly and drop onto a trivet standing in a big pot that contains enough water to cover the ball. Count 20 minutes from the moment the water starts boiling. Then peel your giant dumpling out of the napkin onto a dish where you cover it with bread crumbs browned in butter. Slice it into 1-inch thicknesses when serving and send along with your pork roast, your pot roast or whatever specialty of yours boasts of a rich sauce.

Some like to add refinements to their *knedlíky*—possibly by roasting or toasting the bread, adding baking powder to the flour, a measure of butter or a small cup of fine suet, a bit of dill, or nutmeg. But this is frankly a sturdy peasant dish that is meant to stick to the ribs and to dramatize the sauce it accompanies without asserting itself too much, despite its impressive shape and size.

I Was Called Brave

LOUIS P. LOCHNER

In the long years during which Louis P. Lochner was stationed in Berlin for the Associated Press, he ranked as specialist in news about the Kaiser and members of the Hohenzollern family. While other correspondents climbed over the fence surrounding Castle Doorn, in Holland, to catch a glimpse of the ex-Kaiser, Louis Lochner needed no such stratagem, as may be gathered from his anecdote on the little "court in exile." He writes:

THE FACT that I like mushrooms is responsible for the surprising circumstance that once—and only once—in my life of more than seven decades I was acclaimed a "brave man."

The celebrity who gave me this title had been used to handing out military and civilian decorations by the hundreds, if not by the thousands, during his reign of thirty years.

When I was his guest in 1938, twenty years after his abdication, he was living in retirement, with no authority to confer either decorations or titles. But he still could voice his opinions.

His name was Wilhelm II, last German emperor, who had been banished to Doorn, Holland, at the end of the First World War. The Associated Press had sent me from Berlin to interview him. He so agreed and invited me to stay for luncheon.

We were a small party of a dozen persons. Princess Irene, widow of the former emperor's only brother, Heinrich, was seated to His Majesty's right; his second wife, "Empress" Hermine, opposite him; myself on his left, one of Hermine's children opposite me, the rest of the participants being members of the imperial household-in-exile.

The solemn protocol of Berlin days was still in effect, and Wilhelm II was always served first, then his guest to the right, thereafter the guest to the left (on this occasion myself). I noted that our host did not help himself to the second course, a delicious-looking dish of mushrooms. When my turn came, I unhesitatingly helped myself, for the mushrooms looked fresh and inviting. My host's eyes rested quizzically on me as I ate with obvious relish.

Then came the unexpected accolade:

"Mr. Lochner, you are a brave man," the imperial voice next to me exclaimed, half in admiration, half amusedly.

To my surprised and uncomprehending look the voice reacted: "I wouldn't even touch those mushrooms. Don't you know? My family this morning picked them out in the garden. I wouldn't dare eat them. Tomorrow you'll be dead."

"Empress" Hermine pouted her lips. "*Aber Schatzi*" ["But sweetheart]," she remonstrated.

"I'm not at all sure that my folks know the difference between poisonous and edible mushrooms," the lord of the manor persisted; "that's why I look upon you as a hero, but also as a potential dead duck."

Fortunately for me, the imperial prognostication regarding my future proved wrong and there were no casualties.

When I reported the incident to my German-born faithful spouse and described the mushrooms and the taste of the sauce served with them, she knew immediately how such a dish is prepared. Herewith is her:

RECIPE FOR MUSHROOMS

After making sure that the mushrooms have been cleaned, place them together with consommé and some butter in an earthen pot and let them simmer for about ½ hour. Add a teaspoonful of potato flour, some pulverized zwieback, a bit of fresh lemon juice, salt as desired, and let the whole concoction boil until the gravy thickens, whereupon stir in the yolk of one or two eggs.

"You Gorge Yourself While the Masses Starve," Said Göring

SIGRID SCHULTZ

M Y STORY is from Berlin because that is where I started as a "cub correspondent" of the Chicago *Tribune*, under Richard Henry Little, to become correspondent-in-chief for Central Europe in 1926, and to add regular broadcasting for Mutual Broadcasting to my job at the Munich conference in 1938, much to the displeasure of the Nazis. After Hitler started his war, they had three censors go through my scripts but their blue pencils did little good because with the right kind of intonation and emphasis one could convey more than the gentlemen of the War Office, the Propaganda Ministry and the Foreign Office wanted. They were happy when I went home on leave in 1941—but I returned to Europe to cover the end of World War II as a war correspondent and later to report on the so-called new peace era.

Thus I witnessed the rise and fall of Nazism. In the late twenties I watched the uncouth rowdies and perverts in the first contingent of Nazi deputies to the Reichstag stage their spectacular scenes that were fully as loud and vulgar as those of the Reds. By 1930 there were more than a hundred Nazi deputies and one had to get "to know them." My newspaper "father," Dick Little had warned me: "If a correspondent or politician ever reaches the point where he or she won't talk to an objectionable character to find out what makes him tick, then his or her professional usefulness had ended." This, I did not want to happen.

I sent my half-British, half-German assistant, Alexander von Schimpff, scouting for an influential Nazi with the kind of manners that would make it possible to invite him to an occasional meal, where he could be expected to talk more freely than in an interview. Since the British side of his family was related to the Royal house of England I could rely on his being choosy. As our provider of Nazi news who was to be well fed and sounded out, he picked a definitely rotund ace pilot of World War I, Captain Hermann Göring.

To be on the safe side we tried him out at a luncheon at the small elegant restaurant, Pelzer's, before inviting him to my house. He appeared, flanked by an aide. Though the Nazis claimed to spurn foreign delicacies because their cost "robbed the German economy," our guests devoured vast amounts of very expensive French snails. Göring also showed a gourmet's appreciation of the chef's superb *boeuf Miroton* and a gratifying eagerness to talk.

After word spread that Hitler's first lieutenant had been my guest, my friends among the British and American diplomats kept dropping around to find out what "that man, Hitler's chief lieutenant" had to say. Being accredited to the German government, protocol did not allow them to go after opposition leaders of this type openly, on their own.

When early in 1932 rumors came thick and fast that the Nazis had succeeded in enlisting the help of the Reichswehr General von Schleicher to get Hitler named Chancellor, I invited Göring to the Schultz studio together with my diplomatic friends who were bent on doing their own probing. That evening we knew that Göring's car had been parked all day before the house in which Schleicher lived. When he had his second drink firmly in hand, I asked him point-blank what he had done all day at Schleicher's. He nearly exploded. He pointed an accusing finger at my mother, who stood nearby, charging: "Your daughter has had me watched. She is just like the rest of the *Journaille*. And I'll tell you what that stands for." He explained this was a combination of the word "journalist" and the French *canaille*. Mother just looked at him in frosty disapproval.

Somewhat embarrassed, he wiped his double chin and explained: "It has been a hard day, but I can tell you this: I shall never forgive Schleicher. I'll make him pay for this day." His aide, sensing that something was amiss, came over to check on his boss. Göring quickly put back his mask of polite guest and proceeded to go to work on the British and American diplomats and to try to impress a lovely lady, Catherine Ann Porter, who kept shrinking away to the best of her ability.

The party atmosphere was restored when the guests sat down to dine and, much to their surprise, found themselves confronted with what looked like mere "beef bones." They were marrow bones served the way I had enjoyed them at the Hotel Bristol in Warsaw. They are sawed in inch lengths, salted, garnished with chopped parsley and broiled until the marrow inside is very hot and both ends have a brown, crusty top. The guest loosens the marrow inside the bone, drops it on a small piece of hot Melba toast on his plate, gives it an extra dose of salt and swallows it as a kind of blotter for a tiny glass of aquavit or vodka.

As the dessert, a golden-brown Scotch fig pudding, blazed lustily, Göring, the only fat person in the group, sat back and said reprovingly: "You gorge yourselves while the masses starve." In the silence that followed everybody seemed to stare at his *embonpoint* and wonder whether he was trying to be funny. He repeated his line.

The slender, elegant British diplomat was the first to surmount the temptation to grin and he said: "That sounds like a Communistic line." Göring then proceeded to denounce the capitalistic classes that exploit the working people. He inveighed against the "foreign money lenders" as if he had been at a Red mass rally. Thus we learned that there was nothing accidental in the co-operation between Nazis and Communists in a series of local crises. They were co-operating to bring about the downfall of the Weimar Republic. None of us who heard him that night would ever fall for the myth which the Nazis still circulated in 1960, that Hitler's main purpose was to fight Communism. The Nazis developed it later when they found that their chance of seizing power was greater if they co-operated with the barons of industry. As far as I was concerned, the purpose of the dinner had been achieved: the guest who was to be pumped revealed more than he had planned to.

There is a sequel to this story: On June 30, 1934, the day of the first big Nazi blood purge, all correspondents were summoned to the Propaganda Ministry. Göring appeared in full regalia, with his retinue of officers, strutting as stiffly as he could. In terse words he gave the Nazi version of what had happened, rose and began to stalk out, with his retinue veering in step with him. Then he saw me; he halted; the whole cortege halted; then he said loudly: "And by the way, General von Schleicher was shot, trying to escape." He looked at me piercingly, as if to say: "You see, I've had my revenge." Schleicher and his wife never even had a chance to try to escape. They were shot down in cold blood when the Nazi assassins entered their home.

Göring did not even try to conceal his satisfaction with this and other Nazi crimes. None of us who had listened to his outbursts of hatred in 1932 were surprised by his reaction, though after the Nazis came to power nobody worked harder than Göring to appear as the genial and artistic host. He staged magnificent shows and parties that dazzled many American visitors to the point where our gullible countrymen trusted his honeyed words and resented the warnings of our little group of correspondents and American diplomats trying to tell them about concentration camps and German preparations for war. They preferred to believe the tales of fake and real aristocrats, trained by the Gestapo, who were assigned to them as dates at banquets featuring the most costly dishes chefs could devise.

The guests who assembled at my studio in 1932 to sound out the future Nazi powerholder enjoyed no such fancy fare. In fact, in my efforts to get away from the traditional diplomatic menu, I chose pork for the main course—but it was:

PORK À LA SOUBISE

that can compete with many a more expensive dish. It calls for slices of pork or pork chops with just a little of the bone left on them. For each chop you need:

½ teaspoon of chopped fresh dill
½ teaspoon of chopped fresh borage
¼ teaspoon of fresh sage
¼ teaspoon of minced shallot
Pinch of flour
2 slices of eggplant
4 thin strips of red and green peppers
½ cup of tomato sauce or thinned tomato soup
Salt, pepper, paprika
Optional: tomato slices, topped with part of a basil leaf
Garlic—sour cream

Rub the pork with garlic, a sliced onion and salt. Fry quickly to close the pores. Peel and slice your eggplant into rather generous slices. Dust them with flour, brown them quickly in hot oil. If you appreciate garlic put a toe in the oil, but remove it before you put the eggplant in the hot oil. Mix the herbs and shallots with a pinch of flour.

Pair off each slice of pork with 2 slices of eggplant and tie it with the thinly cut strips of red and green pepper.

If tomatoes are in season you can turn this twosome into a threesome by adding a slice of tomato and a tiny bit of basil before encircling with the pepper strips. Sprinkle the little packages generously with the herb mixture, then pack them side by side in an ovenproof dish. Pour in your diluted tomato soup or tomato sauce and bake in an oven that has been heated to 400° until the meat is well done. If the dish looks too dry for your taste, add some light sour cream mixed with tomato sauce or soup and return to the oven for a few minutes.

POTATO BIRDS'-NESTS

Potato birds'-nests go well with this dish because they are crisp, dry and chewy. For four servings take:

2 cups of grated potatoes, firmly packed
3 tablespoons of butter
1 teaspoon of salt
Fresh-ground gray or black pepper

Start your oven at 450°. Use half of the butter to generously coat a cooky sheet that has a low rim. Peel your biggest potatoes and grate them, using the biggest holes of your grater. There is less danger of grating your skin along with the potatoes if you choose the big ones—and besides, the grating goes quicker. Instead of grating into a pan, grate your potatoes directly onto a kitchen towel using it to squeeze some of the extra moisture out of the potatoes.

Measure 2 cupfuls, then spread the grated potatoes over the cooky sheet lightly, making a lacy but allover pattern. You should get about four thicknesses and salt each of the thicknesses and sprinkle a little pepper as you go along.

Scatter little dabs of butter evenly over the pan, finishing off with salt and pepper.

Slip into warm oven, making sure that the pan gets ample bottom heat for about 10 minutes, when the lowest layer should begin to turn golden. Then broil about 3 inches from the heat for another 10 minutes, when the whole should be crisp and golden brown. Return to the oven if it isn't. When done, loosen immediately with a spatula and cut into pieces. If the potatoes are allowed to stay on the pan while cooling, they stick and are hard to handle.

If, for some strategic cooking reason, you can't use bottom heat and broiler heat for this operation, ready a second cooky sheet, well buttered. When the bottom layers of the first sheet look done, place the second sheet over it and with an elegant gesture, turn the whole potato grillwork into it to give the former top a chance to brown as the new bottom.

You may want to cook your roast in the oven at the same time that you bake your potatoes. If the roast requires a lower temperature than the potatoes, just give them more time.

SCOTCH FIG PUDDING

Figs that have been preserved in syrup make the best pudding, but it can also be made with the more proletarian dried figs.

6½ ounces of pulverized beef suet
10 ounces of figs passed through the food chopper, possibly twice
6½ ounces of bread crumbs or Holland rusk crumbs
5 ounces of brown sugar
1 well-beaten big egg
1 cup of milk

Mix the crumbs and suet. Mix the figs and sugar with the egg and the milk. Stir both mixtures together and pack into a well-closing pudding shape; place in boiling water and cook for 4 hours, adding hot water from time to time.

Serve with your favorite custard sauce, to which you might add, if you like it, some real Dutch curaçao.

If you like flaming puddings, warm some rum, or cognac, put the liquor in a warmed ladle with a few grains of sugar, pour some of it over the pudding, light the liquor in the ladle and dip over your pudding until it catches fire.

BOEUF MIROTON

This is a useful dish because it looks more festive than most pot roasts and yet allows you to use a cheaper cut of meat. Furthermore, if you are the kind of cook who likes to plan ahead, it also gives you a chance to look forward to a specially good dish of plain boiled beef.

Choose a big chunk of beef that has a slightly marbleized look without being too fat and a shape that will make it possible to cut off relatively even slices of meat.

For a party of twelve take at least 6 pounds of beef. Measure out enough water to cover this beef generously and start it toward boiling with:

2 onions stuck with 2 cloves
1 teaspoon of whole peppercorns, bay leaf
2 cut-up carrots
Parsley stalks and some parsley root, some celery root
1 teaspoon of juniper berries
1 sprig of thyme
½ teaspoon of marjoram
Salt
Whatever extra bones you have

Sear the meat just a little on all sides before putting it into the water (with the vegetables) that is nearly boiling. You may tie the meat firmly before doing this to ensure a good shape when it is done. Simmer very gently. This may take 3 hours or 4 hours, depending on your meat. But be sure to remove it before it is really tender. Let it cool a little and cut into even slices, but cover well with broth.

While the beef is cooking, start preparing the sauce. Slice vast quantities of healthy onions very thin. The more onions you prepare, the better your sauce will be.

    4 cups of sliced onions
    1 cup of butter
    ½ cup of flour
    4 cups of clear broth from your cooking beef
    "Four Spices," thyme, marjoram, paprika, pinch of dill, a little very
        sharp pepper, a bit of turmeric, a trace of curry—with as much
        crushed garlic as you would enjoy
    Thin slices of lemon
    Optional: a little sherry or Madeira.

Melt one half of the butter in a pan and add the sliced onions, stirring continuously over a low fire to make sure that they turn into a shiny, off-white, nearly golden pulp. To prevent browning add an occasional tablespoon of warm water or beef broth.

In the meantime brown the flour in another pan, as if you were roasting coffee beans. It must look dark, but not be dark enough to taste burned. When it has the right mahogany-like color, work in the remaining butter, add some of the meat broth until you have darkish paste into which you mix your onion pulp, preferably with a little garlic juice. Add more of the beef broth and then go after the task of flavoring your sauce with the spices mentioned above and cook it to a thickish velvety consistency.

When you are pleased with the taste, and it should be something to rejoice over, whether you add sherry or Madeira or not—pour the warm sauce over the meat slices that have been spread in an ovenproof dish to ready it for the final operation. You must have enough sauce to cover most generously and for an extra load to go in your sauceboat. Spread a few thin slices of lemon over the whole and let stand, preferably overnight, to give the sauce a chance to penetrate the meat. You may find the sauce a little too thin for your taste; then work in some of the pulp of your overcooked vegetables, or if it seems too thick—specially after its resting period—a little clear broth will do the trick, as well as good sherry or Madeira.

An hour and a half before serving start your oven at 400°. Before slipping in the platter with meat push the slices a little closer together, making sure that they are well covered with sauce; leave a space around them.

Cook some really thick macaroni in salted water. Half an hour before you plan to take out the meat, surround it with a *lei* of macaroni that has been well buttered. Check that the meat has enough sauce, but be sure that none lands on the macaroni, which should contrast with the dark meat. Sprinkle with grated Parmesan, a little rose paprika and dabs of butter and finish baking. If the *lei* effect seems too complicated, bake your meat and macaroni separately, or replace the macaroni with whatever starch seems more appealing to you—rice, riced or mashed potatoes.

The secret of

GOOD BOILED BEEF

Many a home cook has tried her hand at this seemingly simple dish only to find that the results of her labors are disappointing! Far too often the beef seems stringy, since none of us can order our beef from farms where the oxen were specially fattened for famous restaurants that are proud of the quality of their boiled beef. One of the amusing sights of the past which I remember with pleasure could be seen every Saturday in Bad Kissingen, a German spa where the wealthy of the world would assemble to take their annual cure under the late, famous Professor Dapper. Millionaires and multimillionaires would line up before the dining room doors opened for lunch to be sure not to miss their favorite weekly gourmet dish: boiled beef. And let there be no doubt in anybody's mind; their judgment was correct; the boiled beef was by far the best in Europe.

It took me a long time to worm the secret out of the late Professor Dapper, but I finally succeeded. The trick is a simple one: you must cook a really big piece of beef to get a succulent slice of boiled beef. Therefore when planning to cook *boeuf Miroton,* get more meat than you need. Cook it all as for the old-fashioned French dish, but reserve a big piece—possibly in your freezer—to serve plain with a parsley sauce, or with Sauce Vinaigrette, or with an egg sauce, or Sauce Diable, with Horse-radish Sauce, plus all the pickles and relishes you have accumulated.

A competitor to *boeuf Miroton* in many a good Paris bistro, is beef cooked à la Flamande, which is also very considerate of the family purse strings. Being Flemish, it goes in for beer.

BOEUF À LA FLAMANDE

2 pounds of beef, cut in even cubes
8 big onions
4 tablespoons of butter
1 teaspoon of peppercorns
Bay leaf
1 teaspoon of chili powder
½ cup of cognac
1 cup of thick sour cream
Salt—1 bottle of beer or a little more

The onions must be sliced very thin and sautéed in 2 tablespoons of butter; when they are transparent add beer, the spices and salt. It takes about 2 hours of cooking until they are reduced to a purée. When the onions have nearly reached the right consistency, brown the beef cubes in the remaining butter; mix onions and meat, add enough beer to cover generously and cook slowly for 3 hours. If the mixture is in danger of turning dry, add a little more beer. Let rest overnight.

Shortly before serving, reheat the meat for ½ hour, add cognac and, as a final operation just after you have taken the pan off the heat, blend in the sour cream. Serve with rice, riced potatoes or mashed potatoes. One of the strange traits of this dish is that none but the smartest of tasters will detect the taste of beer—which does the same job as red wine in the traditional *boeuf Bourguignonne:* it softens the beef.

The Secret of the Roman Proconsul

BELLA FROMM

As a diplomatic and social reporter of the Ullstein press, Bella Fromm, author of *Blood and Banquets*, attended a vast number of dinners and banquets in the days when the diplomatic corps in Berlin and German statesmen were competing with each other in staging the most brilliant parties. She enjoyed the friendship and confidence of many of the diplomats, which was to enable her in time to help many of her friends escape from Germany, when the Nazi persecution of Jews made it imperative for them to try to find a country that would give them a visa. This also gave her an extra good look behind the diplomatic scene, as she tells in the following story:

THERE IS MORE to the diplomatic game than just nego-tiations and formal dinners. The diplomat with a wife who knows how to ferret out the secret about the favorite dishes of politicians or fellow diplomats of her husband is as fine a campaigner as the silver-tongued old pro.

I remember one morning in Berlin when I dropped in to pay a visit to the wife of the Italian Ambassador, stately, elegant Mme. Cerruti. The Ambassador was present and he confided that the dinner which he was giving for Hermann Göring that week was of crucial importance. He had to be put into a superlative mood because the Italians wanted a few of Germany's newest airplane parts.

After he left, Mme. Cerruti summoned the chef and they discussed at length which dishes Hitler's second-in-command had enjoyed most on other occasions. "I know," said the chef. "I remember how he grinned from ear to ear the time we served

OYSTER STEW À LA ORATA

I watched through the door to see his reaction."

Mme. Cerruti agreed that no other hostess in Berlin had been able to emulate that dish, which had been the pride of a gourmet, Orata, a Roman proconsul who lived in 100 B.C. The old Roman had been so fond of this dish that he started the systematic cultivation of oysters in the Bay of Naples.

The chef had experimented until he perfected his own version, which is glamorous indeed: he would try to find a variety of oysters that had a good deal of liquid, counting about six oysters per guest; for Göring he naturally took a dozen. Here is his recipe:

Per serving take:

6 oysters
1 teaspoon of flour
1 teaspoon of butter
4 peppercorns, a trace of grated nutmeg
¼ teaspoon of finely cut lemon peel
1 tablespoon of light sweet cream
1 split of champagne—or if you are not trying to get a few airplanes out of your guest, a good dry Chablis can serve as substitute. Serve champagne or wine with this stew.

Remove the oysters carefully from their shell and sprinkle them ever so lightly with lemon. Take the liquid and the beards and simmer this for half an hour with finely sliced lemon peel, whole pepper, a trace of nutmeg and enough champagne to secure a broth. Blend a teaspoonful of butter and a teaspoonful of flour per serving, add the strained broth, some more champagne and some light sweet cream. Stir until the flour is well cooked and drop the oysters into this lightly simmering sauce.

The Italians got their equipment, thanks to Mme. Cerruti and the chef—and the Roman proconsul.

Adventure in the Alps and the Wondrous Qualities of "Veal Zingara"

HARRY KURSH

THERE are not many full-time free-lance correspondents, a breed of American journalists who will go anywhere, anytime, sometimes at any price, for anyone, to pursue a story.

Harry Kursh, a former business reporter and editor, has been one of the breed for the past decade, and his only regret is that he didn't break his desk-bound chains sooner; but he also regrets that Hollywood has not yet got around to caricaturing the free lancer, complete with bottle of bourbon, trench coat and blonde, because he says he owns a trench coat and a bottle of bourbon but has never been caught in the Orient Express with a blonde. With a little boost from Hollywood, Kursh figures that blondes might start flocking around free lancers. He hopes, however, that Hollywood never uses him as model for caricaturing the free lancer because he says, he's short, hefty, broad-shouldered, barrel-chested, looks more like a wrestler, and wouldn't know what to do with his blonde if he ever found himself trapped again on an Alpine peak, where a bottle of bourbon is handier anyhow.

I T ALL BEGAN in Saint-Moritz on a bright and sunny morning in January. I was lounging rather comfortably and lazily in the arms of an impossibly luxurious chair at the Suvretta House, a picture-post-card hotel where poets come to act like princes, kings check in looking like peasants, and maharajahs come scouting for Rita Hayworths.

Seated by a large lobby window, I was greatly enjoying the scene: an enormous mirrorlike ice-skating rink perched at the edge of a hill, the sounds of laughing children, the gaily dressed men and women and their flashing blades, soft waltz music, and on the horizon a long bank of thick white clouds nestling over the shoulders of an endless chain of Alpine peaks. But more was I able to enjoy it all because I had firmly decided to keep away from my typewriter all day long. In my end of the business, free lancing, this is tantamount to economic heresy, for there is in the world of the free lancer no such thing as a day off with pay.

Suddenly a pair of tall legs stood in front of me. I looked up and recognized Fred Birmann, the genial talented writer and Swiss newspaperman who works for the Swiss National Travel Office and helps foreign newsmen secure information, or a story, any hour of the day, any day of the week.

Birmann smiled. "Well, I found your man," he said. "He's ready for an interview."

"The man" was Freddy Wissel, one of only two men in the world who can fly a ski-equipped light airplane into the Alps and atop an ice-covered glacier, rescue people in distress and take off again. This is like trying to shoot a car at 60 miles per hour into a parking space on a steep greasy hill—only in the Alps the bottom of the hill, in case you miss, is a couple of miles straight down.

Because of his skill and courage, saving people from freezing to death while mountain climbers await rescue by ground forces is Wissel's hobby. He was actually the owner of one of the many small resort hotels that dot the Saint-Moritz landscape so that budget tourists may mingle with the credit-card class in this beautiful land.

Nice contrast. Nice story. "That's great," I told Birmann. "Can you help me set up an interview with Wissel tomorrow?"

"Yes, but not tomorrow," Birmann replied. "I have already spoken with Wissel and he will be happy to give you plenty of time today but tomorrow he will be out of town and you will be gone when he returns."

Once again I was faced with the inevitable choice between indolence and a marketable story, and like any good businessman who has to pay his taxes I chose the latter. I grabbed my topcoat and pencil and hopped into Birmann's waiting car. Birmann looked at me. "No hat, no boots, no gloves, nothing warm to cover your body—won't you be cold?" he asked.

"We're going directly to his hotel, aren't we? Why should I be cold?"

"Oh," said Birmann, "I thought you were going to fly with him into the Alps and see how he does it."

"No thank you," I said. "I'll let him *tell* me about it."

Driving down from the winding snow-packed road leading away from Suvretta House we passed through the colorful village of Saint-Moritz itself and soon parked in front of an unpretentious but impeccable building, the National Hotel. Standing at the door to greet us was Freddy Wissel, a slender, erect man in his late forties, but whose smooth light hair and handsome face and sharp Nordic features gave him a considerably younger appearance.

After introducing us, Birmann left, promising to be back in a few hours to pick me up. Wissel led me to his hotel's intimate dining room, which between meals doubles as an adjunct to the lounge, and there we talked for about an hour. But drawing from the modest Wissel an account of the daring details of his Alpine rescues, the drama, the pathos, and the comedy, if any—all essential ingredients for such a story—was extremely difficult. On the other hand, when I began asking him about the techniques of making his glacier landings in a Piper Super Cub it was like opening a valve in a dam, and he gushed forth with words, all of which went right over me. Sensing that I could not quite understand his flying jargon Wissel, who, like many Swiss, speaks English fluently, said: "Why don't you fly with me and I will show you exactly how it is done. It will be so much better, no?"

"I don't think I shall have the time to wait around until you get a rescue call," I said.

"That won't be necessary," Wissel replied. "The airfield is only a few miles from here. I shall be happy to drive out and take you up now."

"But as you can see," I said, smiling feebly, "I am not dressed for the occasion." That did not help me escape.

"You don't need warm clothes," said Wissel. "I will call the field. They will have the airplane warmed up and by the time we arrive we shall take off in a warm cabin. I will merely fly around to show you the technique."

I considered the compromise generous, plausible—and inescapable. I agreed.

On the way out to the airfield, Wissel told me that he had begun making glacier landings early in 1950, about the same time another famed Swiss pilot, Herman Geiger, accomplished the same feat. All told Wissel had carried out over a thousand Alpine operations (landings and take-offs) during which he had performed more than a hundred rescues. In between, for a nominal fee, he also would make Alpine landings for more intrepid tourists who wanted the excitement of skiing down a mountain without bothering to climb it first.

When we arrived at the airfield, Wissel went to a locker

and donned fur-lined jacket and boots. "But I thought you said it won't be cold in the plane," I said.

"It won't be," he replied. "But I like to be prepared for emergencies, in case I should have to make a landing and get out of the plane on top of a mountain."

"What about me?"

"Don't worry. You will not have to get out of the plane."

Wissel checked in with the flight operations controller to let him know where we were going (in case *we* had to be rescued) and in a few minutes we were off. He headed straight for a series of craggy peaks where there seemed to be no piece of ground, flat enough to land an airplane, no matter how small.

We flew around the peaks in the Bernina range, and Wissel said that as soon as he could find a suitable glacier he'd make a mock landing. As he explained it, a glacier in the Alps is a small strip of ice or snow that clings to the sharp incline of a mountain, like a small white handkerchief on a sharply tilted table. First, he has to determine from the air that the glacier is hard enough for the plane not to sink down to the fuselage when he lands, which would make a take-off difficult, if not impossible. For an emergency, he keeps a pair of skis in the plane to ski down the mountain if he has to abandon ship. But he admitted that not all mountains tolerate skis.

Once he decides that a glacier is right for a landing, and he goes down for a landing, he cannot change his mind. There is no room for error, no room for turning back, slowing down. He must make the landing or settle for a stall that will send him plunging, like a rock, thousands of feet down, or crashing into a crevasse. The same is true for a take-off, only more so. Nearly all glaciers are sur-rounded by crevasses, which are from 50 to 100 feet deep and come to a sharp V-shaped trough, so that if anyone— man or plane—fell into one the chances of rescue, assum-ing one still lived, would be almost nil.

"So that is all there is to it," said Wissel, after we had circled several likely-looking glaciers. Finally, he pointed to a mountain peak, known as the Pers, some 13,000 feet up. "There is a glacier on which I might make a landing."

I could see he was quite anxious to show me the real stuff. "If you've got a few more minutes," he said, "I could make a landing there. Then you will get the whole picture quickly."

"Will I have to get out of the plane?" I asked.

"Oh, no," he said confidently.

"O.K. Let's try it."

"Good!" Wissel beamed.

Suddenly he banked sharply to the left, and circled the Pers, steadily spiraling down and around until he was only a few hundred feet above the glacier. "It looks good," he said, and went straight down for a landing. We made it: in soft snow! The plane came to an abrupt, jolting halt and sunk down to its belly.

Wissel's smile disappeared. "We may be in trouble," he said, grimacing with the understatement of the year.

"How come?" I asked.

"You see, now you have had a perfect demonstration of what I was trying to explain," he said. "I misjudged the texture of the glacier. I thought it would be hard snow."

Now we both would have to get out of the plane, and drag it up to the top of the glacier, about a 150-foot incline, and turn the plane around to be in a position to take off. For the moment, he spared me the news of what would have to be done after that.

He reached back for the skis, threw them out on the snow and then got out, stepping onto the skis, and strapped them to his feet. I jumped out and landed up to my hips in snow. I buttoned my topcoat tight to the collar. Together we began dragging the plane. It was a painful process; we seemed to be making progress at the rate of inches. Within minutes I was a useless helper because I soon began to feel the effects of the thin air and the icy blasts of wind. My hands, freezing without gloves, felt as if the flesh would come off every time I touched the skin of the plane. My feet were numb. My heart pounded so hard that I had to lie down in the snow, time after time, to regain what little strength was left to me. Wissel offered to give me the skis so that I could stand on the snow, but I refused because he, being the expert and the only one who could get us off the mountain alive, could make better use of them.

After a few hours I was completely helpless and Wissel had to drag the plane himself. Once he looked up and said, "We must hurry." A fog was closing in, and if it enveloped the mountain he might not be able to take off at all; then suddenly it began getting darker and colder and I, in despair, sat down in the snow as if there was nothing more to do but wait for the inevitable, a frozen death.

At last, Wissel had the plane in position to take off. He removed the skis, threw them to me and told me to put them on. Why? Then came the news he had withheld. The plane, with both of us in it, would be too heavy for take-off in the soft snow. He would first try a take-off alone, and if he made it he would make several landings and take-offs in the same ski tracks until the snow was packed hard enough for both of us to take off. But if he should fail (never having had to attempt this before) I should try to get off the mountain by skiing down myself.

"That's great," I said. "I not only am wearing ordinary shoes, but I have never strapped on a pair of skis in my life." I placed my feet on the skis but I knew that was all I could do.

Wissel shrugged, as if to say *"c'est la vie,"* and climbed into the plane. I looked toward the inevitable crevasse and saw that Wissel had about 50 or so yards in which to take off. At the moment I could only turn to a selfish thought:

If Wissel were to crash, I was as good as dead. Paradoxically, I could feel beads of sweat on my forehead as I wondered what it was like to die by freezing.

I looked intently at the cockpit and watched Wissel struggling to get the almost frozen motor started again. After a seemingly interminable number of false, spurting, coughing, hacking starts, the propeller turned over, Wissel waved jerkily, and the plane raced downhill, twisting and churning as its skis chugged through the soft snow, and finally the plane was off the glacier, with only a few feet to spare above the crevasse. If I had been with him in the cockpit on the first try, the plane would surely have plunged into the crevasse.

Then Wissel circled and came in for a landing, power on, so that he could drop the plane on target, the previous tracks, turn around and take off again, still in the same tracks. He repeated this process about a dozen times, until each time he was able to take off with additional inches to spare above the crevasse. Finally, he pulled the plane up to where I was standing, told me to get in and said, "Now I think we can take off safely together." By then my body was so stiff from the cold that I could barely move my lips. I think I said something like "I hope so," but between the howling wind and the roaring propeller, I didn't hear any words.

Setting his jaws grimly, Wissel pushed the throttle forward and the plane raced down the glacier toward the crevasse. I fought against an instinct to close my eyes, but somehow I felt as if I wanted to see how the end might come. I looked out just in time to see the edges of the skis touch the edge of the crevasse; then the plane quivered, I shook, and suddenly I felt as if we were air-borne. We were!

For a few moments, Wissel said nothing, apparently uncertain himself that we were still out of danger, then he observed, "Now you have had the real thing. A unique experience, no? Better than just talking, no?"

I wanted to say "No!" but I felt that if I were to open my lips something in my mouth might crack. We returned to the field just in time to stop a search plane from going out to look for us; I thanked Wissel profoundly for the story—for saving my life—and for the experience. Then I went back to the plush comfort of Suvretta House but for the next two days nothing seemed comfortable or warm. I felt as if I would never thaw out completely. I had had narrow calls before, but somehow this episode left me completely unnerved. I could not work. I could not eat. When it was time to catch my Swiss air flight back to New York from Zurich, my good friend, Fred Birmann came to pick me up. He was amazed when I told him that I had hardly eaten anything since the Wissel "interview," for Birmann knew how I always loved my food.

But then in one bright, shiny airport restaurant a wonderful Swiss epicurean meal, enjoyed just before my departure, restored my composure. As always in Switzerland everything was excellent but the entree served at the airport was so exotic, so unique that my taste buds came back to life—all weakness was forgotten! I had three helpings, and finally became so enthused over this unusual dish called steak *de veau Zingara* that I insisted on talking to the chef. Where on earth did he get that recipe? How did he make it?

First, said the chef, salt a nice veal steak that has been rubbed with lemon juice. Then dump it into flour and fry (medium to well) in golden butter in the frying pan. While it sizzles cut the following into slices: boiled beef tongue, boiled ham, truffle, sour pickles and the white of a hard-boiled egg. Heat the tongue, ham and truffle in butter and place neatly on the steak with the garnishing of pickle and egg. Serve with Madeira sauce.

I told the chef it was a superb dish, good for shattered nerves. "How so?" he asked. I started to explain, but cut myself short and said, "Never mind. You'll read about it." I hope he does.

To Alfredo's in Rome

VINCENT SHEEAN

WE like to think of ourselves as a group that does not really fit into any given pattern. Yet there may be a sound criterion for us: when readers and listeners alike reach the point where they feel that they cannot pass judgment on a given situation without knowing what a certain correspondent has to say about it, then said correspondent belongs to the topflight of our profession.

That is where Vincent Sheean belongs. Years before his *Personal History* made literary history, he had ventured deep into Morocco to report to us on *An American Among the Riffi*. Since then he has written novels and roamed the world reporting in depth in war and peace. He has given us a new understanding of great men like Gandhi and Nehru and of the forces at work in our times without ever neglecting the anecdote, the colorful touches that make a period or a local scene come to life. Let him introduce you to one of Rome's favorite characters:

ALFREDO was a man known to every foreign correspondent from the United States who worked in Rome between the two world wars. Indeed, most tourists included his little restaurant on their schedules along with the Vatican Museum and Michelangelo's sculpture of Moses. The widest American public came to know Alfredo first in the novel *Babbitt*, by Sinclair Lewis, in which the upper crust of

Zenith, a midwestern city, graded their own social standing by whether or not they knew Alfredo and his *fettuccine*.

Alfredo himself was a small man with miraculous mustaches waxed into impossible acuity. He spoke bad and ungrammatical Italian as fast as possible so that you might miss the mistakes. He was enamored of Americans (especially rich ones), and film stars and royalty and prize fighters and bathing beauties of all nations. Mary Pickford and Douglas Fairbanks had visited his restaurant on their famous world tour in 1920 or thereabouts, and in gratitude for his wonderful *fettuccine* they had given him a golden spoon and fork for mixing this delectable dish. This golden spoon and fork, subsequently found to be of inferior alloy, were engraved with the names of Miss Pickford and Mr. Fairbanks and a testimonial of their respect for the *fettuccine*.

Not only on the first occasion when I had the *fettuccine,* which was in 1922 on the eve of Mussolini's March on Rome, but at all times thereafter, I was afforded the preparation of the *fettuccine* by Alfredo himself with the sacred fork and spoon bestowed upon him by Miss Pickford and Mr. Fairbanks. His intellect, never notable, had faltered somewhat under the strain of twenty years of fascism. One of his sons had espoused the cause of the Roman Empire and moved with it to Verona, where, no doubt, he perished with it and its Duce. Another son had vowed himself to other views and indeed started another restaurant with *fettuccine*. These political divergences often afflict the heart and soul of the philosopher. However, to the best of my knowledge and belief, nobody ever has impaired Alfredo's pre-eminence in the preparation of *fettuccine*. This incomparable achievement, which owes its perfection to the lavish use of butter, is a far more serious part of the history of Italy in the twentieth century than the conquest of Ethiopia.

The restaurant is in the Via della Scrofa, hard by the Piazza Colonna. On its walls are the inscribed photographs of many celebrated persons, who between 1920 and 1940, visited the Via della Scrofa to eat the *fettuccine*. Many of these have faded from human memory. Of all the commodities, celebrity is the most evanescent. And yet one can recall that rather humorous sourpuss the King of Spain (Alfonso XIII) whom everybody in Italy thought to have the evil eye, and our godlike Charlie Chaplin and the wondrous belegged Mistinguett with her voice like a tonsillectomy. These were the eminent and the permanent. Amongst them were countless flowers and leaves and branches—the signed and certified publicity pictures of the great—whose pretty faces, or other members, have long since gone into that oblivion which awaits us all. And also the sawdust on the floor. It is the sawdust that lasts.

FETTUCCINE

½ pound of narrow egg noodles
2 quarts of rapidly boiling water
1 teaspoon of salt
1 tablespoon of olive oil
1 pound of unsalted butter
Freshly grated Parmesan cheese

Add salt and olive oil to the boiling water. (For some varieties of noodles you may need 3 quarts of water.) Add the noodles, a few at a time. Boil rapidly for about 7 minutes. Stir frequently to avoid sticking. Pour cooked noodles into a collander to drain. Rinse them in cold water.

Melt the butter in the pot in which the noodles were cooked. Put back the noodles. With two forks lift and turn the noodles over and over in the hot butter, adding grated Parmesan, a little at a time. Add 2 or 3 tablespoons of heavy cream, if desired. If you don't plan to serve the *fettuccine* in the pot in which they were cooked, make sure that your serving dish is very hot and that the *fettuccine* are piping hot when they reach the heated plate of the gourmet.

This will serve four hearty appetites.

Part V

ON THE NEWSBEAT IN WARTIME

Lunch with General de Gaulle during the Italian Campaign

RICHARD DE ROCHEMONT

LET Richard de Rochemont introduce you to General de Gaulle, not the tense wartime defender of the rights of France many remember, but General de Gaulle, the kind, relaxed host.

As a war correspondent who served in Africa and Italy Richard de Rochemont can give you a more intimate picture of the man who stands as the symbol of the new France. "Documentaries" are the specialty of our colleague, who gives them extra life and brilliance thanks to his thorough knowledge of backgrounds and trends acquired in years as a close observer of world affairs. He writes:

THE FRENCH, of course, deny that they have a proverb saying, "Never a good meal came out of a clean kitchen," particularly since their postwar cuisine has suffered as much as America's from oversanitation, overrationalization, taste-killing preservation procedures, and the use of plastics for wrapping, for utensils, and even, save the mark, for ingredients, but back in the summer of 1944,

when I was a war correspondent in Italy, the old adage
was still true.

It was a quiet time in the Italian campaign. Rome had
been liberated and the armies were besieging Siena in a
rather desultory fashion. This particular U.S. press camp,
a marvel of comfort in most respects, brilliantly run by
P.R.O.s of talent and imagination, lacked any semblance
of cooking. Bacon and dried eggs, Spam and potatoes,
tinned fruit and an over-all savor of chlorine, potassium
permanganate and Atabrine gave the press mess something
never to be forgotten.

In spite of all the sanitary precautions which the Fifth
Army took, a sadly high percentage of the effectives was
plagued with persistent and acute digestive upsets, owing,
one must suppose, to the lack of natural immunization to
the sprightly bacilli of Italy, more active than those em-
balmed in C rations and Cokes.

Liberating me from institutional food, one day there
came General Charles de Gaulle, who had finally been accepted by the Allies as the only possible chief of the French
forces and as such had come to visit General Mark Clark.
General de Gaulle had invited me to lunch in Algiers
earlier that year, and a very good lunch it was, too, though
not lavish by French standards. As I remember the Algiers
menu, we had clear soup, a bit of cold rockfish with
tarragon mayonnaise, and grilled lamb chops with small
dried African beans of the flageolet type. Salad, cheese and
fruit. Two kinds of Algerian wine were drunk, white and
red, neither very distinguished. The coffee I suspect came
from American stocks, since it was more lightly roasted
than the French like. Cognac was passed, but the General
did not take any. That was Algiers. Then I went on to Italy.

At General Mark Clark's Tuscany headquarters, there was
a slight buzz on the news of De Gaulle's arrival. Clark had
been a key figure in the plans for the invasion of North
Africa, but had never had any direct contact with the man

who had replaced Admiral Darlan (deceased) and General Giraud (shelved) in the master plan, but he proposed, he said, to "lay the cards on the table with him." Though several officers were excellent linguists, there was not much to be said other than the barest amenities. When we were all grouped, military and press, to meet the General, I was pleased to have him stride toward me, hand outstretched, saying, "Ah, here I see an old friend!"

General Clark whispered to an aide, who at once invited me to join the luncheon party in General Clark's mess. It was a great privilege to be there, and as a patriotic American, I prefer not to dwell on the menu. After all, we were at war, weren't we? And one of the proudest boasts of the day was that wherever the U. S. Army went, it brought its own provender, a poor thing, but our own. No G.I. would ever lack for those American symbol-dishes: ice cream and Cokes . . . chocolate bars and, on holidays, turkey with all the trimmings, canned, but much as Mom might have served it if Mom were a mess sergeant.

With General Clark we had steak, possibly cut from the flank of an Alaskan mammoth, frozen for centuries, but cooked to a crisp, with side dishes no worse than those to be found at some of our big eateries along the roads of America today . . . and apple pie à la mode, as I recall.

As a perfect guest, General de Gaulle was amiable, conversational and uncritical. In the few times it has been my privilege to see the General at ease, it has always been when he was with military folk. Like President Eisenhower, he feels most comfortable among those with whom he spent his youth and early manhood, those whom he can trust as having essentially the same values as his own.

When General Clark's luncheon broke up, General de Gaulle said good-by all round. When he came to me, I asked, perhaps a bit maliciously, if he had lunched well.

He replied that he had, indeed. Then, with a slight smile, he asked if I had visited the French Corps, then headquartered at Castel del Piano. I answered no, but that I would be happy to do so at his convenience.

Two days later I arrived, knapsack and raincoat, at the press camp of the French Corps, official guest of General de Montsabert, who bore an uncanny resemblance to the white-mustached little symbol of *Esquire* magazine. Montsabert commanded a free-wheeling division of Moroccans, Senegalese and French colonials who smashed ten-wheel trucks up and down the mountain roads of Italy with complete insouciance and traveled with their own "B.A.C.," two truckloads of veiled beauties who were euphemistically referred to as "the *goumiers'* WACs." The division also did battle, and most fiercely.

Montsabert's personal jeep was souped up to do ninety on the flat, and his driver was a former Moroccan roadracer. No correspondent's jeep ever kept up with him. In charge of the French press camp was Major (eventually Colonel) Lindsay Watson, who, in spite of his name, was French. Watson was reputed to be a godchild of Winston Churchill, and above all he was a *bon vivant* and a man of the world.

The French Corps press camp had no Cokes, no screens, and no Atabrine . . . and no dysentery. Correspondents each had the attentions of an Arab batman, who started the day off with a cup of tea, with or without mint, delivered to the tent. On good days there were *croissants;* on bad days, just bread.

Of the press camp enlisted detail, the majority were assigned to the job of bartering and requisitioning, or, as they liked to call it, "liberating." All things, animate and inanimate, which could bear liberation and help the morale of the liberators and the correspondents accompanying them (*Time* might have called them "the hungriest historians of our times"), came under their purview.

At close of day, when the tired correspondents returned from their duties at the front (with, if lucky, a swim in some not too polluted stream behind the lines), the forces of liberation would already have rounded up a few sheep, a pig or two, perhaps some chickens, and a few liters of wine or spirits. The French Army contributed a certain basic ration, which was astutely traded off with the Italians for artichokes, beans, salad, and at times fruit. No fish was to be had in that region, but the stocks of olive oil were not yet depleted.

Once in a while, "Watson's Raiders" would come upon the cellar of some rich Italian noble or bourgeois, obviously a Fascist and a collaborator, and would turn up some surprising items, such as tins of *foie gras*, and white Italian truffles, French or German wines, and even prewar scotch to be set aside for visiting Britishers or Americans. *Apéritifs* such as Cinzano and Martini vermouth turned up regularly, and once in a while a bit of pernod, but Watson properly disdained Italian gin and imitation whisky as undrinkable and instructed his men to leave them behind.

In all the French press camp there was not a trace of colitis, dysentery, or even tummyache, unless it had been brought in from the outside. The food ranged from the cuisine of the old Foyot's to that of the Djema el F'na, but it was always varied, interesting, and presumably teeming with bacilli of every friendly and some enemy nations. We lived like fighting cocks, growing a bit too fat to fight.

Most of my meals were taken at the press camp, of course, but General de Gaulle (who apparently never forgets anything in spite of the fact that he continues to learn new things, even at an advanced age) summoned me to lunch at the French headquarters. Borrowing a kerchief, since I had no necktie (travel agents never tell you everything), I found myself one noon seated with a brochette of French generals including Juin, de Montsabert, Larminat, etc., and one American brigadier general assigned to liaison.

Our menu was simple. *Hors d'oeuvres du pays*, Italian

sausage and raw vegetables, augmented by some sardines from the ration. Then an excellent *couscous,* perhaps not as classic as a North African Escoffier would have wanted, but light, fluffy and well spiced. Salad followed, with Italian cheese. Then a tart, a bit short of fruit, perhaps, but long on shortening, flaky and delicious. Coffee, black and strong enough for warriors, and a slug of good cognac for our digestion.

De Gaulle was at his best, for although some of the generals round him were newly rallied to his cause, all were known to him as classmates or comrades in arms of prewar days. With them, he was relaxed, cheerful, almost gay, if one can imagine a gay wartime De Gaulle. At that time (the date was June 29, 1944) he knew that victory was in sight, and that his faith and foresight were vindicated.

As the lunch broke up, and my turn came to say good-by, the General smiled and said, "Well, Rochemont, one doesn't lunch badly here, either, *n'est-ce pas?*"

Notes from the Editor and Cooking Experts

If anybody should feel a righteous glow when reading Richard de Rochemont's statement that ". . . wherever the U. S. Army went, it brought its own provender, a poor thing, but our own," may this war correspondent assure one and all that in time a good number of our mess sergeants learned the art of swapping army rations for fresh local produce—not to mention other objects that seemed worth "liberating." A number of higher-echelon officers who would go hunting for deer and wild boar in forests where the battle raged enjoyed great popularity when they shared their game with camp posts and a number of press camps. At times venturesome spirits got into trouble, as did one little band of G.I.s in a small Belgian village. They'd been impressed by the size and number of swans in the local pond, and decided that roast swan would be a pleasant change. What happened to some of those swans in the dark of night is not hard to imagine—but the birds proved so tough and the villagers so indignant and word about this campfire cooking fiasco spread so quickly by the G.I. grapevine that the swan population survived the war in good shape.

As to *couscous*, there are about as many versions of this national dish of the Arabs as there are Arab tribes; Algerians generally use millet as base for this dish, but the Moroccan version made with semolina enjoys wider renown. To get this semolina light and fluffy is a test of artistry and patience. The following is the recipe for a festive *couscous* of which our Arab friends have every reason to be proud. The amounts cited are for a party of eight.

FESTIVE COUSCOUS

For the semolina base take:

1 pound of semolina
2 teaspoons of salt
3 cups of water
¼ cup of butter

While some advocates of short cuts pour boiling water over the semolina as a starter, most chefs hold that you get a lighter produce by using cold water. They spread the semolina in a wide basin, moisten it with a little of the cold water, into which they have put the salt, then mix it gently by hand to fluff it, continuing to add the water until each grain seems saturated and swells. Pour off the driblets of water that may be left; then put the semolina in the top of a steamer to cook above the meat and vegetable mixture. After it has become warm during the cooking stir in the butter. Stir the semolina three times with a fork during the cooking.

MEAT AND VEGETABLES FOR THE
COUSCOUS:

1 3-pound chicken
3 pounds of lamb shoulder
3 little squashes or eight chunks of pumpkin cut in 2-inch squares
3 tomatoes
8 medium-sized onions, cut in slices
8 young turnips
3 artichoke bottoms or Jerusalem artichokes
1 cup of fresh broad beans or fresh Lima beans
3 small hot peppers
2 small sweet peppers
4 ounces of chick-peas that were soaked and are half cooked
8 small carrots cut in two, lengthwise
2 cloves of garlic
4 ounces of cardon—if you can get it
1 tablespoon of salt
2 cloves
¼ teaspoon of cinnamon
1 teaspoon of caraway seed
1 teaspoon of red Spanish pepper
Optional: 1 small cabbage cut into 4 pieces

Cut the chicken into small chunks with the bones and cut the lamb shoulder into 1-inch cubes. Season lightly with salt and pepper and brown this meat very quickly in hot oil or chicken fat.

Place in the bottom pan of a steamer with the squash or pumpkin, tomatoes, onions, turnips, artichoke bottoms, broad beans, hot peppers, sweet peppers, chick-peas, carrots, garlic, cardon, salt and spices. Pour over a little less than 4 quarts of water. Place your soaked *couscous* in the top of the steamer, making sure that the liquid does not touch it. Cover and cook on a slow fire for 2 hours. When done, make sure that the semolina and the meat mixture are properly salted.

Pour off some of the broth in which the meat and vegetables have cooked to serve separately as extra sauce, to which you may add some cayenne pepper if you like highly spiced food. Ladle the meat into a wide serving dish, arrange the vegetables on it in a pleasing symmetrical pattern and surround with a ring of the semolina scooped out with a tablespoon to form balls.

The preceding *couscous* might be described as a Europeanized version. We are grateful to Miss Halima Embarek Anegay, Cultural Attaché of the Moroccan Embassy in Washington for her recipe for an:

AUTHENTIC MOROCCAN COUSCOUS

for a party of six to eight. Take 2 pounds of fine-grained semolina. Dampen it with slightly salted water until it is sticky. Place in the upper half of a steamer and steam for 30 minutes without cover. Then sprinkle again with salted water and work with buttered hand until the grains are moist and well separated. Set aside.

While the semolina has been steaming prepare the following items:

    4 pounds of lamb cut in cubes
    6 tablespoons of cooking oil
    Salt and pepper to taste
    1 cup of chopped coriander, or 2 tablespoons of powdered coriander
    1 cup of chopped parsley
    3 pounds of carrots, scraped and quartered
    3 pounds of turnips, scraped and quartered
    3 large onions, finely chopped
    3 pounds of tomatoes, scalded and peeled or 1 No. 2 can
    2 pounds of zucchini squash, scraped and quartered
    6 green peppers, seeded and cut in strips
    1 pound of chick-peas, soaked overnight
    2 quarts of water

Place the oil in the bottom part of a large double boiler. Sauté the onions, parsley, coriander and spices for 5 minutes. Add the meat and brown slightly. Add the water.

Place the buttered *couscous* in the top steamer over the meat and cook over a steady flame for about 90 minutes. Remove the *couscous* and work again with salted water and butter. Place the carrots, green peppers and turnips with the meat, add more water if necessary and cook 20 minutes. Then add the tomatoes and zucchini and return the *couscous* to the top steamer. Cook for another 20 minutes.

Put the *couscous* in a large serving dish, arrange meat and vegetables in center and pour the broth over all.

Since the Moroccans are justly proud of their sweets, Miss Anegay has also given us the recipe for a popular cooky that goes under the name of:

KAAB GHAZAL

which naturally may be made in smaller quantities than she listed, though she adds that these pastries keep well. They call for:

> 2 pounds of almonds
> 2 pounds of sugar
> 2 tablespoons of cinnamon
> A little rose water.

Blanch and grind the almonds. Mix them with the sugar and cinnamon and grind again. Add rosewater and mold into small crescents of about 3-inch lengths by hand.

Then prepare a dough with:

> 2 pounds of flour
> 1 tablespoon of melted butter
> 1 egg yolk

Mix all well together and roll out very thinly. Cover each crescent with dough and bake in a medium oven for 10 to 15 minutes.

If you want an amusing North African salad to follow the *couscous*, you might try:

MUNKACZINA

Peel 2 oranges and slice very thin
2 medium onions, sliced very thin
4 ounces of black, stoned olives
2 tablespoons of oil
Salt, pepper

Whisk the oil, salt and pepper together and pour over the oranges, onions and olives.

And if you want a Tunisian equivalent of a British savoury, there is:

THETCHOUKA

18 fillets of anchovy
½ teaspoon of ground nutmeg
1½ teaspoons of minced mint leaves
Toast fingers

Scrape the fillets of anchovy to remove all salt and oil; mix the mint and nutmeg and roll the anchovies in this mixture before placing on small, narrow slices of toast.

The Admiral Was Grateful

ROGER HAWTHORNE

IF THE time ever comes when Antarctica is listed as an extra continent, Roger Hawthorne may well claim to know all six continents of our world. As one who served on the U. S. Antarctic Expeditions, he wrote a book about *The Exploratory Flights of Admiral Byrd 1939–1942.* He covered the Coronation in London for the New Bedford *Standard-Times;* he covered the Washington beat for the Washington *Times-Herald* and the Associated Press and he was stationed in New Zealand for six years. Thus he was well qualified to utter the "well-chosen words" expected at a friendship banquet given by Chile to honor Admiral Byrd. He remembers the occasion well:

THERE ARE many different types of embarrassment but I suffered one of the worst while returning from Little America with Admiral Richard E. Byrd in 1940. The Admiral was being wined and dined by the Chilean Navy at a very formal dinner in Punta Arenas on the Strait of Magellan. As P.R.O., I was sitting below the salt. Because I had a bit of Spanish the Admiral tipped me off that when it came time for afterdinner toasts I was to do the proper thing when he signaled from the head of the table.

It had been a good dinner, with much red, white wine and liqueurs. The hour was late, the ladies were lovely, the food had been delicious and everybody was mellow when I got the Admiral's nod.

The Admiral had loaned me a castoff dinner jacket for the occasion to replace my Antarctic rig. It was tight but adequate make-do, and as I rose, glass in hand, all was right with the world. Curiously enough the magnificent floral centerpiece began to move slowly toward me. Several large plates crashed to the floor. To my further amazement, suddenly all the electric lights went out. Only as the guests left hurriedly did I discover that a button of my borrowed jacket had become ensnared with one of the hidden light cords attached to the centerpiece and the entire electrical system. On our way back to the ship the Admiral quieted my shaken ego by saying: "That was the quickest way to end a dinner that I ever saw. Thanks!"

The dish I remember is:

ARROZ VALENCIA

a cousin of the famous Spanish *paiella*. For six you need:

1 3-pound chicken
1 pound of fresh shrimp, cooked
½ pound of ham, cut in strips
½ cup of olive oil
1 large onion, finely chopped
2 green peppers, chopped
5 tomatoes or a can of tomatoes
A few canned artichoke bottoms or cubes of Jerusalem artichokes
4 fair-sized garlic toes
1 cup of chicken broth
2 bay leaves
1½ cups of uncooked rice
½ small can (3 oz.) of pimentos or the equivalent in fresh pimentos
Tiny twig of saffron

Bone the chicken; cut the chicken meat in cubes and use the bones either to make a fresh cup of chicken broth or to improve the canned chicken broth you plan to use. Pass the garlic through a press and give it a good chance to flavor the chicken broth.

Heat the olive oil and sauté the onions and green peppers until they are tender. Brown the chicken cubes and the ham in onion-peppers mixture. When they are golden, add the cooked shrimp, the tomatoes, the pimentos and, if you have them, the artichokes. If you intend to use Jerusalem artichoke cubes hold them back. Transfer the chicken, shrimps, tomatoes and sauce into an ovenproof dish that has a well-closing lid. Pour in the chicken broth, add the bay leaves, saffron, salt and pepper; cover and bake very slowly. When the chicken is almost tender and needs only a few more minutes add the artichoke chunks, together with the rice boiled *al dente*. Make sure that you fork it in lightly to avoid packing or crushing it.

A Lunch for a Man's Freedom

SIGRID SCHULTZ

THE TIME had come to serve the most filling meal we could devise—despite wartime shortages—to a high-ranking Nazi. "We" in this case stands for a small, close-knit group of correspondents on duty in Germany in 1940. The Germans had just invaded the Netherlands; in Berlin they had arrested most Dutch correspondents including a member of our group who shared some of our most reliable news sources. By chance we found out that a few fanatical Nazis in the Propaganda Ministry and the Foreign Office were working with the Gestapo to try to stage a big trial against him because he was one of the best-informed correspondents. With some consummate lying and a bit of perjury, the Nazis hoped they could brand him as a spy. If the Gestapo went all out, it might discover the identity of a number of Germans who had honored us with their confidence. This would mean desperate trouble for them, and the little officials who considered us most undesirable characters would certainly try to rope us in, in the course of the operation.

To queer the game of the lying fanatics we had to

have a chance to present our evidence against them, discreetly, effectively to a more intelligent higher-up. The only way to do it was in the course of a long, leisurely, thoroughly satisfying lunch in the presence of a few friends from the American Embassy. Our target was a roly-poly Rhinelander, who loved his food and was smart enough to know that the underlings were acting out of personal spite. Furthermore, loving his food, he was having a thin time since rations were skimpy in those days—even in the fanciest restaurants. The Germans had not yet gained control of the supplies of Holland, Belgium, occupied France that were to fill the larders of the Nazi bosses later.

We organized a kind of minor international plot to corner enough edibles for a truly filling lunch. We succeeded.

Luckily the Foreign Press Association had put over a deal with the Nazis when they started rationing that allowed us to receive a weekly small package of eggs, butter, bacon, cheese from Denmark, if it were paid for by our families or offices in our homelands. I'd hoarded part of this wealth for an emergency and my maid did some fancy bartering, basking in the happy conviction that we were going to all this trouble merely to please a high-ranking Nazi. Had she known that our purpose was to trick the Gestapo, she would have balked.

Our roster of helpers included the American diplomat who gave us flour so that I could bake bread and a cake, which I did, toward dawn, after all news cables were filed. The Swiss parted with some extra good kirsch for a fondue to be made with Danish cheese; the Norwegian had a few tiny cans of spicy *gaffelbitter*, to go with the cocktails; the elegant wife of the Yugoslav diplomat gave us canned apricots and extra eggs; the Czech had a most welcome package of raisins and nuts for the cake. The Rumanian diplomat, who, like the other non-Americans, did not even come to the lunch, was the most generous of all, donating caviar that he had just brought from Bucharest as well as

part of a bottle of Napoleon brandy, since he deemed my
three-star variety not potent enough for this "save a soul
operation." My wine cellar was up to the requirements of
the day, since I had bought a good deal of wine from Bella
Fromm, who was to write *Blood and Banquets* after she
reached America. She had gone into the wine business when
she lost her job as a reporter because she was Jewish. I
had also bought some wine from a relative of Einstein's
secretary, who had found an emergency income as a dealer
in wine.

At the luncheon our diplomats set the tone, giving the
correspondents ample opportunity to present their case.
The Rhinelander was bent on appearing as the jovial, well-
informed man, ready to belittle "regrettable errors of over-
zealous underlings." The fencing never stopped but it did
not reduce anybody's appetite or thirst.

What did we serve? With the pre-lunch drinks we had
the Norwegian bites and stuffed, baked mushrooms. Then
came:

Caviar, on small, flat "Berlin" potato pancakes
Scotch barley soup à la Printanière (which was green)
Ham à l'Arlésienne, with riced, browned potatoes and almonds—a
   red and brown dish
Green salad
Zabaglione on whole canned apricots and "Daily Telegraph" cake
Swiss fondue
Coffee and liqueurs

I have rarely seen more surprised faces than when a fat
little wooden board, surmounted by a hot brick was placed
before each guest. On that brick went a ramekin of the
Swiss fondue, which kept bubbling to the last bite. Fondue,
I felt, was to give this meal the required all-time caloric
high, but this being a kind of "daggers drawn" lunch, it
could not be served in the traditional communal dish. The
bricks solved that problem and gave the men a good chance

to wag their heads, which they find fully as enjoyable as women do.

After most guests left, a thoroughly sated Rhinelander, Wallace R. Deuel of the Chicago *Daily News* and I sat quietly by my fireplace enjoying the Napoleon brandy. We wanted to make sure that our guest had gotten the point. He had. His reaction showed that the little fellows had started the Gestapo machinery. The evidence we had presented during the lunch had convinced him that we knew of their intrigues and that a staged trial would do the Nazis more harm than good.

We had chosen our target well. The next day our Dutch colleague was released from prison—and the Nazi underlings found it necessary to be polite to us—for a while at least.

What more could one ask of a meal?

We never told our Dutch friend about this session. He had enough trouble with his country being invaded. He survived to become a high official at the court of the Queen of the Netherlands. Our Rhinelander, being smart, stopped working for the Nazis after Hitler declared war on America. Today he is a wealthy businessman. The little officials who had plotted against us and our friend out of Nazi fanaticism have influential jobs in West Germany, and assure one and all that they never were Nazis. But they run fast when they see any of the correspondents who knew them in the days when they were in cahoots with the Gestapo.

Some of the dishes I mentioned could well grace American menus, because they are good as well as practical. Take, for instance:

BAKED MUSHROOMS

Choose mushroom caps that are just big enough to provide one good bite. The day before you plan to serve them, stuff them with *beurre d'ail*, the same garlic butter you use for snails. Keeping them in the refrigerator overnight gives the various tastes a chance to blend.

For the final preparation toast one side of little squares of bread that are to serve as base for the mushrooms. Place them on a baking sheet or in a fireproof glass dish, top them with a mushroom cap, with the broad side up so that the butter does not run out too much, sprinkle a few breadcrumbs on top. Slip into an oven that has been heated to 350°. Bake for about 15 minutes, turn on the broiler to brown them just a little, serve very hot.

Instead of garlic butter you can fill the caps with a mixture of mushroom stems, diced ham and minced parsley and possibly some chopped, browned walnuts.

POTATO PANCAKES WITH CAVIAR

Frankly I prefer good caviar on a little bed of beefsteak tartare, made of carefully grated beef, a little onion pulp, paprika, capers and salt. But there was no hope of getting the right kind of beef and, besides, this was to be a "filling" lunch.

For the plain potato pancake, grate big, healthy potatoes into a sieve that rests in a pan filled with water. Toward the end of this operation you will, when you lift up the sieve, see that a white sediment of potato starch has settled at the bottom of the pan. After you pour off the water make sure that the grated potatoes are pretty dry and add the potato starch. Salt this mixture, drop it by spoonfuls into a frying pan filled with sizzling butter or oil or lard or shortening, depending on which frying medium you prefer. Flatten the mixture immediately, baking on both sides.

When the pancakes are crisp pile on your caviar, possibly a little onion pulp, squirt a little lemon juice on it, or serve with a slice of lemon.

Some cooks like to add eggs to their potato pancakes on the theory that it makes them lighter. It does, specially if you beat the egg white. But the plain potato pancake has a texture of its own, a chewiness that is a good contrast to the soft caviar. You can also serve the pancakes as dessert, with applesauce, quince jelly or cranberry sauce.

SCOTCH BARLEY SOUP À LA PRINTANIÈRE

If you are for short cuts, take a cupful of barley, wash it well, drop it into 2 quarts of salted boiling water to which you have added 1 tablespoon of butter. Cook until soft; add 2 quarts of beef broth, or chicken broth or mutton broth, and extra bouillon cubes, salt and pass through a sieve. Sprinkle with some chopped parsley before serving.

That is the routine soup, which can be quite good if your broth is satisfactory. A better result, I believe, is achieved if you use:

2 cups of washed barley
6 quarts of cold water
Soup beef bones with meat on them
Small lamb bone (it should be big enough to give some strength, but not big enough to impart too much of its particular flavor.)
2 tablespoons of cut-up celery root
2 stalks of celery
Parsley root
2 carrots
2 onions stuck with 2 cloves
1 leek
1 bay leaf
Peppercorns
A few juniper berries
Handful of spinach
1 tablespoon of parsley
2 tablespoons of sorrel

Cook all this except the minced parsley, half of the spinach and the sorrel. Cook slowly for 3 hours. Pass through a sieve. The soup should be of a smooth, thickish consistency. If it is too thick add some clear bouillon. If it seems too thin mash in some of the barley pulp. This will serve eight.

You may feel that this sounds like putting everything in except the kitchen sink, but famous chefs go even further. Savarin, for instance, recommends the addition of a little piece of milt, to obtain a soup that really tastes of beef. Chefs at Vienna's famous Sacher urged their apprentices to use a piece of liver instead. A friend of mine who knew Boulestin claims that he usually smuggled a small piece of beef kidney into the heartier-tasting soups. I have tried all three and they are helpful, provided you show restraint. That is where your artistry comes in.

To achieve the "à la Printanière" effect, cut up spinach leaves and sorrel leaves (less their ribs), add a little chopped chervil and cook this in butter, adding a little broth until you have a soft green mash which you pass into the soup through a sieve; this is to provide the needed green springtime color.

A soup of a similar consistency but with a slightly different taste can be made by using what the French call *Blè vert* and the Germans call *Gruenkern* instead of barley. These are kernels of grain, picked while still green and dried. Use them instead of barley, saving a few spoonfuls of the cooked grain to add to the soup you have passed through a sieve. It thickens it a little and gives everyone a chance to do some guessing at this strange filler.

HAM À L'ARLÉSIENNE

The great advantage of this dish—besides being delicious—is that a little meat will go a long way.

Take thin slices of cooked ham. Spread them at the bottom of a big fireproof platter that has been rubbed with garlic and buttered or oiled. There really should be only one layer of ham at the bottom of the dish. Cover this ham with your favorite tomato sauce that has been well spiced and let stand a while, possibly overnight to allow the flavors to mix. When getting your meal ready surround the meat with a ring of riced cooked potatoes, into which you stick a few slivers of almonds. These potatoes should be put in lightly—not packed. Cover the whole with a light snow of freshly ground Parmesan, dot with butter, brighten with a little Hungarian paprika, slip into the oven, bake until really warm, then turn on the broiler to brown a little.

Serve an extra dish of tomato sauce with this.

If you are short of enough big platters to bake the ham slices in single layers, you can let the pieces overlap, making sure that each piece has its full quota of sauce.

The potato wreath around the ham may displease purists who know that it does not really belong to a dish from southern France. They are right, but slightly browned, with the few slivers of almond standing up in them, the riced potatoes are a pleasant accompaniment. So is rice.

TOMATO SAUCE, PROVENCE STYLE

Naturally the tomato sauce should be as close to the Provence version as possible. The cook on the Riviera will cut ripe tomatoes in four or more pieces, place them on a bed of finely cut onions that have been half cooked in olive oil with a garlic toe. To make sure that the sauce is not too tart, she cooks some grated carrots with it—just enough to mask the tartness of the tomato. She adds a few leaves of basil, chervil, bay leaf, thyme before pouring in enough water to prevent the mixture from sticking while it simmers gently. Savarin was in favor of pounding this purée in a mortar until it was smooth, finally slipping it into a pan and mixing it with some fresh butter. A more modern way is to put it into the blender with a little butter, after removing the bay leaf, and give it a quick turn to smooth the sauce.

In a separate pan, cook some finely cut green peppers until they are almost soft and add a few spoonfuls to the tomato sauce. Add salt and freshly ground pepper. The juice in which the peppers were cooked may be added to the sauce in case it seems too thick. It should be relatively thin to get into the pores of the meat and to remain light and creamy after the dish has been baked.

Some chefs add a little *roux* sauce to the cooked tomatoes, but the flour in it deadens the flavor that should remind one of the sunny shores of the Mediterranean.

Since most men feel cheated without a dessert—though they'll rarely admit it—I used my last eggs to make a Zabaglione to be served in small sherbet glasses, with a canned apricot and some crushed macaroon at the bottom. Zabaglione has the advantage of keeping nicely overnight in the refrigerator and requiring no last-minute fuss.

ZABAGLIONE

Put six egg yolks in a pan with 6 tablespoons of finely powdered sugar. Start whipping and gradually add a cup of white wine, or preferably marsala. Place above a pan in which water is boiling gently, and continue beating until the mixture is fluffy and set. If you have used white wine, you can flavor with rum, or whatever liqueur you prefer, before pouring into small glasses or a serving dish. The canned apricot or peach or pear that may have been soaked in the same liqueur with which you have flavored the Zabaglione adds to the festive quality of this dessert.

Being very light it needs the company of a macaroon, or some fancy cooky, or a slightly dry piece of cake such as:

THE "DAILY TELEGRAPH" CAKE

This is not its original name. But sometime in the twenties the London *Daily Telegraph,* which had an excellent food editor, published this recipe. I tried it and I have found it truly worth while. The cake keeps for several weeks without getting too dry, which is a great help when yours is the kind of household where guests drop in unexpectedly.

    2 cups of flour
    Pinch of salt
    2 teaspoons of double-acting baking powder
    1 cup of butter or shortening
    1 cup of sugar
    1 cup of seeded muscat raisins
    ½ cup of chopped walnuts and a few nice halves
    ½ cup of candied fruit
    2 eggs
    1 tablespoon of rum, water or sherry

Several hours before you plan to bake, or even the night before, separate and soak the seeded muscat raisins to give them a chance to puff up. Dry them well before using.

Chop part of the nuts, keeping back a few nice halves. Cut the butter or shortening into small pieces in a mixing bowl. Sift together the flour, salt and baking powder. Then sift it into the bowl with the fat and work with the tips of your fingers or with 2 knives until the mixture is like coarse sand. Add the sugar and stir lightly, preferably with a fork. Work in the nuts, the raisins, the candied fruit, stirring lightly after each addition to make sure that the newcomers are well coated and won't bunch together.

Beat the 2 eggs lightly with the water or rum. Pour into the bowl. It will seem insufficient at first, but if you stir swiftly with a fork, all parts will be moistened by the egg mixture. Again use the fork to drop the dough into 2 buttered bread pans to avoid packing too tightly. Decorate the tops with halved walnuts, walnut pieces, candied cherries or little strips of angelica.

Slip into an oven that has been heated to 350° and bake for 1 hour. Test with a skewer to make sure that the middle is really done.

The original recipe called for lining the cake pan with buttered paper. This has its advantage when you plan to keep the cake for quite a while or want to send it away as a present. For everyday use one can pass up the paper operation.

FONDUE

No one can give better advice for making fondue than the Swiss cheese specialists. Most cheese stores have their booklets. For my taste most of their recipes call for a little too much flour. If the fondue is to be used as main dish, as the Swiss often do, you need, for six people:

1½ cups of firmly packed, shredded Swiss cheese
3½ teaspoons of flour
1 clove of garlic
3 cups of light dry white wine
Salt, pepper, nutmeg, paprika
9 tablespoons of kirsch or 6 tablespoons of cognac
Long loaf of French or Italian white bread

Dredge the shredded cheese in the flour. Rub the earthenware pan or chafing dish in which the mixture is to be cooked with the garlic until it seems to melt away. Pour in the wine and place over a low fire. Watch until air bubbles begin to rise to the surface. Stir with a fork, add handfuls of cheese, giving each handful a chance to melt into the wine before adding the next.

Keep stirring. When the mixture begins to bubble add a tiny bit of salt, grind a more generous dose of black pepper over it, give it a discreet dusting of paprika as color effect; you may or may not add the nutmeg. Then stir a little more, while adding the kirsch or cognac.

If yours is the kind of party where guests will enjoy sticking torn-off bread—not cut bread—onto the tines of their fork and dipping and twirling it in the cheese, one after the other, the communal dish can be fun—specially if those who lose their bread in the cheese while twirling have to pay a fine. For more formal parties fondue can be served in very hot ramekins.

Should the fondue start to act sluggish and become too thick, pour in some heated white wine that has been kept in readiness for this emergency, stirring to restore the right degree of "gooeyness."

The real cheese lovers will be on the lookout for the final crust that forms at the bottom of the bowl. It can be lifted out in a single piece and broken up among the various claimants.

Strong, hot coffee is a vital necessity after fondue—accompanied for the gourmet by a little glass of kirsch or cognac depending on which of the two was used by the chef. One last reminder: You may succeed with other cheeses, though Swiss or Gruyère or a mixture of Swiss and Gruyère are best, but the kirsch or the cognac must be good imports!

A Wedding near the Battle Line

PEGGY WILHELM

IF ANYBODY tries to tell you that the Army has no understanding
for young love, don't believe it! Men who had been in the grim
Battle of the Bulge and had thrown back the German attack were
still scanning the skies nervously in fear of V bombs in that icy-
cold January of 1945. Our armies still had to fight the battles of
the Roer, the Ruhr and the crossing of the Rhine but in Maastricht, in the press camp of the Ninth Army, officers, G.I.s, mess
sergeants and Dutch officials plotted together to stage a real wedding party for young Peggy Maslin of the Red Cross and John
Wilhelm, correspondent of the Chicago *Sun*.

Major Barney Oldfield (now Colonel), P.R.O. of the Ninth
Army Press Camp, who later was to shepherd the first contingent
of American correspondents into conquered Berlin, gave the bride
away. In his book *Never a Shot in Anger*, he remembers gleefully
how the Mayor of Maastricht, Mynheer van Kessenich, with
typical Dutch outspokenness, lectured the young couple on getting an early start on a family, boasting of his ten offspring—and
how the *Life* photographers "shot the whole wedding affair in
detail, including some twenty-five military men and war correspondents kissing the bride, a picture story which *Life* eventually
ran."

That the wedding party was a grand success you can see by

the way ex-war correspondents and "military men," who were at Maastricht reminisce about it at reunions, clustering around young Peggy as if she were their own daughter or little sister. Today John Wilhelm is director of McGraw-Hill *World News* and he has completed a first stint as president of the Overseas Press Club. He has detailed Peggy to describe the wedding party given under the auspices of the U. S. Army.

I T WAS in Maastricht, Holland, near the German border, just a short drive from the battle lines where the U. S. First and Ninth armies were pushing back Hitler's *Panzer* units after their almost successful push through Belgium in the Battle of the Bulge.

John Wilhelm was a war correspondent for the Chicago *Sun* and I, Peggy Maslin, was with an American Red Cross clubmobile unit driving a coffee and doughnut truck when we met in Verdun, in the summer of 1944. We became engaged in Spa, Belgium, where the First Army Press Corps was comfortably ensconced in the charming holiday town to which the prewar royalty of Europe used to flock to take the baths. And we planned to be married there, until that bitter Christmas Eve when the Germans strafed the town, drove the press corps back into Holland, and killed Jack Frankish of the United Press who was to be our best man.

Since both our families were very unavailable, the U. S. Army, in the personable and popular figure of Major Barney Oldfield (now Col. Oldfield of SAC), who was then press officer in Maastricht, assumed charge. Our bans were duly posted in the town square; the burgomaster, Baron Willem van Kessenich, donned all his badges of office for the first time since the Germans had invaded his town so long before; the village florist cut his precious white cyclamen plants for the bride's bouquet. After a frantic search enough coal to heat ancient St. John's Church turned up, and most of the townsfolk and all the press corps and Red Cross girls came out in the snowy cold for the event. *Life* magazine's Bill Vandivert and George Silk were on hand to photograph the affair.

The climax of the day was the wedding supper served in the main dining room of the Hotel "of the Greyhound and Black Eagle" where the Ninth Army Press Corps was living for the moment. The innkeepers, the Van Eggersholts, provided their best linens and china, hidden away during the German occupation, and their cut-glass goblets were filled time and again with prewar vintage wine, dug out from behind walls where it had been hidden from the Germans. Some may laugh at the menu, but the army mess sergeant had done his best with the supplies on hand: pork chops and applesauce, mashed potatoes and sauerkraut! No gourmet would rave about it but, to our Dutch guests who had been desperately short of food for years, it seemed lavish.

The final course proved spectacular. Our mess sergeant himself appeared bearing a bride's dream of a wedding cake, a three-tiered, white-iced beauty topped by a tiny bride and groom (where he found them remains a mystery to this day). The hotel chef, not to be outdone, provided a Dutch wedding cake, too beautiful to be cut, and almost too rich to eat. It was a Christmas tree of spice cake and fruits, covered with bright candies and macaroons, the whole edifice coated in a melted sugar glaze. In those days of near famine for our Dutch hosts, it was a monument of ingenuity and generosity.

SPICE WEDDING CAKE

Here is the recipe for which our Dutch chef must have used many substitutes in those days when potatoes and apples were the mainstay of the Dutch diet and such luxury items as appeared in the cake were practically unheard of:

1 pound of almonds
3 pounds of currants
1 pound of mixed sliced peel
3 pounds of raisins
2 cups of cognac brandy
4 cups of sifted flour
2 teaspoons of baking soda
2 teaspoons of cinnamon
1 teaspoon of cloves
1 teaspoon of nutmeg
1 pound of shortening
1½ cups of firmly packed brown sugar
16 eggs
3 drops of wintergreen
1 cup of molasses
1 cup of sour cream

Blanch and shred almonds, let stand in closed jar with fruit peel and brandy several days. Mix and sift flour, soda and spices. Cream shortening, add sugar, beat in one egg at a time, then wintergreen and molasses. Add flour mixture and sour cream, mixing well, then brandied nuts and fruits. Place in a greased mold, cover tightly with waxed paper and steam 2 hours. Bake in 250° oven 2 hours, uncovering last half hour. This will stay fresh indefinitely if stored in tightly closed container. For a cake such as ours, decorate with colored mints and small macaroon cookies, pour sugar glaze over all.

Saved by the "Savouries"

FRED B. BARTON

FRED B. BARTON of Akron, Ohio, author of *Let Yourself Go* and many magazine stories, started what you might call "save the reputation of savouries" movement among food-minded friends and colleagues! Here is his wartime meeting with a "savoury":

THE BRITISH—I know some of them, and love them—have their peculiarities. For instance, when you expect dessert you may come upon a device called a "savoury."

You spell it with that totally unnecessary "u."

Well, sir, late in 1943 I thumbed my way from Londonderry, North Ireland, to Reykjavik, Iceland with the R.A.F. My invitation was hearty enough; my friend Bob Brown, who was P.R.O. (press relations officer) for the United States Navy at Londonderry introduced me to a British admiral, a submariner just back from Malta, who headed the Royal Navy at that base. He must have taken a shine to me, for he sent his assistant over to see the Royal Air Force, in my behalf. You see, I wanted to get some stories about B-24s, the Liberators. And all the B-24s in that area were doing duty off Iceland.

So, without travel orders of any kind—and that annoyed the U. S. Army boys considerably—before long I was flown in a B-24 with a returning vacation crew from Londonderry. We made a stop in the Hebrides, and blew a tire. So we stayed all night. That suited me: I was getting acquainted with these R.A.F. lads and enjoying their company. And writing the first of a couple of pieces for *"Plane Talk."*

Lunch was terrible, and I wasn't getting enough to eat. Then came what the British called the savoury. The five R.A.F. men took a cautious nibble and pushed it aside. I tasted mine: macaroni and cheese, and cooked almost as well as at home. I ate six portions of it and felt wonderful. That day I blessed the British institution called a savoury.

Defenders of the "Savoury" Speak Up

Obviously the mess sergeant at Londonderry bestowed the title of "savoury" on macaroni and cheese when, plagued by wartime shortages, he was trying to find filling substitutes for his lads. Let one of our popular London hostesses, Mrs. DeWitt Mackenzie, whose husband was stationed in London for many years for the A.P., tell you about real savouries.

The traditional savoury is a small hot and generally spicy bite, that is supposed to surprise you and give you an extra lift right after the "sweet," which is the British equivalent of our dessert—and it is served before the fruit and nuts. Not so long ago many of the leading families had their own traditional savoury recipes and guarded their secret most jealously. Bits of game birds, fancy sauces, surprises from India and the far-flung colonies figured in them.

Coming after comparatively rich courses, the purpose of the spicy savoury is to clear the palate for the full enjoyment of the afterdinner drinks, the port aged in wood, the whiskies or brandies.

Because they pave the way for drinks, you might want to try some savouries as hors d'oeuvres or cocktail bites. There is, for instance:

SCOTCH WOODCOCK

For six to eight persons take:

Yolks of 2 eggs
½ cup of cream
3 teaspoons of anchovy paste
Toast, butter, cayenne

Cut the buttered toast into 2-inch squares, spread them with anchovy paste. Season the yolks with a little cayenne and salt. Beat them slightly and then beat them into the hot cream. Continue to stir over the fire until the mixture thickens and pour over the toast.

SAVOURIES OF FOIE GRAS

While we usually serve our goose liver cold, for a savoury it must be warm. Prepare your toast, butter it and cut slices of the goose liver in the same shape as your pieces of toast. Place the goose liver on a plate, which you put over a saucepan of boiling water. Cover with a lid or another plate, and keep the water boiling hard until your little slices are warm, but not too soft to transfer to the hot pieces of toast.

FISH ROE

Fish roe—from herring roe to cod roe and, in our country, shad roe—figures in many savouries.

For eight persons take:

10 ounces of roe
8 crusts
3 tablespoons of butter
½ teaspoon of minced shallot
½ teaspoon of minced chives
½ teaspoon of minced parsley
Pepper, cayenne
8 wedges of lemon
Optional: ¼ teaspoon of dry mustard

Wash and drain the roe. If it is smoked, soak it for a while if it seems hard. If it is fresh, cover it with boiling water to which you have added a little vinegar and simmer for about 10 minutes. Let cool and cut it into eight slices, which you fry in part of the butter. Fry the shallot, chives, parsley in butter, adding the mustard, if you plan to use any. Spread on the fried crusts, top with the slices of roe and a dab of butter. Pass under the broiler and serve, very hot, with a lemon wedge.

On a cold night some will enjoy:

MARROW CRUSTS

For eight take two fair-sized marrow bones. Remove the marrow carefully and soak it in lukewarm water for 1 hour. Shortly before serving time, cut the marrow into inch lengths, place in cold water, bring to a boil, pour off the water immediately. Spread on very hot buttered toast, sprinkle with a little minced parsley, lots of salt and a little black pepper. Pass under the broiler.

Anchovies do as well in savouries as in cocktail bites. If you belong to the group that does not relish vast amounts of salt, let your anchovies spend a night in lemon juice and follow it up with a bath of your best olive oil. For the real southern French savoury:

ANCHOÏADE

make a cream of anchovies by pounding them in a mortar with a little olive oil and vinegar. Spread this cream on slices of a firm-textured white bread. Cover with slices of hard-boiled eggs and over the eggs spread a kind of veil of very thinly sliced onion. Scatter a few dabs of butter, a little black pepper over the whole and brown quickly under the broiler.

If you are lucky enough to find very big anchovies, you can enjoy:

FRIED ANCHOVIES WITH ONION

Fillet the anchovies. Soak them in milk for several hours. Roll them in flour. Then roll them in a mixture of wine vinegar and water. Give them a final coat of flour. In the meantime fry a garlic toe in olive oil and when the oil is really hot, fry the anchovies in it until they are golden brown. Add a little flour to the olive oil in the pan to make a thinnish sauce which you pour over the fish that you serve with a crusty roll, and if it fits into your menu, two rounds of raw onion.

Another defender of savouries, Mrs. Webb Miller, whose husband was one of the stars of the U.P., suggests that you might try:

MALAKOFFS

which require:

1 cup of flour	Rose paprika
¼ cup of warm water	1 tablespoon of olive oil
3 eggs	Pinch of salt
2 tablespoons of butter	8 slices of Swiss cheese
	(⅛-inch thickness)

Mix the flour, salt, water, olive oil to a smooth paste with a wooden spoon. Beat the 3 eggs to a good foam and fold into the paste. Coat the slices of cheese with this batter and fry them in the melted butter until they are brown. Sprinkle with a little paprika and serve immediately.

Who Had the Best Laugh?

T HERE is one point on which lovers of food, throughout the world, philosophers and doctors agree unanimously: laughter is by far the best accompaniment to a memorable meal, though it is not always the kind the host expects!

Take, for instance, the experience of WALLACE R. DEUEL, author of *People under Hitler*, and EDWARD BEATTIE, author of *Freely to Pass* who were on duty in Germany during the Nazi regime, the one serving the Chicago *Daily News*, the other the United Press. They were invited to a party by Hitler's chief of the Labor Front, Robert Ley; and ever since the Duke and Duchess of Windsor had come to Germany as his guests, Ley liked to think that it was up to him to introduce a new uppercrust social style for his "master race."

He was somewhat handicapped in his attempts at elegance because it was new to him, because he drank heavily and because he had a speech defect that made him spit in all directions and sprinkle whoever was foolish enough to come close to him. In his search for refinement, he learned that Americans love oyster cocktails. He knew only too well about cocktails. And oysters were expensive in Germany, which suited him fine.

To surprise his two American guests, the sputtering Ley

cornered them, talking his head off while they tried to keep a little further away to avoid the drenching. At his signal a bartender came over bearing three glasses filled with a grayish mixture.

"This is in your honor," beamed Dr. Ley; they dutifully took the glasses offered them; the host grabbed his own, said *Prosit* and the equivalent of "down the hatch," and downed the mixture. The boys had to follow his example. With Ley sputtering and spitting, leaning over close to see how they enjoyed the treat, they gulped and laboriously swallowed the contents of the glasses, filled with nothing but the biggest, fattest oysters that could be found on the Berlin market—and the Danes sell some fancy big ones to their Berlin clients!

That was the food experience these two correspondents remember as a perfect example of "international misunderstanding" in the gastronomic field.

Coffee Not Understood

GEORGE SELDES, correspondent and author of many a book and of the spectacular new collection of *The Great Quotations*, tells of a linguistic misunderstanding that afforded quiet fun to correspondents of World War I. He remembers how:

IN THE last American campaign in 1918, General Pershing moved his press section (G-2-D, A.E.F.) to Bar-le-Duc, where, for the first time, we joined an officers' mess with the French. The menu had previously been printed only in French, and for some unknown reason every day for years the printed menu bore in ink (alongside the words "Menu 2 fr. 50") the words, *Café, non compris, 25 centimes.*

When the American war correspondents arrived, the French printed the menu in both languages. Alongside the English version they wrote in ink: "Coffee, not understood, 25 centimes extra." How true, how true!

One war later young Americans in uniform, on duty in England, enjoyed the blessed relief of a good laugh at the expense of a general who did not know mess-hall "protocol."

A Practical Joke on General Eisenhower

ROBERT KAYE was in London at the time working for our secret radio station that beamed news to Europe in six languages. Its poetic sounding name was ABSIE, which stands for American Broadcasting Station in Europe. Robert Kaye writes:

IN LONDON, in 1944, the most mouth-watering place anyone could eat in was not one of the little Greek restaurants in Soho. It wasn't the Savoy or Claridge's. It was the giant basement ballroom of the Hyde Park Hotel that had been turned into a huge officers' mess where meals were served cafeteria-style. Not only was the food extraordinarily good by wartime standards (and I wish I could lunch in a place like it in midtown Manhattan, today), but the efficiency and good fellowship contributed to make luncheons at this mess an outstanding experience.

Guests walked along what seemed like a usual cafeteria-style counter. From behind mountainous piles of delicious food attendants offered visitors everything—steaks, chops, roast or fried chicken, vegetables such as one never saw elsewhere in England, condiments, beverages, and superb desserts. At each steaming table guests were urged to accept a generous helping. One could go through the entire line and load enough food for a platoon. The tariff was still the British wartime minimum for a meal, five shillings.

There was only one hitch. It was considered exceedingly bad form to accept more food than one could eat. And if a guest overestimated his appetite or capacity there was no way out but to finish everything on his tray.

Occasionally, in that summer of 1944, I took the short walk from my flat in Grosvenor Square and arrived at the Hyde Park mess in time for lunch. One day there was quite a flurry. Word had gone out that General Eisenhower was coming—his first visit to this mess.

I entered the queue directly behind his party and, because of another tradition of this mess, I sat at a table two feet away. It was mandatory not to roam at will about this vast cavern in order to select a table of one's choice, but to fill tables on the periphery of the group of diners already seated. Thus, I was a witness to what was probably one of the best practical jokes of the war. The officers who had brought General Eisenhower to the mess had apparently neglected to inform him that etiquette demanded he consume everything on his tray. This situation was complicated by the fact that all the attendants at the steam tables insisted upon piling high the plate of their distinguished diner. Thus, General Eisenhower came to his table with several pounds of food. When he had had his fill he complimented his fellow officers on the excellence of the mess and remarked that he had already eaten much too much. Thereupon, he was told that it would be in very bad taste not to finish his tray.

That is how I saw General Eisenhower consume what was probably a week's ration at one luncheon.

ROBERT I. QUEEN saw army cooking from a lower-echelon angle. He relishes the memory of "Soapy Soup":

WHILE in training as a private in the United States Army at Camp Croft, S.C., I found that the first sergeant had posted me to kitchen police duty.

During the afternoon, the various men started playing catch with a piece of G.I. soap. A wild throw and the soap landed in a vat of soup the mess sergeant had placed on the stove.

Since no one was brave enough to mention the incident to the sergeant, this soup was served to the men of Company B, 36th Battalion.

The men who had served on K.P. that afternoon refrained from having soup and looked questioningly at everyone who accepted it. Many asked for seconds and thirds.

The climax came when the Commanding Officer came by and complimented the mess sergeant on the excellent soup!

Part VI

COMPETITORS IN INTERNATIONAL
POPULARITY

Lowly Staples Rate High in Epicure Circles

EVERY country on our globe seems to boast of its own special dish of dried peas or beans, be they white, pink, red, brown, yellow, black, gray or mottled. Connoisseurs the world over appreciate them, as may be gleaned from T. R. Ybarra, former correspondent of the New York *Times* and *Collier's*, author of *Young Man of Caracas;* from John Alius, one of the chief correspondents of United Press International; from stories by the late Wythe Williams and Floyd Gibbons; from Betty Wason, who at times was correspondent for C.B.S., Transradio, and *Newsweek;* from Juliette Elkon, who reported from Spain during that country's Civil War; and from Anna Geist, who came to Europe to keep house for a brother in the diplomatic service and who felt there was much Europeans could learn from us.

T. R. Ybarra was and is a master in the art of brightening the most routine meetings with the quick spirit of his Latin ancestors and the sense of humor and proportion of his Massachusetts forebears; he also has the real gourmet's ability to discover the best restaurant within reach where there might be a story. He likes to refer to the anecdote he remembers for us as "the King and I."

MANY YEARS AGO, when I was London correspondent of the New York *Times,* I was a patron of a Spanish restaurant in Air Street, off Piccadilly, run by Señor Martinez, a Spaniard. When King Alfonso XIII of Spain came to London on a visit, much secrecy surrounded his movements, as is usual in the case of traveling royal personages, for security reasons. But Señor Martinez, at whose restaurant Alfonso was to take lunch, promised to let me know on what day and at what hour the King would be there. He kept his promise.

Scrambling into a taxicab, I dashed to Air Street. Sure enough, at a nearby table in the Spanish restaurant on that thoroughfare, sat the King of Spain, in the company of several Spanish and English dignitaries. A waiter came to the side of my chair.

"What would you like to eat?" he asked me. Then and there I had a glorious brainstorm.

"What is the King eating?" I inquired.

"*Cocido à la española* [Spanish boiled dinner]."

"Bring me *cocido à la española*."

"What would you like to drink?"

"What is the King drinking?"

"The finest Rioja wine that Señor Martinez could find in all London."

"Bring me the finest Rioja wine Señor Martinez could find in all London."

You see, I had figured out that whatever Alfonso was eating and whatever he was drinking must necessarily be the best stuff in the place.

Spanish boiled dinner and Spanish Rioja wine were brought to me. Both were super-excellent. The newspaper game teaches those playing it all sorts of useful tricks.

Since recipes and cooking stoves intimidate T. R. Ybarra, we are lucky that Juliette Elkon has a real *cocido* recipe for us which you will find later in this chapter.

LIKE KING ALFONSO in his day, the President of Brazil relishes his country's national dish made with lowly staples, as you will read in the following account by John Alius, United Press International Manager for Brazil at the time this was written.

B RAZIL'S President Juscelino Kubitschek de Oliveira has always been a friendly, simple man. And it is characteristic of him that on the day it became evident that he was elected president of the biggest of Latin-American nations, he should have had for dinner nothing other than the plain but immensely nourishing Brazilian national dish of *feijoada*, seated at a table in his modest house in the city of Belo Horizonte with his family, the few well-wishers who could be crowded into the little dining area, and a U.P.I. reporter.

After the meal, Kubitschek, like every other Brazilian who has just eaten *feijoada*, relaxed a while with a tiny cup of scalding hot, inky-black coffee, and talked of his plans for giving Brazil "fifty years' progress in five" (i.e., the term of a Brazilian president's office).

In numerous lines of endeavor, Kubitschek has succeeded—in road building, automobile manufacture, etc. And it was a tough job.

Making *feijoada* is easier. This recipe serves about eight:

FEIJOADA

3 pounds of black, dried beans
6 strips of bacon
1 onion
Polish sausage
Smoked tongue
Salt pork
Ham shoulder
Garlic, salt

The beans are soaked in lightly salted water overnight to soften them. Next morning, left in the same water, they are cooked for about 2 hours, by which time they have become reasonably soft. At this point, fry 6 strips of bacon, take out the bacon, and put into the fat several spoonfuls of the beans. Mash the beans, mixing them well into the bacon fat. Blend in very finely chopped onion, and a touch of garlic. When this has turned into a smooth purée, pour it back into the bean pot. Cut up the Polish sausage (or peperoni, if Polish sausage is not available) into 1-inch pieces and toss into the pot. Ditto salt pork, the smoked tongue, and the ham. Let the whole brew, simmer for 5 to 6 hours. (Go easy on salt, since the pork contains plenty.)

The beans should, when served, be in a rich sauce, rather like chocolate before it sets. If the brew seems watery, take another few spoonfuls of beans, and repeat the process of mashing them into bacon fat.

Feijoada is served with cooked rice and orange slices. Most Brazilians put the rice on the plate first, then pour *feijoada* over it. The orange slices are served separately, and provide a very refreshing chaser for the rather "heavy" taste of the *feijoada*.

No sane Brazilian with a sedentary job eats *feijoada* at noon; it's by no means an easily digested dish.

"The Tiger" of France, Clemenceau, used to be a firm addict to southern France's national bean dish:

LE CASSOULET

When I asked his biographer, Wythe Williams, one of the founders of the Overseas Press Club, how it had been possible for him, in his young days, to become so close to the political leader of France, he grinned: "We loved the same kind of food and we had many a good *cassoulet* together!"

This was naturally not the full truth, but the addiction to some special dish or drink can form an amazingly strong tie between people. There used to be a small, unpretentious-looking little restaurant on a side street near the Place Pigalle in Paris in my childhood, where almost every famous painter of the time would turn up on Thursday for lunch to enjoy the *cassoulet,* made by a real Toulousain. Students of Académie Julien would slip in too, to have a good look at the successful masters of the old school while they relished their meal.

In theory, the *Cassoulet de Toulouse* is made only with goose, but even the authors of that impressive work of art, *L'Art Culinaire Français,* point out that a very acceptable *cassoulet* can be made with the leftovers of a goose, or of lamb or mutton. Duck will do equally well.

For a party of twelve you need:

½ of a goose or one duck
2 pounds of dried white beans
½ pound of pork rind
¼ pound of bacon or salty ham in one piece
2 pounds of pork
5 toes of garlic, chopped
2 sprigs of thyme
1 bay leaf
2 tablespoons of salt
1 onion, chopped
Pepper, cloves
Bones of a roast duck or roast goose
3 carrots
¼ cup of tomato paste
Sausage with garlic

Soak the beans overnight. Drain them, put them into a kettle with 5 quarts of cold water, the pork rind, bacon or ham, the carrots, onion, garlic and spices—and if you have them, bones from a roast duck or goose. Start cooking very slowly, and simmer for about an hour. Remove the bones and replace them with the firm little sausage, similar to the sausages of southern France and cook for another half-hour. Make sure not to boil too hard; if you do, the skins of the beans will break.

If you don't have the traditional kind of sausage, broil 1 pound of fresh sausage. While the beans cook, brown ½ of a goose. Moisten with some of the broth of the beans and cook until almost tender. This operation is naturally not necessary if you plan to use leftover goose or lamb.

Cut the pork in big dice and brown them in goose fat, adding the juice from the pan to the beans.

Take an ovenproof casserole, put a layer of beans at the bottom. Cut the goose in just enough pieces to provide at least one for each guest. People with bigger appetites can fish for pieces of the other meats! Discard the pork rind and sprig of thyme, replace with the browned pork, the sausage and bacon or ham, cut in slices. Cover with the beans and the water in which they have cooked and a lid.

Bake the *cassoulet* for about 4 hours in a very slow oven at 250°. Serve with French bread and red wine.

For the *cassoulet* with lamb and pork, which *L'Art Culinaire Français* calls "truly simple and good," treat the beans as mentioned above, using lamb instead of goose; roast a little piece of pork and fry or cook the sausage. Bake the beans with the mutton pieces and slices of sausage and bacon buried in them. In the last half-hour of baking, add slices of the roast pork to warm them properly or serve them alongside the *cassoulet*.

Floyd Gibbons, who for years had his headquarters in Paris, felt that Italy was the only country with a bean dish that could compare with our American baked beans: *minestrone*. In Rome he had a favorite little *trattoria* that did not look in the least impressive. He loved to describe it as the finest place in Rome to newly arrived "visiting firemen," bent on meeting blue bloods. When he took them there, he would gleefully watch their initial disappointment at the shabbiness of the place and their delight when various princes and dukes, princesses and duchesses who were dining in the place were pointed out to them. Now they could go home and say: "When I had dinner with the Duke and Duchess of So-and-so in Rome . . ." Luckily there usually were a few genuine blue bloods in the place, often dining at Floyd's expense, to enhance the glamour of his favorite haunt of the moment.

MINESTRONE

was solid fare, but bright as a picture—equally satisfying to the eye and the inner man. For a party of 12, you need:

3 pounds of young cabbage, that is, shiny green
2 cups of navy beans
6 young carrots, and a spare older one
1 green pepper, cut up
2 small white turnips
2 toes garlic, crushed with a wooden spoon
4 stalks of celery
4 tomatoes, cut up
A handful of spaghetti
1 bay leaf, parsley, basil, salt, pepper, sprig of thyme, oregano, paprika, optional: one small hard sausage
4–5 cups of half tomato juice, half bouillon

Soak the beans overnight with one of the crushed garlic toes. Start 2 of the pounds of cabbage, the aged carrot, 2 stalks of celery, part of the green pepper, in 5 quarts of cold water with some coarse salt. Also the turnip, bay leaf, thyme, parsley and possibly the sausage. Cook until you have a strong-tasting stock. Strain and cook the beans in this stock slowly for about 1½ hours, until the beans are nearly soft. Add tomato juice and bouillon.

In the meantime shred the remaining cabbage, slice the celery, carrots, green pepper; snip some parsley and basil.

Pour off some of the broth in which the beans have been cooking, bring to a boil and cook the cut-up vegetables in it. When they are nearly done, dump them and the broth in which they cooked into the bean pot. The purpose of this double operation is to have fresh-looking and tasty vegetables and to avoid overcooking the beans. Add the cut-up tomatoes. When the soup is boiling, break in a small handful of spaghetti or vermicelli that will cook quickly. After about 10 minutes the soup should be ready to serve, together with the *pesto*. If you want to include sausage, slice it thinly and add it to the soup as decoration.

Much of the success of this course depends on the:

PESTO

which is served with it in a sauceboat and every guest stirs a spoonful of it into his soup plate.

The classic *pesto* is made of:

1 cup of parsley leaves
1 cup of basil leaves
6 cloves of garlic
½ teaspoon of salt
½ cup of olive oil
½ cup of freshly grated Parmesan or Gruyère

Cut the greens roughly, crush the garlic and put this into an electric blender with the salt and oil. Run the blender until the mixture is finely minced. Then add the cheese and oil. Check on the taste and add more salt or garlic if need be. Put into a jar with a lid and keep in the refrigerator for a few hours or days to give the *pesto* a chance to ripen. Serve at room temperature after making sure that it has the consistency of mayonnaise; if it seems too dry, blend in some more oil.

If you like your *pesto* to be stringy, use Romano cheese.

If you have no fresh basil leaves, a teaspoon of dried basil will do, but then you must use a little more oil.

Some French cooks prefer to use one-third of parsley, one-third of chervil and one-third of basil. Swiss cooks like to add a few young leaves of lovage, which they also call the "Maggi plant," because it has a slightly meaty flavor. Incidentally, lovage is a fine helper in the making of stews because of this particular taste.

If you know that some of your guests don't like garlic, mince some of the greens separately and blend them with olive oil and cheese. Send them along to the table in a separate sauceboat. It won't be real *pesto* but why make guests suffer in the name of authenticity, when it is easy to circulate two sauceboats instead of one?

Italians are so fond of *pesto* that they also use it on their pasta or with fish. When they mix it with their macaroni or spaghetti they sometimes blend in some anchovy as a dramatic touch.

Garlic enthusiasts like to serve:

GARLIC BREAD

with their *minestrone,* though it generally goes better with a plain soup that needs a little pepping up. Take:

1 long loaf of French or Italian bread
4 blanched cloves of garlic chopped very fine
½ cup of melted butter
½ cup of finely chopped parsley
Pinch of salt

Try to prepare your garlic-butter-parsley mixture the day before you plan to use it. In a tightly closed jar in the refrigerator, it becomes a little smoother in taste.

Shortly before serving, cut or saw your crusty bread at 1-inch intervals down to the bottom, being careful to keep the bottom whole.

Have your mixture at room temperature and spread it evenly over the cut surfaces. Roll the whole loaf into thin aluminum foil and bake in a hot oven (400°) for 20–30 minutes.

For big slices of this bread, cut it on the bias; for smaller slices, cut straight down.

To MAKE a less complicated bean dish, you might take the advice of Betty Wason, a former war correspondent, who wrote *Miracle in Hellas* and remembers:

THE LITTLE Greek village perched on the mountainside was far enough from the front line in that winter of 1940–41 to be quiet but close enough for its citizens to be jittery. I reached it with other correspondents with the sound of crashing bombs and front-line mortar exchanges still echoing in my ears.

As we drove through the village's one street in a car bearing both American and British flags, a man came rushing out from a small tavern to stop us. He was the owner and he was inviting us to lunch. His tavern was small. The kitchen was even smaller. All the food was simmering on a single black cast-iron stove. But the odors were divine.

There was no bill of fare. The owner, who said he had run a hotel in Wisconsin for nine years, suggested that he could give us beans "prepared the Greek way," some lamb and some greens. The food was brought to us on thick plates, the type common in "greasy spoon" joints, but it was superb.

I have prepared beans this way a good many times since, and the dish is always an enormous success—especially with men. But I offer it with a certain apology, for it cannot taste as good as the Greek dish we enjoyed in that tiny village.

BEANS À LA GRECQUE

1 pound of dried white beans
½ cup of olive oil
3 or 4 garlic cloves
4 or 5 medium onions, thickly sliced
4 to 6 garden-fresh tomatoes, peeled and diced, or 1 large can (1 lb. 14 oz.) of tomatoes
¼ teaspoon of marjoram or oregano
¼ teaspoon of thyme
1 bay leaf, crumbled
2 tablespoons of minced fresh parsley
1 teaspoon of salt, or more to taste

Soak beans overnight in water to cover. Drain thoroughly and wash with cold water. Heat good olive oil, the best quality you can buy, in a heavy iron pot or Dutch oven. Add crushed or minced garlic, the onions and the herbs. Let cook in olive oil until onions are soft but not brown. Add chopped fresh tomatoes (best when local tomatoes are available, but the rest of the year canned tomatoes are preferable). Let simmer until well blended and saucelike. Add drained beans and enough water to reach just to top of beans. Bring to a boil, then turn heat as low as possible and simmer, covered, for 1 hour; then add salt, remove cover and simmer 1 hour longer. Makes four to six servings.

Your TRUE Spaniard will insist that *cocido* be served with saffron rice, which in its own right deserves a good place in the amateur chef's collection of recipes, because it can add dash to an otherwise indifferent piece of fish, veal or chicken.

For Juliette Elkon, world traveler and author of *The Belgian Cookbook*, there is pathos in the memory of Spain and its famous *cocido*. She remembers:

As THE SIEGE of the Alcazar was drawing to its close in September 1936, doctors and nurses were busy rounding up lost or orphaned children. With them I reached the village of Noves. It was almost deserted after a heavy bombing. A kindly, dignified gentleman, a retired school teacher, agreed to give us quarters but said we'd have to take our meals in the canteen.

The *cocidos* it provided were meager and we were fed up with *garbanzos* and rabbit. To make matters worse we'd be greeted by a delicious smell of *chorizo* garlic whenever we reached our lodgings. We invariably found the old gentleman carefully removing the crumbs from the tablecloth with the beatific expression of the sated. We began to suspect him of hoarding and talked loudly among ourselves about the slow tortures which should be inflicted on hoarders. The man's face never once changed.

On the third day of our stay, we found the señor lying under the table in a dead faint. We searched the house for something to revive him only to find the wine jar filled with water and the bread hutch empty but for a few toasted crumbs. But in a small pan there was a slice of bread absorbed in a little oil and garlic that had obviously been fried over and over again. There was absolutely no other sign of food or drink. The gentleman's belly had been bloated with hunger rather than high living. When asked why he had not told us of his plight his reaction was that of the proud Spaniard of the old school. "I could not let my guests know that I was in need of help."

Thus, with one little slice of bread he conjured up for himself and for us the dream of a real *cocido*. This is how it should be made:

SPANISH COCIDO

2 pounds of beef (boneless neck)
Small ham hock
If possible the leftover bone from a leg of lamb; if not possible, a
    fresh lamb bone
1 fryer, whole
1 can *cecci* with liquid, or ½ pound of chick-peas (soaked over-
    night and pre-cooked)
1 cabbage
2 leeks
2 tomatoes, peeled and seeded
1 carrot
2 cloves
2 "knackwursts," sliced thick

Cover beef, hock, and lamb bone with 4 quarts of water.
Bring to a boil. Skim. Reduce the heat and simmer for 2
hours. Brown fryer on all sides under the broiler to sear the
meat and seal the juices. Place it in the pot. Bring to a boil.
Skim carefully. Add rest of ingredients. Bring to a boil.
Skim again. Reduce heat and simmer 25 minutes or until
chicken is tender. Meanwhile prepare a saffron rice. Remove meats to a heated serving platter. Cut into serving
pieces. Cut cabbage and add vegetables and sausages,
Serve rice, meat, and vegetables in a soup plate and moisten
with broth from the tureen.

SAFFRON RICE

1 teaspoon of saffron
2 quarts of water
1 tablespoon of salt
1½ cups of rice, unwashed

Use a tall pot into which your sieve will fit, or a steamer.
When the water has reached a rolling boil, throw in the
rice and saffron all at once. Boil for 8 minutes (for wild and
brown rice, 20 minutes). Pour contents of pot into a sieve.

If necessary, add a little cold water to the pot to catch the last grains. Place sieve with rice in it under a faucet of cold running water. This will wash away extra starch. Place 2 cups of hot water in the same pan. Bring to a boil. Place sieve with rice in it over boiling water so the rice will not touch water. Cover with a clean kitchen towel folded several times and gently steam the rice for 45 minutes over low heat.

Rice can be done this way in the morning of a party and reheated in the same manner 30 minutes before serving. It will be perfect. Serves four.

Editor's Note:

Let us return to beans: We shall have to by-pass scores of recipes from all lands of the world, but we would be displaying a kind of gastronomic inferiority complex if we failed to turn to the United States of America and a version of baked beans that deserves loving care because of its excellence. Unlike its international competitors this variety of baked beans won't remind you of its goodness for hours to come or provide an alibi for an extra siesta.

In the days between the two wars, Americans on duty in Berlin could sample food in that capital's best restaurants. When on special assignments in Paris, Brussels, The Hague, Warsaw, Vienna or Prague they knew where to go to enjoy good fare. Nevertheless, when Anna Geist, sister of one of the consuls, Raymond Geist, sent out word that she was preparing a baked beans party, no one, from ambassador down would fail to heed the call—unless a big story were brewing. She was from the Middle West but her specialty was:

NEW ENGLAND BAKED BEANS

2 pounds of white navy beans
1 teaspoon of soda
2 middle-sized onions
½ pound of bacon, cut in small pieces
1¼ cups of sugar
1 tablespoon of dry mustard, salt and pepper

Wash and soak the beans overnight. In the morning parboil with a little salt until the beans are soft but not broken. Add the soda and let rest for 5 minutes, turning out the fire. Wash thoroughly in cold water three or four times.

Cut up the onions and place in bottom of bean pot, then add the beans and distribute the bacon. Mix the sugar, the mustard and a little pepper with hot water; pour over the beans and add enough hot water to cover them. Bake, covered, in a very moderate oven for the first 8 hours; remove the cover and bake in a slow oven until nicely browned. Add enough water during the cooking to obtain a nice thick sauce.

If you prefer a stronger addition of meat, cook a Polish sausage, slice it and sink the slices into the beans for the final browning operation.

The only time these beans failed to get an enthusiastic reception was the time when Polly Abbe and her three youngsters, who wrote the best-seller *Around the World in Eleven Years*, were given a bean party. Why? They'd been terribly hard up out West, when Polly, the one-time Follies Beauty, and the kids decided to try their hand at writing about their trek through Europe. "All we could buy was beans," said they, "and we used the bean bags as writing paper for our first drafts. It will take a long time until we can look another bean in the face," which was comprehensible but definitely exceptional and should not be held against one of our prized national dishes!

Suckling Pig Might Win
International Popularity Contest

IF AN international gastronomic popularity contest were held, our beloved American steak or turkey might well be defeated by suckling pig. Spain's Prince Don Carlos, Yugoslavia's Marshall Tito, Swedish, Polish, Hungarian gourmets, Chinese mandarins, democratic leaders in the Philippines and lesser mortals, are bound to disagree in the political field. When it comes to eating, they rate suckling pig as real party fare.

We have witnesses to prove it.

Let us start with Jean Colbert, director of Women's Activities, at Station WTIC, Hartford, Connecticut, who can testify for the Spanish side. She writes:

WHEN I was in Segovia, that town which looks like an illustration for fairy tales, high on a hill in the Guadarrama Mountains, I learned that its people have a legend which they treasure. According to it, every monarch who ever ruled Spain since the sixteenth century appeared in their main square and went to have a meal in the Casa Cándido before he came to power.

Today, the folks feel certain that Don Juan Carlos will be Spain's next ruler because they saw him in the square and they saw him enter the *casa*, where they serve Spain's most famous suckling pig and where I interviewed him.

This is the oldest restaurant in Spain; partly built in a cave, it retains all the color of the old days. The waiters are dressed in the traditional costumes of the past: red velvet jackets, green corduroy pants, white shirts with brilliant scarlet cummerbunds and green scarves around their necks. They wear sombrero-like hats of maroon velvet with two big velvet buttons. One of the bosses is an old bullfighter called Felix Colonno, who sports an even more colorful outfit than the help.

Flanked by his constant companion and diplomatic aide, the Marquis de Cantanar, young Don Juan Carlos, answered my questions, without revealing that he knew of the legend of which Segovia is proud. I also tasted the restaurant's prized dish, roast suckling pig, known as *lechóncito asado*. This is how it is made:

ROAST SUCKLING PIG À LA SEGOVIA

Clean suckling pig, stuff, truss, make long gashes through the skin of the back and put on rack of roaster, with the front legs and the hind legs folded under as if it were cowering. Brush with melted butter (or oil), sprinkle with salt and pepper. Pour 2 cups of boiling water around the rack. Cover with buttered paper and sear in a very hot oven.

During the cooking process, make sure that no blisters form on the skin. If it looks as if one were starting, prick with a big darning needle or a skewer. Reduce the heat slightly and cook for about 2½ hours, if the suckling pig is big enough to serve eight to twelve people. If it is smaller, the cooking time will be less. When it is tender, remove the paper and brush all over with cream or butter. Remove to serving dish and garnish with apples and water cress.

The stuffing that Segovia cooks put into the piglet calls for:

1 large chopped onion
4 large chopped carrots, cooked
2 large chopped sour apples
2 diced sausages of the long and spicy variety
2–3 cups of bread crumbs
4 tablespoons of oil, or butter
1 cup of milk
Salt and pepper

Brown the chopped onion in oil or butter. Slice the sausages and brown lightly. Mix with carrots, apples, salt, pepper. Simmer for 5 minutes, add milk to the bread crumbs and put into the cooked mixture. Stir thoroughly and stuff the pig.

Our second witness hails from Poland.

Halina Tomaczewska was a war correspondent attached to the American forces in World War II. A "free" Pole who fled from her country when the Nazis invaded it, and who can't return to it as long as it is under Red control, she works in Paris. But on important holidays homesick Poles will get together to enjoy "suckling pig with Polish stuffing." She writes:

W HILE French and American cooks will incorporate the pig's liver into the stuffing, the Polish chef uses the liver for a sausage or a pasty, but piglets, like stuffed pork roasts, capons or turkeys, rate a more fancy treatment.

POLISH STUFFING

4 minced chicken livers
½ cup of finely minced, mild onions
1 teaspoon each of minced dill, marjoram
Sprig of tarragon

1 tablespoon of minced parsley
A little grated celery root
¼ cup of melted butter
3 cups of chopped mushrooms, cooked in butter (the tasty, dried
 European kind)
1 chopped apple
½ cup of cooked chopped chestnuts
3 beaten eggs
Enough soaked and dried bread crumbs, fried in butter or olive oil,
 to help fill the cavity
2 tablespoons of brown sauce

If the suckling pig is heavy, and requires more time to cook, the mushrooms need not be fried before mixing them with the other ingredients. This stuffing with its wealth of herbs makes the meat of the pig seem all the more delicate in contrast.

The "free" Poles are not the only ones to whom a plate of suckling pig is like a taste from home! During World War II young Norwegians would undergo harrowing experiences to flee from their country to join the allied forces fighting the Germans. Some made it sailing in tiny boats; others crossed all of Russia, China, India to reach Toronto's "Little Norway" where they were trained as flyers. One of their protectors was the Norwegian shipping magnate, George Vetlesen, who'd see to it that on occasion the young lads had a treat of:

SCANDINAVIAN-STYLE SUCKLING PIG

For this the suckling pig is cut into serving portions. Cover them with cold water. Cook slowly until the meat is tender. This takes about 2 hours, depending on the size of the animal. Salt is added shortly before the cooking is done —not before. The cooked meat is served ice cold (which makes it easier to slice), together with horse-radish sauce.
The bottle of aquavit or vodka usually stands on the

buffet right close to the cold suckling pig, which, being fat, provides the inside "blotter" experts know will make it safer for them to down the stiff drink in one swallow—followed by a formal bow if you respect Scandinavian rites.

In Yugoslavia when Marshall Tito entertained visiting chiefs of state, from Emperor Haile Selassie to Nehru, to U Nu, to Khrushchev, to Nasser, suckling pig held the place of honor on the menus, according to Helen Fisher who was stationed in Belgrade for the United Press and who reports:

Tɪᴛo's gala state receptions are generally given in the gardens of the official presidential residence, the wedding cake White Palace, which Prince Paul built between the wars in one of the most beautiful settings of the world. Weather permitting, tables are set up at the end of the formal gardens beside a reflecting pool for Tito, his wife and their official state guests.

For the others, long tables flank the four walls of the big ballroom and are set up along the wide terraces from which a broad sweep of stairs leads to the garden.

Besides the brown, shiny suckling pigs, roasted on spits, the guests would also enjoy Adriatic *langoustes*—huge creatures with their meat concentrated in one succulent chunk inside the shell.

Suckling pig is really the national party dish in Yugoslavia. No wedding, christening or other important family occasion would rank as a feast without it. The roasted pig is chopped into chunks at the table. If you happen to be considered the guest of honor—visiting foreigners generally are —you will be presented with the tender cartilage of the pig's ear, deemed the supreme delicacy.

For lesser festivities the local citizenry repairs to open-air gardens, where they will find a delicacy that may well rival the best of suckling pigs:

ČEVABČIĆI

Pronounced "chevabchitse," and about the size of a thumb, it is made of equal parts of veal, pork, beef, sometimes venison, chopped together with onion, garlic, thyme, marjoram, then marinated for 2 or 3 days. The marinade has a base of *kaymak,* which is a cousin of yoghurt and of sour cream to which the cook adds the herbs, spices and some wine.

When meal time comes it is shaped into little patties, which are broiled quickly and served with big piles of chopped raw onion.

While the patties are broiling, the guests start with plenty of *rakija,* the plum brandy which is also known as *slivovka,* and they wash down the patties with white wine. Long before the meal is over someone will have brought out a guitar and started to play folk songs with everybody present joining in with the same gusto with which they enjoyed their *čevabčići* and *rakija.*

Go to the Philippines for Real Suckling Pig.

Hopping around the map comes naturally to our tribe. Dr. Gregor Ziemer, former Chicago *Tribune* correspondent, author of *Education for Death* and director of publicity for the Association of the Blind, will tell you about Sergio Osmeña, who was President of the Philippines from 1944–46 and dishes he and his bride enjoyed on Cebu in the Philippines. Dr. Ziemer writes:

WE HAD just arrived in Cebu from a small town in the Middle West as honeymooners to become government teachers. This we felt would be a fine start to see the world. We found the town in a frenzy of excitement because its famous son, Senator Sergio Osmeña, was coming home for a visit. Later he was to become President of the Philippines (1944–46) but he was already famous. We looked forward to this, our first contact with a great man.

The American colony of this tropic Visayan city joined with Filipino officials to put on a welcoming outdoor reception for the slender, soft-spoken statesman who was proud of being half Chinese.

It was a stimulating experience to meet this dignified, forward-looking Senator Osmeña, who had such great faith in his nation and the United States, too.

As if he knew of the struggle to face the free world in the following years, he said: "We are the outpost of Democracy in the Orient. There are difficult times ahead. Let us hope and pray that your country and mine will always be friends. If not, Democracy will die out here." Thanks to men like him, democracy can survive.

Dancing to a native orchestra under Chinese lanterns helped us work up an appetite for a magnificent buffet—a display of food beyond description. To mention a few items: golden mangoes, fragrant papayas, bright yellow breadfruit, ten varieties of bananas, scores of different meat dishes, colorful desserts and fine mellow cigars.

Two delicacies intrigued us especially: *lechón* and *sorbete*. *Lechón*, we discovered later, was suckling pig—but not the British kind with an apple in its mouth.

This suckling pig was roasted over a slow fire in a deep pit, fed with coconut husks and palm leaves and sweet-smelling *nara* wood—hard as iron. The pig, stuffed with white rice and fresh, juicy coconut meat, was wrapped tightly in green banana leaves, probably the forerunner of aluminum wrap. The suckling was scraped so clean that even the crisp rind was delicious.

The meat was not cut, but gently plucked off the bones and eaten off more banana leaves. It must be tasted to be believed.

And then there was the delicious, aromatic dessert:

SORBETE

Young coconut meat in the milky stage was scraped out of its shell, mixed with an equal proportion of coconut milk and goat's milk, and sweetened with unboiled cane juice. A banana was mashed into it. The whole was frozen gently.

Try it sometime.

Part VII

TIPS GALORE

From the Notes of an Apprentice at Sacher's

NORA HODGES

MOST OF US who picked up our favorite cooking secrets while on overseas assignments could never lay claim to one of the top white caps which only real chefs have a right to don. The one exception is Nora Hodges.

When, at a very tender age, she decided to leave her native Vienna and to try to become an American reporter, her grandmother ruled that she would have to learn a real trade before she left for far-away lands. The grandmother was a friend of Vienna's famous Madame Sacher, whose restaurant was the mecca of all gourmets traveling to Austria. She prevailed on her to allow her granddaughter to serve an apprenticeship in the Sacher kitchens.

Nora became a successful correspondent who reported from many lands but she still has a big fat book of notes about some of Sacher's most famous recipes. They are written in German and Nora Hodges translated some of them for us. She writes:

THE NOTE which I appreciate most was written out for me personally by one of the Sacher chefs. It provides the authentic recipe for the famous:

SACHER TORTE

You will need:

1 scant cup of butter
3½ ounces of softened, best-quality chocolate
1½ cups of very fine sugar
¼ cup of flour and
5 eggs

Cream the butter and stir in the softened chocolate. Add half the sugar and stir in the egg yolks one at a time, beating steadily. Beat the egg whites with the rest of the sugar and fold into the mixture. Sprinkle the flour over the whole with a light hand. Mix swiftly and fill a well-greased pan dusted with flour. Bake slowly for 45 minutes, when the cake tester should come out clean.

The chef would make his icing out of:

5 ounces of chocolate
5 ounces of lump sugar
½ cup of water

cooking until he could spin a thread, then stir at the edge of the stove until it "had the temperature of the lips." This icing would be poured over the baked cake that had been cooled, given a good coating of melted apricot marmalade.

I find other useful notes. For instance:

To make shrimp or lobster bisque and other dishes that improve through the addition of shrimp or lobster paste, we learned to make lobster or:

SHRIMP BUTTER

Well-washed shells in which the shrimps or lobster were cooked are pounded in a mortar with a little butter. When the shells are almost like a paste, add just a little broth or water and pass through a sieve, discarding the more recalcitrant little pieces. Continue to pound until you actually have a paste; add its full weight of butter, pound some more, then heat until the butter foams—but don't let it get brown. Pour in some cold stock or cold water and set aside. When the mixture is cool a lump of red butter will be in the pan, ready to be used for whatever purpose you choose—be it to finish a bisque or to turn a plain fish into a gastronomic surprise by coating it with red butter before baking it in the oven.

Since the Viennese like their veal, as they should since it is excellent, the apprentices cooked it in many ways, besides the traditional *Wiener Schnitzel* or the *côtelettes de veau en papillotes*. There was:

VEAL CUTLET, TURKISH STYLE

which was soaked in lemon for a little while, fried in butter, served on rice with ham and radishes.

Lovers of meat on skewers will appreciate the

ÉMINCÉ DE VEAU

String small flat pieces of tender veal onto a skewer alternately with good bacon, sprinkle with salt and pepper, roll in bread crumbs and broil. Sacher would have scorned the following suggestion, but the truth is that our veal is not as tender as that bought in Vienna's best shops. If you doubt your meat's tenderness, marinate your veal in a mixture of light sour cream and white wine, with a dash of soy sauce—just enough of the latter to tenderize, not enough to impose its taste.

FILET À LA WELLINGTON

was a dish with which the apprentices could earn their caps. It can be made with eye-of-round or a similar piece of tender beef that should be roasted quickly in a V-shaped rack over a shallow roasting pan. Before it is quite done, it is salted and peppered and given a first coat of *duxelles*, chopped parsley and, if possible, some meat *glacé*. Then it is rolled into a sheet of your favorite dough. The dough is given a brushing of egg beaten with a little water. The whole roll goes into a pan with the seam at the bottom and is baked for ½ hour in a very hot oven. (The French *pâté brisée* does well for this dish.)

The sauce that goes with the roast à la Wellington is made of the drippings in the pan, *duxelles*, tomato paste, and Madeira wine.

SACHER DUXELLES

is simpler than most French *duxelles*. It is made of finely minced onions, fried in butter to which finely chopped mushrooms, salt and pepper are added and the whole is fried some more. To give cohesion a light smuggling in of arrowroot or flour blended with broth is helpful.

RUSSIAN BEEFSTEAKS

Cut and fry onions, ham, sauerkraut, dill pickles; cook until you have a tasty paste. Take slices of beef and pound them thoroughly. Fill them with the mixture, tie them firmly, brown them and finish cooking them slowly in a cream sauce.

Sacher's famous boiled beef was served with a great variety of sauces, starting with:

DILL SAUCE

For this, Sacher's apprentices melted butter and flour in a pan; they added minced onions and minced dill, frying the mixture a little more without letting it get brown; then they added some vinegar and the whole was brought to a boil, passed through a fine sieve, enriched with some cream and flour, cooked a little more and given a sprinkling of finely chopped fresh dill.

SAUCE SOUBISE

is for lovers of onions. The onions are cut into "thin leaves" and boiled in water until soft. When the water is boiled down, flour mixed with butter is added. This mixture is reduced a little more and given its final cooking with a good portion of milk.

HORSE-RADISH SAUCE À LA SACHER

Soak a pinch of saffron in hot beef or veal broth—preferably the Austrian or French kind—not the strong-tasting Spanish variety. Soak crustless bread in another cup of broth. Cook a light mixture of flour, butter, broth, chopped parsley and a few mushrooms. Pass through a sieve and whip this into the combined soaked saffron and bread with a wire whisk to make it very light. Add fresh grated horse-radish and finish by bringing close to a boil.

BRAISED DUCK À LA GRIOTTE

Cut up greens, scraps of bacon, of veal, adding thyme and bay leaf, and your equivalent of *Quatre Épices*. Start by browning this in a pan; when it is good and hot add the duck. As soon as the duck has an artistic brown color, take it out, let the fat drip off, dust with flour and roast it; pour over it a mixture of red currant jelly liquefied with cognac, red wine, cherry liqueur, making sure there is enough of it to provide a kind of shallow bath. Let the duck steam in this mixture until it is tender. Pass the sauce in which the duck steamed and serve with cherries.

For:

CANARD À L'ORANGE

the Sacher apprentices merely replaced the cherry liqueur with an orange liqueur and replaced the cherries with oranges.

SOLE À LA EDWARD VII

Chopped shallots, mushrooms cut into thin leaves, peeled tomatoes, a pinch of tarragon are all sautéed together and put into a fireproof dish to form a bed for the filet of sole. Cover the latter with a Béchamel Sauce, sprinkled with Parmesan, and bake *au gratin*.

One of the tempting dessert sauces in the notes of this apprentice is called:

GIL BLAS

Roast and pound 3½ ounces of hazelnuts and blend them into melted chocolate. To thin the sauce add some cognac. If the sauce is to be used on *crêpes*, it needs an addition of vanilla sauce.

And should someone be tired of rich food:

GRIESSCHMARN

can serve as a soothing inner poultice: an equal amount of semolina and boiling milk are mixed together with butter, some of the inside of a vanilla bean, sugar, possibly some lemon peel and raisins, and the whole is given a cover and baked in the oven, to be served plain or with raspberry or apricot sauce.

Notes from the Editor and Cooks

Some may find "spinning the thread" for the genuine Sacher Torte too risky an undertaking. As a substitute for it you might try the following, using:

⅔ cup of apricot jam
3 ounces of chocolate that is less sweet than the one baked in the cake
¾ cups of confectioners' sugar
2 tablespoons of hot water
1 egg—1 egg yolk
5 tablespoons of butter

Melt the jam in a cup placed in hot water. Spread on top of the cake that has been cooled a little. Let rest for about 20 minutes. Melt the chocolate with the water and beat in the sugar. Whisk in the egg and continue beating. Beat in the egg yolk and when that has been fully absorbed, work in the butter that has been creamed, spoon by spoon. Spread evenly on the cake.

Its success depends on the cook's ability to choose two kinds of chocolates that complement each other well. Some like to use bitter chocolate for the icing but the Sacher chef would probably disapprove, finding that it is too harsh a contrast to be distinguished!

Since Nora Hodges mentioned the Viennese version of Horse-radish Sauce, we might take a quick look at some of its counterparts from other lands, such as:

ENGLISH HORSE-RADISH SAUCE

Soak the horse-radish in cold water for at least 1 hour. Then scrape it very fine. Thereafter mix:

2 tablespoons of horse-radish scrapings with
1 teaspoon of dry mustard
½ teaspoon of salt
1 egg yolk that has been blended with
3 tablespoons of olive oil and
3 tablespoons of vinegar

Stir energetically and serve as is, if the sauce is to accompany cold meat or fish. If it is to go with a warm dish, place a container with the sauce in a pan with hot water, but don't let it come to a boil!

GERMAN HORSE-RADISH SAUCE AND APPLES

Grate:

6 tart apples, and add
2 tablespoons of sugar
½ cup of wine
¼ cup of wine vinegar
1½ cups of grated horse-radish

CZECH HORSE-RADISH AND WHIPPED CREAM

Whip:

4 tablespoons of heavy cream. Then add:
2 tablespoons of white wine vinegar
1 tablespoon of sugar
1 tablespoon of salt
1 cup of grated horse-radish

Mix both of these two last sauces just before serving; otherwise they become soggy and lose their looks and taste. They go very well with many kinds of fish. If the cook is tempted to use the prepared bottled horse-radish, she'll have to cut down the amount of vinegar mentioned in these recipes. This will reduce the amount of work involved. It will also reduce the quality of the sauces.

Notes from the Editor and Cooks

There is one dish you will find all over Vienna and Eastern Europe possibly because it gives the chef a chance to smuggle in some leftovers.

POZHARSKY KOTLETY

are really a traditional Russian dish which Sacher and other Austrian chefs incorporated into their menus, dressing them up on occasion with an addition of finely chopped truffles or a tiny bit of freshly chopped dill.

The following is the recipe of Mrs. Alexander Kipnis, wife of the famous Russian-born basso who starred at the Metropolitan, at the Berlin and Vienna operas, in London and in South America. It calls for

7 slices of enriched white bread
3 tablespoons of milk
1 pound of cooked veal, finely chopped, or 1 pound of finely chopped chicken meat
1 finely chopped onion
2 tablespoons of butter
1 egg
1 egg beaten with 2 tablespoons of water
1½ cups of fine, fresh bread crumbs
1 cup of bouillon
1 4-ounce stick of butter
Salt and pepper

Remove the crusts from the bread slices and soak them in the milk. Fry the onion in 1 tablespoon of butter slowly until it is well done but not brown. Squeeze the bread until it is dry and mix it with the meat, the egg, the cooked onion and season to taste.

Shape this mixture into 6 even-sized chops. Let them dry a little in the air, then dip them into the beaten egg and roll them in the bread crumbs.

Melt the butter until it is nearly bubbly and fry your fake chops until they have a thin, attractive crust. Turn down the heat and continue cooking until the chops are well done, but not too dry.

While they are frying, heat a casserole into which you place them while making the two sauces that are their traditional escorts. For the first one, pour the bouillon into the pan in which they have been fried. Add the butter and scrape carefully to get a shiny sauce which you pour over the chops in the casserole. Then a

MUSHROOM SAUCE

of a thickish consistency is made with

½ pound of finely sliced mushrooms
2 tablespoons of butter
1 tablespoon of flour
½ cup of bouillon
Juice of ½ lemon

Heat the butter, add the mushrooms and cook for 2 minutes; sprinkle the flour over the mushrooms, add the lemon juice. Cover and simmer for 10 minutes. Serve with the *kotlety* that have been kept warm in the casserole in the oven until ready to serve, and to satisfy three diners.

From Peanut Butter to French Pâtés

MRS. HENRY CASSIDY

AMERICANS who are old enough to remember the many hours spent poring over reports from Paris, Moscow and Washington or listening to broadcasts before, during, and after wars, will recognize the name of Henry Cassidy as that of a trusted, welcome old friend. For years he was a correspondent with the Associated Press and later of N.B.C. only to return home to resume newspaper work on our shores.

During most of his overseas assignments, his wife Martha was with him. So was young Constance after she arrived in this world. Martha Cassidy is the one who took pen in hand to give you a glimpse of Americans in Paris after "Liberation" and a few choice recipes:

HOSTESSING Sunday afternoon at-homes in the late fall of 1945 in our home in France included providing a bizarre menu.

When Henry, our seven-year-old daughter Constance, and I returned to France in October, we were one of the first American families to go back after the end of the war. On the outskirts of Paris we found what had once been a lovely ten-room villa with about an acre of garden, complete with tile pool, fountain, boxwood hedges, poplar trees, etc. The property had been abandoned for six years, but after a month with painters, paper hangers, plumbers and moving men, it became what seemed to be a typical American home to our French friends, and brought back nostalgic memories to the United States Army boys we had met in the Hotel Scribe.

By jeep, bicycle and train, invited and uninvited, our guests arrived regularly on Sunday afternoons—most of them accompanied by friends! But there never was a crowd who was less trouble. The routine was the same every week: a gin rummy game on the terrace; someone playing the piano in the salon and couples dancing wherever there was space; and in the comfortable easy chairs and on the sofas, the young soldiers curled up with the comics from the Sunday papers which Connie's grandparents collected and sent to her weekly from America.

For refreshments, there was no choice and the menu never varied: green-tasting French Armagnac (which was all we could find at the time), saltines (the dining-room steward on the troopship on which we had gone to France had given cartons of these to Connie the last day aboard—he was afraid she'd go hungry in France) and peanut butter (which we'd taken over with us). Sounds awful, doesn't it? But had we been able to serve *pâté de foie gras* with truffles on toast strips and champagne cocktails, it couldn't have tasted better to those homesick boys.

After the guns ceased fire and a measure of peace returned, matters changed. The more venturesome boys who stayed on in Europe after the big exodus of fighting men began to check on local customs and to go on reconnoitering expeditions of their own. Tired of army food, they went looking for little *bistros* run by cooks with imagination who knew how to make the best out of the little they had. The more successful *bistro* bosses usually had some relatives in the country who could be induced to part with some of their precious produce in complicated barter deals, involving everything possible from socks to soap, etc., in a country despoiled by four years of German occupation.

Two of our enterprising young Sunday guest sergeants had struck up a friendship with a *patron* who had no car, but whose in-laws had a farm within reasonable reach. On their day off, they'd drive out to it, load up their jeep with mysterious-looking packages for the *patron's* wife, Madame la Patronne. She in turn would go to work to reward the boys with some fine meals. They soon had favorite dishes, including *pâté de veau et jambon*—a ham and veal *pâté*, that was the traditional specialty of the house.

To show their gratitude to their wartime hostesses, the two sergeants took Connie and me to this favorite hangout of theirs. Madame la Patronne bustled about, apologizing profusely that she had not been able to scare up a few truffles to lend an extra artistic touch to her *pâté*, but even without truffles, the meal was delicious. She wrote out her recipes for us and here they are:

HAM AND VEAL PÂTÉ

For the dough of the *pâté*, known as *pâté brisée*, you need:

3½ cups of flour   2 eggs
1 scant cup of butter   1 ounce of salt
    ¾ cup of cold water

To fill the *pâté*, you need:

1 pound of big, thin sheets of salt pork
2 pounds of veal
1 pound of ham
½ pound of twice chopped beef
3½ ounces of bread soaked in water or bouillon and squeezed dry
1 egg
Grated nutmeg, pepper, thyme, garlic, marjoram, chopped parsley, a very little chopped celery, a bay leaf

Prepare the dough and the filling the day before you plan to bake the *pâté*.

To make the dough, sift the flour onto a board to form a volcano-like hill in the center of which you drop the softened butter, the two eggs, the salt and cold water. Mix well and knead the dough until it is as smooth as silk. Wrap it in paper and place in the refrigerator for at least 12 hours. If you prefer to use lard instead of butter, melt the lard and warm the water before mixing.

Have your butcher cut a big, square piece of salt pork into very thin sheets with his machine—not the way bacon is sliced, but parallel to the rind to give you bigger pieces. The day before baking put a few bits of dried thyme and marjoram between the sheets to flavor them. Cut neat little pieces of veal and ham, of ½-inch thickness, that have neither fat nor gristle, until you have 1 good pound of veal and ½ pound of ham pieces. Sprinkle salt, pepper, grated nutmeg on the veal, keeping in mind the degree of saltiness of your ham and salt pork.

Take the tough parts of the veal and ham that you have not cut up and pass them through a food chopper with ½ pound of ground beef. Mix this meat carefully with the bread that has been squeezed dry, an egg, finely minced parsley, celery, crushed garlic, pepper, thyme, marjoram, to achieve a kind of sausage meat. In fact you could use sausage meat instead of making your own mixture, but as a rule the commercial sausage meat is so fat that it spoils the delicate flavor of the *pâté*.

When ready to bake, butter a 10-cup-size fireproof dish or 2 fireproof glass bread pans. The advantage of using two pans is that if your guests don't eat as much as expected, one of the two *pâtés* may survive to serve as main course a few days later; whereas remnants in the big dish will look like leftovers—good ones it is true—but why give anyone a chance to use that word?

Sprinkle the buttered dishes with bread crumbs and line

them with the dough that has been rolled out to ¼-inch thickness, allowing it to hang evenly over the rims by about ½ inch. Reserve enough dough to form lids.

Next, line this dough with sheets of the salt pork, fitting them neatly all around. Then pack a layer of your sausage meat at the bottom and sides of the dish over the salt pork. Put in a layer of your meat pieces, a thin layer of sausage meat, and continue to the top layer which must be sausage meat. Cover the top with a last sheet of salt pork, and place a bay leaf in the middle of it. Roll your last dough to form a well-fitting lid. Place it on the salt pork, sprinkle water around the edges of the dough, bring them back onto the lid, press down with a fork, forming a little pattern with it to make sure that the *pâté* is firmly sealed. Cut out a small round the size of a quarter in the middle of the lid to form a chimney, through which the steam escapes. Surround the chimney with a ring made of the dough, gluing it on with a little water.

If you have energy left you can paint the top with egg yolk mixed with a tiny bit of water, which gives you a shiny crust; but this is not really vital because the *pâté* gets its own beautiful golden color when baked for 1½ hours at 375° if you have made one big pâté, or 1 hour if you have made two smaller ones. Test the doneness with a skewer or toothpick passed through the chimney.

Whether served hot or cold, in the dish or out of it, the ham and veal *pâté* is a thing of beauty, and a treat, specially if it is served with *la patronne's:*

SAUCE CUMBERLAND

Because it is so good, chefs of many lands have created their own versions of this sauce, an international classic. Basically, it calls for:

3 tablespoons of red currant jelly
1 tablespoon of wine, or port wine
2 tablespoons of orange juice
1 teaspoon of dry mustard
1 teaspoon of paprika
½ teaspoon of ground ginger
1 tablespoon of finely slivered, orange rind
1 tablespoon of finely slivered lemon rind

Start by cutting up the colored part of orange rind and lemon rind—to obtain 1 tablespoon of tiny slivers of each after they have been soaked in cold water and have been brought to the boil to soften them.

While they drain and cool, melt the red currant jelly over a low flame, without letting it get very hot. Add the wine, or port wine, mix the spices with the orange juice and add to the jelly-wine mixture, bringing the whole close to the boil to blend thoroughly. Finish up by adding the orange and lemon rind julienne and a mere hint of salt. Serve very cold.

The *patronne* did not think highly of "modern" short cuts but she felt that when pressed for time one might substitute a cousin of Sauce Cumberland:

OXFORD SAUCE

The difference between the two is that the quota of lemon and orange julienne is cut in half and it is obtained merely by grating the rind of the lemon and orange instead of slivering and cooking it. This saves time and effort, but it deprives the gourmet of the fun of chewing on the surprising little pieces and trying to identify them—and when the guest tries to identify an ingredient his or her taste buds are ready to do their share to help the party.

Cumberland Sauce is a friend of the cook in another way: it survives longer stays in the icebox, and it will dress up many a dish of cold or hot meat from ham, veal to venison.

Give it the company of a few spoonfuls of raisins that have been puffed up in hot water and rubbed dry and you have an enjoyable sauce for boiled tongue. Blend it into the drippings of your hamburgers and they'll seem more festive than usual.

JELLIED CUMBERLAND

Cumberland will also do things for a platter of slices of a veal roast or a beef roast that turned out to be drier than expected and are in danger of being dull eating. To perk them up, place the slices neatly on a platter and put it in the refrigerator for a while to get the whole well cooled. In the meantime take

1 tablespoon of gelatine
1½ cups of beef broth
3 tablespoons of Cumberland Sauce

Soak the gelatine in ¼ cup of the cold beef broth; bring the remainder of the broth to a boil; stir in the soaked gelatine, heat a little more to make sure that it is well dissolved. Beat in the Cumberland Sauce. Cool it a little, then pour over the cold meat slices, coating them evenly.

Very thin little wedges of lemon or orange can be placed on some of the meat before the gelatine mixture is poured on and allowed to set. For an extra dash of color, firm some of the gelatine in the refrigerator and cut in tiny squares as edible garnish. Some prefer to use wine instead of meat broth to make the Cumberland glaze.

After our hosts showed that they had learned to mix the salad at the table in the French manner, Madame la Patronne herself brought in the dessert. Had there been gold in the goblets she carried, she could not have looked prouder. They contained a Norwegian lemon pudding that she had learned to cook for some wild young Norwegian painters in the gay days before the war. This was the first time she'd had enough eggs to cook it, thanks to the extra supply which her young American friends had wheedled out of her mother-in-law. She had chosen this:

LEMON PUDDING

partly because one of the sergeants, who was tall and very blond, reminded her of her prewar Scandinavian friends. She slapped her ample hips in glee when he admitted that this tasted just like the pudding his Norwegian grandmother had cooked for him on gala days! "Extravagant people, those Norwegians," she muttered; "you need five eggs for just four people!"

For one pudding you need:

1 package of gelatine
½ cup of cold water
5 eggs, separated
1 cup of sugar
Juice of 1 big lemon or 2 small ones
1 tablespoon of grated lemon rind
Pinch of salt

Dissolve the gelatine thoroughly in the cold water; if necessary place it over boiling water, but cool to lukewarm. Beat the egg yolks until they are very light in color. Gradually add the sugar, beating all the time. Add the lemon juice and rind and finally the cooled gelatine. Don't stop beating. Add salt to the egg whites and beat until stiff. Fold into the mixture. Pour into goblets or into a bowl that holds about 1½ quarts. Cool in the refrigerator, or if you like a more sherbet-like consistency, put it in the freezer. Just before serving top with a little sweetened whipped cream. If you have it, cut a tiny strip of candied angelica as a final touch of color.

Short Cuts for Epicures

POPPY CANNON

THE FAMOUS, popular correspondent had cooked the Christmas turkey to perfection and everything he served with it was delicious. His colleagues and their wives were full of admiration for his culinary achievement. The husbands pointed to this or that special touch of artistry of the amateur chef, until one of the wives could not resist the temptation of moaning about the hardship of cooking meals on 365 days of the year.

The host sat back in his Early American captain's chair and ruined his popularity with the ladies for months to come by saying: "I really don't see why women make such a fuss about cooking. All one has to do is learn to master a few basic tricks, search for some dishes that are different and go to work to find a way of making them with a minimum of fuss."

The girls were cross; they wanted to know just how he could manage with a minimum of "fuss." He countered: "Why don't you read the articles of Poppy Cannon, the Epicure Editor of *House Beautiful* and take her advice and that of others like her?"

The correspondent-chef is not the only one who appreciates Poppy Cannon's advice, as may be garnered from her two stories:

BEFORE I went off to Ghana for the Independence cele-
brations in 1957, a message was transmitted to me
through a mutual friend that Prime Minister Kwame
Nkrumah had suddenly developed a new and overwhelming
interest in cooking and would I please bring him some
books, preferably on French cuisine and perhaps give him
a few pointers.

In a gush of enthusiasm, I arranged to have an electric
blender dispatched to him at Christianberg Castle, and
upon my arrival in Accra, let it be known (through chan-
nels, of course) that I was prepared to begin the lessons.

During my ten-day stay, all Ghana was rocked by the dis-
covery of an alleged plot against the government. Within
the same week, Guinea and Ghana agreed to merge. The
Prime Minister did find time to talk to me, but he talked
about life in the United States, about the possibilities of
developing tourism in Ghana . . . about a great many other
topics. But how does one keep a Prime Minister's mind on
his cooking? I couldn't do it.

However, when I left, his Excellency had the blender and
also, among others, this recipe for making one of the most
famous of all French sauces: a HOLLANDAISE, which is
easy as melting butter. For that's *all* you have to do in the
way of cooking.

You will need:

Butter	Cayenne pepper
Egg yolks	Salt
Lemon juice	Blender

In a small saucepan, heat ½ cup (1 stick) of butter to
bubbling but do not let it brown. Into the container of the
blender put 3 egg yolks, 2 tablespoons of lemon juice, ¼
teaspoon of salt and a pinch of cayenne. Cover the container

and turn motor on high; immediately remove cover and quickly pour in the hot butter in a steady stream. The moment all the butter has been added, turn off the motor. Makes ¾ cup Hollandaise Sauce—enough for four servings. For larger quantities, use 4 egg yolks, 1 cup of butter and 4 tablespoons of lemon juice.

At Serving Time:

Serve immediately or keep warm—over but not touching boiling water. It is a Dream-Thing to serve over cooked broccoli or asparagus or cauliflower or with poached fish or over poached eggs. If you mount said egg on a paper-thin slice of ham, set upon a toasted English muffin half and mask it with Hollandaise you have nothing less than Eggs Benedict.

Editor's Note

The short cut which Poppy Cannon devised for the Prime Minister of Ghana may help other cooks to cope more easily with some of the great "classics" in the sauce world: Béarnaise Sauce and Sauce Medici.

For Béarnaise, cook 2 chopped shallots and parsley, whole peppercorns, tarragon, vinegar in water until soft and reduce to 2 tablespoons. Put this mixture in the blender with a pinch of salt and proceed as for the Hollandaise.

And if Sauce Medici would look good on your menu, add tomato paste and a bit of basil to the base for Béarnaise and blend it all happily with a hint of garlic into a sauce that is bound to impress even the most critical boss, or the boss's wife, or the in-laws.

Poppy Cannon also remembers this:

WHEN the young King Baudouin of Belgium came to the Overseas Press Club after his tour of the United States, he allowed as how he had been subjected to a kind of shock treatment at the hands of the American Press—bombarded on all sides by questions which he might earlier have considered indiscreet, "particularly questions about young ladies." So we elbowed our way through the crowd.

And we said to the King, said we, "There is a question that is not indiscreet, but it might seem startling."

"Do please ask it," said the King, thus giving us an opportunity to get a really good close-up look at him. He is a slim young man, not quite but almost six feet tall. His eyes are blue but they look darker under his round owlish spectacles. His hair is brown, but it too looks darker because it is so carefully slicked down. He has the appearance of a junior Madison Avenue executive, almost the typical young Man in the Grey Flannel Suit, except for his collar. Even on that very hot afternoon in early summer it was a high stiff collar, so white and shiny that it looked as if it must have been buffed.

"The question is about eating," we said apologetically . . . what did he remember most vividly about his meals in the United States? He smiled and then he laughed. Visibly the collar bent.

"Chicken," he answered without a moment's hesitation, "chicken, chicken, everywhere."

His aides agreed that the King had been deluged with chicken in all forms—Southern fried, barbecued, roasted, fricasséed. His favorite among all of them was (though we admit it does sound almost too pat) chicken à la king that was served to him in Texas. It seems to have been a very special à la king, for according to the description by members of his entourage, the dish was richly gilded with egg yolks and had a lively taste of onion and the sparkle of lemon juice.

QUICK AND REGAL CHICKEN

American cookbooks contain many classic recipes for dishes of this type. But there is a new way to achieve a dish that is wondrously similar to the one that made the King's eyes shine.

You will need:

Chicken à la king, canned or frozen
Egg
Lemon juice
Instant onion
Mushrooms

Begin with a package of quick-frozen chicken à la king. Add 1 (4 oz.) tin of sliced, broiled-in-butter mushrooms complete with liquid and ½ teaspoon of dehydrated instant onion. Heat slowly. Remove from fire. Beat 2 egg yolks or 1 whole egg slightly with a silver fork. Add 1 teaspoon of lemon juice to the egg and beat again. Stir 2 tablespoons of the hot sauce from the chicken into the egg. This method will prevent the egg yolk from curdling. Then add the egg to the chicken à la king and stir. Heat again but do not allow to boil after the egg has been added. Keep warm over hot water in a double boiler or in a chafing dish.

At Serving Time:

Place on toast, or even rice. Or, better still, serve on flaky-hot baking powder biscuits. (Could be the ready-to-bake type.) This amount makes two king-size servings.

Quickies avec Chichi

JOSEPH QUENTIN RIZNIK

IT HAS BEEN said at times that the gay young blades who earned their journalistic spurs on the Paris edition of the Chicago *Tribune* in the twenties had an extra talent for picking the bright side of life. Joseph Quentin Riznik was one of them. He proves his optimism by describing his contribution to the *Overseas Press Club Cookbook* as "quickies," but being a sound reporter he carefully adds *avec chichi,* and it is this little "extra fuss" entailed in his recipes that provides the enjoyable tang and flavor to his recipes.

Joseph Quentin Riznik writes:

FOR CHANGE of pace and palate a quickie section of some chichi dishes and sans name-dropping. A quick list of some simple oddments of amateur cooking in the home kitchen or kitchenette or serving pantry and meant to be served forth at an Overseas Buffet in which the O.P.C. cookbook host may take a dozen guests on a jetflite around the world of tastes and flavors.

POMMES À L'HUILE

Six good-sized potatoes boiled, sliced while warm into a shallow bowl, salted lightly and dusted with fine-ground white pepper, a heaping cupful of finely minced fresh parsley lightly mixed with the potato slices, the whole drenched with peanut oil—and drench is the word for it. That's it. And you might try a thick slice of onion, finely chopped, tossed in and/or a squeeze of lemon juice.

EGGPLANT GAS STOVE

Armenian, Balkan, Arabic, Syrian—whatever designation you care to give it, the essence of the matter is a gas stove. On the stove or gas plate, place a live eggplant, just as it comes out of your shopping bag without washing or preparation of any kind, on the ring of the gas stove. Light the gas and turn it up full blast. Burn one side black—maybe 5 minutes of burning—turn the gas off and grabbing the stem carefully turn the thing over. Relight the gas and do the same thing to the other side. Remove the miserable-looking charred thing to a plate, cut longitudinally to lay the insides open. Allow to cool for fifteen minutes or so, scoop out the *ikra* (caviar, that is) of the entire eggplant, being careful not to include any of the outside charred skin, and when you have the outscooped stuff in a shallow bowl, use the edge of the bowl of a tablespoon to chop the mound of stuff coarsely. Drench with a first-quality French olive oil or with peanut oil, lightly chopping the oil into the *ikra*. Now and only now salt lightly and use fine white pepper or coarse black pepper to taste. A few minutes before serving, mince a good-sized onion finely and stir into the *ikra*. Serve in a bowl at warm room temperature with small squares of fresh white bread handy to be piled by your guests with *ikra* and eaten out of hand. Don't confuse this with the chilled tomato *ikras à la Russe*. If perchance there is some *ikra* left over, it converts into a pungent relish by mincing two fat cloves of garlic into the leftover, adding a big splash of vinegar and a heaping spoon of sugar.

NAHIT NIBBLES

Cecci beans done with lower East Side Manhattan chichi. Drain a can of chick-peas, add ½ can of onion soup or 1 tablespoon of onion soup mix. Bring to a boil. Let cool in the broth. Drain thoroughly. Place in a shallow bowl in a warm oven for a while, sprinkle generously with coarse black pepper. Pile into a bowl to be eaten hot or cold like shelled peanuts.

HORSE-RADISH-JUST-HORSE-RADISH

Freshly ground horse-radish root is a rarity to track down and purchase. But the whole root you'll find easily by asking around. Soak it overnight in water to cover either before or after peeling. Use the coarse-fine side of your grater and be prepared to weep copiously. Yep, cooks cry for it. For a frankfurter budget, serve the grated horse-radish as is, without any tampering, with piping hot frankfurters. The method of eating is to bite off the end of the frankfurter, then dunk the juicy end into the grated horse-radish. The amount that sticks is just the right amount for the next bite. Dunk and bite until you've run out of frankfurters or the horse-radish or both. For the roast beef budget, whip up a bowl of whipped cream, *naturelle*. Fold in the dry grated horse-radish. Serve it with roast beef.

FRESH COCONUT GOODIES

With an ice pick or screw driver puncture the eyes of the nut, pour the milk into a bowl. Crack the nut open, remove the meat. Peel the brown skin from the white meat. Use

the coarse side of your grater and when you have a mound
of fresh grated coconut you are in business. To whipped
cream cheese add an equal part, in volume, of the grated
fresh coconut, blend well.

What you're going to make out of this basic mixture is
coconut balls, each the size of a large hazelnut or small
walnut. Try an assortment the first time out by flavoring
small batches of this basic mixture. Use separate small
bowls. Add curry to one bowl; a can of anchovy paste to
another; onion salt with a sprinkle of sage to another.

A San Francisco favorite is to add a fat clove of garlic,
squirted into the bowl through the garlic press, with five
drops of olive oil and fine white pepper. Allow each bowl
to "age" in the icebox for several hours before fashioning
into coconut balls. Serve forth each flavor separately on a
chilled serving plate. The coconut milk may be used to
moisten the whipped cream mixture to the proper consistency.

Whatever your favorite flavor of coconut and cream
cheese—and some like the mixture sans flavor—it makes an
elegant stuffing for chicken breast. Depending on what axis
the chicken lies, it has an east and west breast or north and
south breast. Whatever your orientation, loosen the skin of
the chicken breast, working down from the neck. Stuff the
resulting pocket with as many coconut balls as it will ac-
commodate. Sew up with needle and thread. Pat the stuffed
breast dry with a towel, but gently, dust with a suspicion of
flour and fine white pepper, fry golden brown in copious
amount of unsalted butter, place in hot oven for 8 minutes
when pan-browned. Remove thread before serving forth on
a slice of white bread which has been fried in the well-
buttered pan. Yes, this is a variation on the classic chicken
Kiev, but then woman is a variation on that classic—man.

Who Has the Hottest Steak?

COLUMBIA ROSSI

COVERING assignments in Spain, Latin America, Italy and the Caribbean for the American News Service and others, Columbia Rossi has her own recipes for our national dish: steak. She writes:

D ID YOU ever see a terrific bullfight where the bull ends up as the hero? Well, I did. And did you ever eat the luscious steak of a valiant bull? Well, I did.

A quaint butcher shop in Mexico City around the corner from the American Embassy is owned by an *aficionado*, meaning a bullfight fan. Oftentimes I cooked the meat of the brave bulls who had fought in the *corrida* the Sunday before. Don Pedro, a rotund man with a twinkle in his eye, makes eating steak from a bull a *pièce de résistance*.

It was a Monday morning as I sauntered into the shop. A crowd of women was standing around the counter. Don Pedro was gesturing and describing the great *corrida* of the day before. While doing this, he hugged a huge carcass.

As he spotted me, he halted and slapped the carcass with gusto and affection. Then he called out to me while all eyes turned: "*Señorita, mi amiga Americana,* did you go to the bullfights yesterday?"

I nodded. Indeed I had. How could I forget that a near riot was caused by the fifth bull—a bull who refused to be dominated; a bull so brave and defiant that he won the *oles* and cheers of the onlookers; a bull that put to shame the famous matador who was fined incessantly by the judges in the box who ordered the trumpets sounded indicating the *multas* or fines. These fines are charged to the bullfighter who fails to kill the bull in a certain time limit.

The matador's *muleta* failed to hit its mark. Each time the bull successfully shook the sword out and at one stab the *muleta* bounced into the air falling down dangerously near the irate bullfighter. The crowds jeered the performer while they cheered the bull. Finally, peons and other toreadors had to help put an end to the frenzied bull. The people stood up in ovation to the animal, waving kerchiefs and shouting *Oles*.

For a moment I was lost in the crowd at the arena when Don Pedro awakened me to: "*Señorita,* what would you say if you eat the meat of that famous bull?"

Understanding and appreciating his emotions, I smiled in acquiescence.

"Then, listen everybody," he said, holding the carcass affectionately, "this treat is on me. I was the highest bidder at the *corrida* for this brave bull and now I will honor him by giving it all away free."

I hated to see him lose money, but at the same time I could not offend him. Then too, I had never tasted freshly cut meat and I asked Don Pedro how to prepare the steak he cut for me.

"Mix some olive oil and red vinegar and salt and pepper. Then some *orégano*. Drop the steak in. First one side, and then the other. Then broil it to taste. After it is done, mix some chili and tabasco and pour on top. *Señorita,* you will like it."

I did. It was delicious and I can recommend steak à la Mexicana. Some may feel that a Chinese steak can be pretty hot too, as you can gather from the following recipe:

TONG-YAN YOKE-PAR

that has all the flavors of the Far East to delight just two diners:

1½ pounds of sirloin steak
½ cup of sliced mushrooms
1 teaspoon of light soya sauce
2 tablespoons of oyster sauce
1 teaspoon of Chinese sweet vegetable sauce
1 teaspoon of monosodium glutamate
1 teaspoon of mustard
1 tablespoon of cornstarch
½ cup of water
Garlic—1½ cups of soup stock

Mix the spices, cornstarch and water, stirring well. Broil the steak. When one side is done, sprinkle with garlic on both sides. Broil until medium done. Slice.

Pour 1½ cups of soup stock in the skillet from which the steak has been removed. When it boils, add the mushrooms, salt and the mixed sauces. Stir until thick and pour over steak.

Would You Like Perle Mesta's Hors d'Oeuvres?

KATHRYN CRAVENS

PERLE MESTA'S fame as a hostess is undisputed. Kathryn Cravens, author of *Pursuit of Gentlemen,* actress, news commentator and correspondent who traveled through twenty-two countries on various assignments, will tell you about some of the hors d'oeuvres served at a party of Madame Ambassador and hint at how she secured the recipes.

IT WAS going to be Madame Perle Mesta's most fabulous party. Following her return as Ambassador to Luxemburg she made plans to see that folks sat up and took notice. And they did. Replies came back from all over the world accepting her invitation.

Newspaper columnists hinted that in addition to a few members of reigning royalty, three out-of-a-throne kings would appear. Even the President of the United States might drop in. It finally became simpler to count by the dozens the number of ambassadors, governors, senators and congressmen expected. Hollywood stars promised to entertain. The hotel where Mrs. Mesta lived assured that the buffet tables, laden for one thousand guests, would look like paintings.

I flew to Washington from New York the day of the big affair. The city was crowded. Mrs. Mesta had made a reservation for me in her hotel and I felt lucky to have a room waiting, even if it had turned out to be off the back hall, rear.

To my surprise, I was ushered into a tremendous suite, suitable for the harem of a sultan who wanted lots of company. I telephoned and asked the desk clerk about the apparent mistake. It wasn't, he assured me.

"But the price," I blurted, remembering our Texas wells spout dust instead of oil, and I had counted five baskets of fruit in as many bedrooms.

"As a special favor," the clerk said, "and because you will probably remain for some time after the party is over, the suite will only cost you $150 a day." I was too weak to thank him for the bargain.

It seemed stupid to waste all of that space and not show off my Washington home, which I could afford for only one night. So when Mrs. Mesta came by to see if I were comfortable, I invited her to tea, knowing that a few other guests could be rounded up. She accepted and said that she had intended to invite a few of the Hollywood stars up to her apartment for cocktails but her secretary would get in touch with them and we could all meet at my place.

My party was going fine. People enjoyed the well-stocked bar that had been set up. Mrs. Mesta, her sister, Mrs. George Tyson, and Celeste Holm actually wanted tea. But none came. Neither did the fancy hors d'oeuvres I had ordered.

Demanding service, after several pleas, I got an assistant chef on the phone. "It is impossible," he groaned. "Mrs. Mesta's party has us crazy. We are decorating *her* hors d'oeuvres . . ."

That gave me an idea. And because I promised never to

tell, I can't reveal how it happened, but within a few moments several waiters rolled in tea wagons laden with delightfully decorated delicacies. Smugly, I thought, although small in comparison, this party will also be remembered.

Perle took one look and exclaimed, "Why, Kathryn, how on earth did you manage to get some of my special hors d'oeuvres up here?"

With great composure, I answered brilliantly, "Er-ah-er!" And my glass crashed to the floor.

The next day, when I went to say good-by to the assistant chef, he explained a few secrets—the recipes of the canapés that gave me away. They are:

AMERICAN BEAUTY STUFFED EGGS

12 fresh eggs
Pickled beet juice

Hard-boil eggs, cool in cold water and peel. Drop whole eggs in beet juice and let stand until they are ruby red. Dry them and slice in half lengthwise. Remove yolks.

CAVIAR FILLING

Russian caviar   Orange juice
Lemon juice   Paprika

Season caviar with lemon and orange juices and fill the halves of eggs. Grate egg yolk over top and dust with paprika. Any stuffing can be used to alternate on platter.

RADISH ROSES

Radishes—uniform size

Wash and cut down thin strips of red peel almost to the stems to form petals. Then place in ice water. The peel will curl back like rose petals. They can be served as part of hors d'oeuvres tray or to garnish.

OLD-FASHIONED RADISH BOUQUET

24 large radishes
⅔ cup of Bleu cheese
1 tablespoon port wine
Paprika

Proceed as in Radish Roses, but remove inner part, leaving only the petals. Return to ice water. Mash Bleu cheese well, add port and stir. Force the mixture through a fine-meshed sieve, then place in a pastry bag. Use small rose design tube. Fill the cavity of each radish, which has been drained and dried, and dust each with paprika. Arrange all 24 on top of water cress in an old-fashioned bouquet. Allow water cress to just peep out beyond "roses." Serve chilled.

CHEESE APPLES

2 8-oz. packages of American cheese
1 cup of chopped pecans
24 tiny pickled onions, chopped
Paprika
Whole cloves

Mash cheese with fork until it is soft and add pecans and onions. Mix well. Shape into small round balls, and roll each ball on one side in paprika. Stick a clove for stem in each "apple."

STUFFED PICKLE FLOWERS

Dill Pickles (B&G Dwarf Brand)

Cut off one end of each pickle and remove center with apple corer. Stuff them carefully with filling, chill for ½ hour. Slice thin. Arrange on cold platter in shape of a five-petaled flower. The stem can be made of a long match-wide piece of pickle.

PICKLE FILLINGS

1. Mix equal parts of Bleu or Roquefort and cream cheese
2. Cream cheese with chives 3. Cheddar cheese mashed
with a little grated onion 4. Ground ham with cream cheese
and dash of onion salt

PÂTÉ DE FOIE DE POULET

1 pound of fresh chicken livers
1 small onion
1 stalk of celery
½ teaspoon of salt
3 whole peppercorns

Wash livers, drain, and cover with water in saucepan.
Add onion, celery, salt and peppercorns, and bring to a
boil. Simmer for about 20 minutes under lid, then drain
and cool. Grind livers only through finest meat chopper
blade and mash. Then mix:

4 tablespoons of grated onion
1½ teaspoons of salt
1 pinch of cayenne
2 teaspoons of dry mustard
⅛ teaspoon of mace
⅛ teaspoon of powdered cloves
5 teaspoons of French brandy
1 cup of softened butter or rendered chicken fat
¼ teaspoon of anchovy paste or 1 finely chopped truffle
3 drops of Tabasco sauce
Fresh parsley—decorate
Sliced green olives—decorate

Add all these ingredients to ground liver and blend together until smooth. Pack into a crock or mold and chill in
refrigerator overnight. Turn out on cold platter and decorate. Serve with crackers, toasted rounds or French bread.

Part VIII

FROM THE SHORES OF THE BALTIC
TO THE ADRIATIC AND THE
SEA OF MARMARA

A "Treat" at the Ritz in Budapest

FARMER MURPHY

FARMER MURPHY, who scored many a scoop for the papers he represented as an overseas correspondent, has a typical story of feast and famine. From his hilltop home in New Canaan, Connecticut, he goes back to the days of the Bela Kun revolution in Hungary during 1919.

He writes:

As I was then stationed in Vienna for the Chicago *Tribune*, it was only a short quick jump by car to Budapest. There I found myself among half a dozen or so other correspondents. We discovered at once that our most pressing problem, after that of gathering news, was "When do we eat?" The question of where we should sleep was fortunately and surprisingly easily answered. We discovered that with the coming of the Communists, or Bolsheviks, as they are usually referred to, the propertied class pretty generally fled the city and the managers of hotels simply deserted them.

The new government put a Bolshevik soldier on guard at

the hotel entrance and he usually took only a casual interest in his job. The correspondents found that to get sleeping accommodations they needed only to wander into the hotel, select the room of their choice and settle down. They selected the Donau Palast, known as the Ritz.

However, the food problem was difficult. The normal sources of supply had dried up after the Bolsheviks took over, partly because transportation had broken down, partly because of fear.

But the British had sent along an officer to watch developments. He knew where there were stacks of the standard prisoner-of-war packages left on hand at the end of the war. They contained a can of bully beef, a portion of bacon, apple butter, tea, hard biscuits, a small square of salt pork and a package of cigarettes. He let us have some of them. The kitchen help and waiters, who had no place to flee to, had remained in the hotel and they gladly went to work to concoct meals out of these supplies and to scout around to see what could be bartered in the way of additional food by forays into the near countryside.

One morning as I was about to leave the hotel, I ran into McCarthy of the London *Times*, who was talking with a rather tall, erect man of middle age and distinguished bearing. His well-tailored suit was rumpled and showed recent hard usage. McCarthy introduced him as his friend, Count — and I recognized the name as that of one of the Hungarian families that were as well known as the Esterházy or Károli, but which escapes me after forty years.

McCarthy explained that the Count had been in hiding in the woods, with almost no food. He was desperately hungry. Did I have anything to eat in my room? I thought there might be something in my prisoner package. I took the Count to my room. All we found was the square of raw salt pork and some hard biscuits. I apologized to my guest for making him walk up several flights, without having any real food for him, and I said I would scout about for something better. But the Count would not permit it. Taking out his pocket knife, he cut off slices of raw salt pork and made what he called a good meal out of it with hard crackers. He looked as if this were a real treat for him.

Raw salt pork, in a crisis, after a long fast, may seem palatable. But I was to learn, on that same trip, that it is held in high esteem in parts of Hungary. We happened to drive through a small village about fifty miles from Budapest that was all agog over a peasant wedding. Seeing our foreign car, the celebrants insisted that we join in the party being given by the bridegroom's wealthy father. In a big, almost square room long tables were set up along the wall where the guests ate and drank, while in the center of the room gay couples danced to the tune of the local band. The food was plentiful and delicious, and the host poured Tokay with a lavish hand, as if there were an unlimited supply of it.

Every little while some guest would get up from the groaning table and propose a toast to the bride and bridegroom, glasses would be refilled and emptied fast as required by tradition. In between, couples would get up and dance to shake down the food and drinks and to return to the table for more solid and liquid sustenance.

The food served at the wedding party by trim young girls in swishing wide, brightly colored skirts, tight bodices and fancy headdresses was a joy after the lean days in Budapest. I was particularly impressed by a cold soup which, to my surprise, was made of a fish of which we usually think very little: carp. While the host himself carved roast goose, his wife pointed with pride to a concoction baked in a beautiful earthenware dish which turned out to be her own homemade goose liver *pâté*. Her pride was absolutely justified.

After about seven hours, as the sun was rising, the Hungarian who had insisted on our joining the party, invited me to breakfast at his house.

When I sat down at the table, I saw a plate in front of me and on this plate, as a starter, there was a slice of fat, raw salt pork and beside it, a glass of brandy.

Try this for a morning-after headache!

Note from the Editor

I am glad to state that a good many years ago a lovely blond Hungarian movie star, Camilla von Hollay, taught me the secret of the:

HUNGARIAN CARP SOUP

which can be served hot or cold, and what is more, it can be prepared the day before you plan to serve it. For ten guests take:

1 6-pound carp
1 bay leaf
Big bunch of soup greens, including leek, carrot, celery root, celery stalk, parsnip, parsley and parsley root
5 lumps of sugar
1 teaspoon of paprika
Salt to taste
Thin slices of lemon
Optional: wine or vinegar

Boil the soup greens, bay leaf and paprika for 4 hours in 5 quarts of water, a good part of which will evaporate. When the broth has finished cooking, pass it through a sieve, mashing a little of the vegetables into it.

While the greens cook, cover the carp with coarse salt. Rinse off the salt when the broth is nearly done. Cut the carp into slices, of a little less than 1-inch thickness, except for those near the tail which can be a little thicker to secure a fair division. Place in the hot broth you have salted and tasted and simmer until done, but not tender enough to fall apart.

If you like to cook with wine, add a little to the broth before cooking the fish. If you suspect the fish of tasting a little muddy, a tablespoon of wine vinegar can be helpful.

Place a slice of fish on each soup plate, with a sliver of lemon, possibly a few pieces of carrot for color effect, then cover with the broth in which the fish was cooked. If you want to serve this soup cold, put the plates in the refrigerator, preferably overnight. After about 8 hours the broth will be like fine jellied consommé. Try to resist the temptation of discarding the head; it ranks as a delicacy among Europe's connoisseurs who can take it apart with the dexterity of a surgeon.

Florida red snapper and similar fish lend themselves to this same Hungarian treatment.

In normal times, a roast suckling pig would have figured at the village wedding—but in 1919, as in many a tragic lean year thereafter, the delicious little Hungarian porkers, which are among the best in Europe, were worth their weight in gold. In the days after World War I there was little that an astute farmer could not get in exchange for them, from a piano to a fancy fur coat.

Geese ranked as a substitute in the countryside where youngsters under school age and the very old shared in the task of keeping the flock together in patches of greenery that other farm animals disdained. The goose fat takes the place of butter for weeks on end, while the goose liver will be baked in earthen dishes and kept in a cool cellar in readiness for a festive occasion.

Here is the Hungarian recipe that rivals many a commercial *pâté de foie gras.*

HUNGARIAN PÂTÉ DE FOIE GRAS

1 good-sized goose liver, sprinkled with thyme and marjoram
2 tablespoons of goose fat
¼ teaspoon of salt
⅛ teaspoon of "rose" paprika
2 tablespoons of water

Place the goose liver in a fireproof dish and pour the warmed fat and water over it. Add salt, pepper and paprika. Cover the dish and cook for ½ hour at 350°. To brown the liver slightly, increase the heat to 400°, after removing the lid. To be sure that the liver does not get dry, put a few slices of bacon over it as protection.

If it is to be kept for a short while, pour liquid goose fat, or best-quality lard, up to the rim of the dish in which the goose liver has cooked and store in refrigerator.

Sign Language Has Its Dangers

JOSEPH PETERS

ONE of the lucky correspondents is Joseph G. Peters—lucky because he returned to his prewar beat and can view present-day developments with the wisdom that comes from intimate knowledge and experience. His headquarters are in Belgrade, Yugoslavia, where he carries on reporting tasks which he started in the middle thirties, covering stories from Vienna, Trieste, Prague, all over the Balkans down to Saloníki.

This is an area where languages present a real problem. Even sign language has its pitfalls, as revealed in the story of our gay, debonair—and food-loving—friend, who usually can cope with all kinds of situations thanks to a fine sense of humor.

NOSING around for background stories in the Balkans early in 1936, I found myself one day on a train bound from Bitolj in Yugoslavia to Saloníki in Greece.

At the speed of a snail, our train crawled through the rugged mountain country of northern Greece where apparently nothing moved but some goats and lizards. The ancient wooden coaches that made up our train looked like a string of turtles, head to tail, each one swaying its own way, yet obediently following its cinder-spewing leader through the barren canyons.

The entire rail line was about a hundred miles long. It took us just about ten hours to make it—from 8 A.M. to 6 P.M. Not really so bad, considering that it took the average Macedonian three times as long to ride this distance on a jackass. But when you get practically nothing to eat all the way . . .

Well, that's the sad gastronomic story I really want to tell before I start chewing up my own metaphors.

For a couple of days I had been well fed in Bitolj on such succulent dishes as *musaka,* suckling pig, *pita* with chopped meat or with spinach, and barbecued lamb. So before boarding my train that morning, I had only coffee and a *croissant.* I never gave a thought to food during the trip, expecting for sure to be able to grab a bite at some station restaurant along the way. It didn't work out that way though.

An Albanian, a businessman I guess he was, shared my nondescript first-class compartment. He looked like a pleasant guy. We grinned at each other from time to time, since we got nowhere conversationally. I tried every language I could say a word or two in, but my friend understood nothing but Albanian. And Albanian, of course, has no common roots with any other modern tongue. It's supposed to be derived from the ancient Illyrian, and that was one of the languages, aside from Assyrian and a few others, that I had missed in my classical education. How did I know my boy was an Albanian? I pointed a finger at him and said "Bitolj?" He said "Tirana."

Every few miles our train would stop at a station, and it looked as if everybody rushed out to the water pump and filled up earthen jugs or bottles. After I had watched this rush at a few stations, the novelty wore off. By noon I also got bored looking at the desolate countryside between stations where apparently nothing grew but rocks. And with boredom came hunger. So at the next station I got out with the water boys in search of food. Except for some sticky candy and soda pop, there wasn't a thing to buy. The same luck at the next couple of stations. Now I was really getting hungry. Then it happened.

My Albanian friend pulled down from the rack above him a good-sized wicker basket. When he opened it, there was the finest assortment of food I had ever seen. No soup or nuts, but everything in between and around. Tiny smoked fish, olives, snow-white sheep cheese, scallions, hard-boiled eggs, well-smoked garlicky sausages, *slivovitsa*. That was the hors d'oeuvres. The main course consisted of a luscious *bourek-pita* (my favorite Balkan meat pie), a couple of golden-brown breaded spring chickens, a jar of eggplant and green pepper salad, a big, round loaf of white bread, and a couple bottles of clear red wine. For dessert he had some *baklava*, bunches of yellow grapes, tangerines, and red apples. My mouth was watering. (It still is now while I write about it.)

After my Albanian displayed all this epicurean wealth, he grinned and made a motion asking me if I'd like to partake. Perhaps a bit greedily, I nodded my head up and down. Alby grinned, started to eat with gusto and made no move to give me anything. I was puzzled. Was the guy playing a game with me? As he gobbled away his stuff he would turn to me at times and grin. Once he offered me some wine by pointing to the bottle. Again I nodded—and nothing happened. He filled his glass and had the nerve to raise it with a big smile, giving me the toast. My return grin was a sick one this time. Finally, wiping his hands with a big white napkin, he once more turned to me offering his food. Again I nodded eagerly. Alby just shrugged his shoulders, closed the basket and put it back up on the rack. This really floored me. What in hell was this wise guy trying to do to me? Tease me to a hunger death?

Maybe I was stupid not to get up and grab some of that food while he offered it. Maybe I should wait now until he gets out of the compartment and swipe some of the stuff. Maybe . . . and I fell asleep. Then someone shook me by the shoulder. It was Alby. He grinned from ear to ear and waved good-by. We'd arrived in Saloníki.

It was about a week later, down in Athens, that someone enlightened me about the strange behavior of my Albanian pal: gestures mean different things in different parts of the world. When an Albanian says "yes," he wigwags his head from side to side. In our sign language that's "no." And when an Albanian says "no," he nods his head up and down (accompanied by a slight click of the tongue), which to us means "yes" (without the tsk). Well, when I nodded my head, my pal interpreted it correctly in Albanian as "no." So I got no food, no wine, no nothing.

But don't let this discourage you. Here is how you can make a

BOUREK-PITA

This is one of those delightful Balkan dishes that not only has a wonderful taste but can be made with ingredients to suit your own palate. As a matter of fact, you can find dozens of varieties in Yugoslavia alone where the *bourek-pita* is practically a national dish. Mainly there are three kinds: with spinach, with cheese, and with meat. The latter two break down into several sorts, depending on the kind of cheese or meat used. We'll take a *bourek-pita* with beef and pork mixed.

First of all, you need a strudel dough for pastry. If you are an expert and have a lot of time, you'll make the dough yourself, as the Yugoslavs do. But you can buy ready-made strudel leaves anywhere, so why bother. Other ingredients:

1 pound of ground beef
1 pound of ground pork
3 large onions finely minced
Shortening or oil; salt and pepper
Thyme, marjoram and a little ground bay leaf

Put 3 or 4 layers of the strudel pastry in a long, well-greased pan. Brush each layer liberally with melted shortening or oil. Mix the beef, pork, onions and salt and pepper until thoroughly blended. Break off small pieces and sprinkle over pastry. Cover with a few more layers of the pastry, each brushed with the shortening or oil. Put the pan into a fairly hot oven and bake for about 1 hour until the pastry is crisp and brown. Cut in about 4-inch pieces and serve warm. This is enough for about six people as a main dish. The Yugoslavs use the dish often as an appetizer. You can do that also by cutting the dish into smaller pieces. And it goes just fine with cocktails. The danger is, the *bourek-pita* being so good, you'd eat so many of those smaller pieces that you'll skip the main dish. So you better make the *bourek-pita* the chief part of your dinner.

As a main dish, *bourek-pita* is accompanied by a wonderful sauce that is a Balkan specialty. It's base is *kaymak*, a yoghurt-like mixture. It consists only of the skin which forms on top of the milk resting in big vats. Daily it is skimmed off carefully and ripened in a wooden tub. The Yugoslav and other Balkan cooks add their herbs and meat drippings to it and obtain a velvety sauce with a delightfully baffling flavor that has none of the cloying heaviness of plain cream.

From Peacetime Warsaw to Wartime Istanbul

BETTY WASON

MY FIRST bona fide assignment, with expense account, reached me in Prague in the summer of 1938. I was to travel to Poland to interview a young Captain Bursynski who was preparing a spectacular balloon flight, strictly for scientific purposes.

I had gone to Europe with nothing much but a burning spirit of adventure and free-lance credentials. Now that I had a real assignment I decided to be wise and "make" something on expenses by traveling third class. Until then I had always traveled third class, and lived third class, to make my meager finances stretch as far as possible. But it had been on big international routes. This time I had to travel through poor provinces. The powers that be held that the oldest carriages were good enough. They were alive with insects of all kinds, and the traveling peasants were noisy and boisterous. At the end of what seemed an interminable night the train pulled into Warsaw. I decided I'd done enough slumming and had better enjoy my expense account. There were few better places to enjoy it in pre-World War II Europe than Warsaw's Hotel Bristol.

Because of that night ride, I felt as if I were in another world when hours later I sat in the sumptuous dining room of the hotel, at a white-clothed table near a tinkling fountain, listening to gentle chamber music from the orchestra. The food was superb and never to be forgotten: crayfish in aspic, as beautiful to the eye as to the palate, flavorful morsels of red crayfish in a wine-flavored jelly, interspersed with pale green-white spears of asparagus. Next came *côtelette à la Kiev*. I have enjoyed this culinary masterpiece on other occasions, but I honestly believe this surpassed them all. The white chicken meat was incredibly juicy and tender, bathed with melted sweet butter; the crisp outer coating was crunchy, golden brown yet light as fine pastry.

My captain was not in the capital. I finally found him near the Polish-Czech border in a small resort in the beautiful Tatra Mountains. Despite the language barrier I managed to get his story and file it on time. The flight was scheduled for October 1, 1938. That was the day Hitler had set for his march into Czechoslovakia. After the details of the Munich conference became known, the balloon and equipment mysteriously went up in flames. Europe no longer had time for scientific research.

But I had enriched my gastronomical knowledge as I was delighted to do in my other assignments, as for instance in wartime Istanbul.

The year was 1940. Neutral Turkey, in those jittery days, was a meeting ground for diplomatic personnel and journalists of many nationalities, all eying one another suspiciously and all in turn watched even more suspiciously by the Turks. Outwardly life for the hotel set was very gay. At a swimming party one day I met a Soviet vice-consul who began asking me out.

In the hope that I might pick up material for a story, I accepted his invitations only to be offered a job as a spy, at $300 a month. I assured the gentleman that I was strictly a journalist and not interested in making money by any other means—but I would be glad to give him any information I happened to come across *if* he would do the same for me. I knew no answers to the questions he asked me about American production but why not dream some up? The vice-consul took notes and invited me to another lunch at an excellent restaurant run by White Russian exiles.

The meal started off well enough, because the food was so wonderful. We had finished the soup and *piroshki* course and were started on the Caucasian *shashlik* when he told me with a curled lip that the information I had given him about American production was all wrong.

With a straight face, he went to work to feed me the Red party line to the point where it even spoiled the succulent *shashlik* for me. Regretfully I thought of the cheesecake that had been ordered, the smooth, creamy *pasha* that I had enjoyed at the restaurant on other occasions. But his propaganda fare was more than I could take. I told him so in no uncertain terms and marched out.

If you try my *pasha*, you'll know that I had to be real mad to pass up the end of the meal. You'll also enjoy my other recipes gleaned in Warsaw and Istanbul.

POLISH RAKI W GALARECIE
(CRAYFISH IN ASPIC)

1 pound of shrimp in the shell*
12 asparagus spears (fresh, frozen or canned), cooked, diced
1 or 2 carrots, cooked, diced
2 cups of vegetable stock
Sprig of fresh dill, or ⅛ teaspoon ground dill seed
1 cup of very dry Spanish sherry
½ teaspoon of salt (or to taste)
1 small onion, peeled
2 envelopes of unflavored gelatine
¾ cup of mayonnaise

The vegetables are cooked first and the water saved as stock for the aspic. If canned asparagus is used, save the liquid from the can for the same purpose. Measure 2 cups, adding water if necessary. Combine this with ½ cup of sherry, the peeled onion and salt, if needed (taste to determine), and the dill. Bring to a boil, and when boiling briskly, add shrimp in the shells; bring again to a boil and cook just 3 minutes or until shells are bright pink. Cool. Remove shrimp, peel, strain stock through cheesecloth or very fine sieve. Measure liquid; add remaining ½ cup sherry to make 2½ cups altogether. Soften gelatine in 2 tablespoons of cold water; dissolve by adding boiling-hot stock. Arrange a layer of shelled shrimp in bottom of well-rinsed 1-quart ring mold. Cover with a film of clear gelatine; chill until firm. (To speed up, place in freezer just 5 minutes.) Mix remaining gelatine mixture with the mayonnaise, beat with rotary beater until smooth. Arrange diced asparagus and small pieces of carrot over shrimp; cover with layer of mayonnaise, chill until firm. Chop remaining shrimp in small pieces; place a layer of chopped shrimp over the firm vegetable-mayonnaise layer; add remaining mayonnaise until mold is filled to brim. Chill in refrigerator until

---

* Since crayfish are not generally available here, shrimp will do.

very firm, at least 2 hours. Unmold on lettuce. This is enough to serve six generously.

CÔTELETTES À LA KIEV

(To serve 6)

6 whole chicken breasts
¼ pound of butter
Flour
2 eggs, well beaten
1½ cups of fine, dry bread crumbs
3 pounds of fat or 3 pints of oil for deep-fat frying

The breasts are boned and skinned, with the collarbone left on. The butcher will do this for you on request, but it's easy enough to do it yourself with a sharp knife. Cover the meat with waxed paper and pound mercilessly, using the edge of a plate or back of a cleaver. Meantime, form butter into pieces the "size of pigeons' eggs" and chill thoroughly by placing in a bowl of ice or in the freezer until very firm and hard; then roll in flour. Place one of these in each pounded chicken breast; then pound the meat together to seal all the way around. Dip each breast in beaten egg, then in bread crumbs, taking care to brush egg around the edges of the meat to seal thoroughly. Chill thoroughly, then repeat the egg-and-crumb process. Chill again. Heat the fat or oil in a deep saucepan, preferably in an electric fryer or electric saucepan with fryer basket. If frying thermometer is used, heat to 375°; in electric saucepan, set control at 360°. Fry one *côtelette* at a time, until crisp and golden on each side. Keep fried *côtelettes* in oven heated to 400° until rest of meal is ready to serve, but no more than 10 minutes. When *côtelettes* are cut into with fork, melted butter oozes out in a golden stream over the tender white breast meat.

CAUCASIAN SHASHLIK

3 pounds of lamb from rump or leg, cut into cubes
2 or 3 onions, thickly sliced
2 peeled garlic cloves
1 cup of dry white wine, or ½ cup of vinegar and ½ cup of water
⅛ teaspoon of allspice
1½ teaspoons of salt
1 or 2 very small eggplants
Olive oil
1 lemon, sliced

Place lamb in bowl, cover with minced garlic and a few slices of onion. Combine wine, allspice and salt, heat to boiling, pour over meat. Let marinate several hours or overnight, then pat meat dry with paper towel.

About 1 hour before meat is to be cooked, cut eggplant into thick slices, leaving skin on. Get the smallest eggplants you can find, for these seem to have more flavor. If medium-sized eggplants must be used, cut into squares about the same diameter as onion slices. Douse the eggplant with plenty of olive oil, and let it stand long enough to absorb the oil thoroughly. Then lace meat on skewers alternately with eggplant (salted before placing on skewers) and onion slices. Broil over a hot charcoal fire or on the spit of an electric rotisserie until meat is well browned.

Serve slices of lemon with the meat, the lemon juice to be pressed over the meat with the tines of a fork. This is enough *shashlik* to serve six.

PASHA

1 pound of pot cheese, well drained
½ pound of softened butter
½ pint of sour cream
1 cup of confectioners' sugar
¼ cup of chopped or ground blanched toasted almonds
¾ teaspoon of vanilla

Put cheese through food mill or sieve or beat in electric blender until smooth. Combine with butter, sour cream, sugar and vanilla; beat until smooth and creamy. Fold in almonds. Line a 1-quart mold with cheesecloth and press cheese mixture into it, pressing down hard with back of wooden spoon. Cover with waxed paper, then with small plate. Cover plate with heavy stone or some other heavy object. Chill in refrigerator 24 hours; to unmold, pat outside of mold with towel wrung in hot water, turn out on platter and carefully remove cheesecloth. Serve with Sauce Sabianoff.

SAUCE SABIANOFF

In a medium-sized bowl, place 2 unbeaten egg yolks, 2 tablespoons of confectioners' sugar, the grated rind of ½ lemon and ¼ cup of amontillado-type Spanish sherry. Place bowl over hot water in saucepan and beat constantly with rotary beater or portable electric mixer until mixture is smooth and thickened, about 5 minutes. Add 1 teaspoon of lemon juice and 1 tablespoon of rum, beat about 30 seconds longer and remove from hot water. Makes about 2 cups of sauce.

Part IX

MEET MAHARAJAHS, MAORIS, PATHAN
SOLDIERS, TYCOONS, PEKING DUCKS
AND SURPRISES FROM JAPAN

Curry with the Maharajah
—by Proxy

LAWRENCE G. BLOCHMAN

WHENEVER a book or a novelette of Lawrence G. Blochman appears there is rejoicing in the ranks of the lovers of mystery stories.

As a correspondent who reported from Tokyo, from Hong Kong, from Calcutta, from Paris and Nice, from San Diego and Guatemala, who was stationed in England and France during and after World War II, this former president of the Mystery Writers of America really knows the weird characters and their backgrounds with which he entertains and baffles us.

As author of *Here's How!* the O.P.C.'s Round-the-World Bar Book, Mr. Blochman is a seasoned guide in the art of drinking, and the following story will reveal him as an expert in the art of preparing curry:

I T IS a long time since His Highness Tukoji Rao Holkar III, Maharajah of the Indian state of Indore in the 1920s has been in the news. When he did make the cable desk, he did it in a big way. His penchant for marrying American girls (one at a time; His Highness bowed to the curious customs of the bride's country rather than insist on the polygamous prerogative of an oriental potentate); his fondness for Hollywood and French cuisine; and the murder of a Bombay merchant by nine officers of his cavalry bodyguard, which led to his abdication, once made him the darling of tabloid editors. When I first met him in May 1923, however, he was only a very rich and rather obscure ruler of one of the 500-odd native states of India.

I had been working on a newspaper in Calcutta, and went to Indore to present letters of introduction to the family of a classmate of mine at the University of California, a Mahrati Brahman named Gogate. His influential family promptly arranged for me to be guest of state. As a result I had an interview with the Maharajah, and since I had no formal occidental attire, I borrowed some Mahrati court clothes—turban, skin-tight white trousers, a gold-edged gossamer scarf, and all.

The interview turned out to be a fencing match. I tried to get His Highness to express views on the future of India— while His Highness was more interested in prohibition in America, in the attitude of the United States at the impending Lausanne Conference, which was to establish peace in the Near East, and the art of shooting birds. (He offered to arrange a *skikar* for me, but I begged off.)

Next morning I was informed by the Household Officer that His Highness expected the interview to be strictly confidential and off the record. I probably couldn't have sold the story anyhow!

As I lived in a second-class guest house, protocol prevented His Highness from inviting me to dinner. However, the Household Officer, who lived right next door to one of the Maharajah's many palaces, did invite me to share a meal with His Highness by proxy. The proxy host, the court physician, and I reclined on rugs and pillows on the Household Officer's lawn, listening to court musicians and watching the blazing stars which were beginning to appear overhead. Red-turbaned *khidmatgars* brought dinner from the palace kitchens—huge brass trays, each containing twenty small nickeled bowls, most of them curried or chilled vegetables of various kinds, and because His Highness was not a Brahman, two meat curries, both mutton. As the cow is sacred in India and the pig eschewed by Moslems, the only curries you can find in India, outside of lamb and mutton, are chicken, shrimp, eggs and vegetables.

My personal preference for a curry is veal because its bland nature serves as an excellent background for the bright taste-coloration of East Indian spices. This is, of course, something you will never eat in India. But that's all right, too, because no actual curry ever tastes the same outside India. My own cook in Calcutta used to buy the spices fresh in the bazaar every morning and grind them himself. I'm sure the Maharajah's chef used at least fifty spices in various combinations.

If you insist on making your own curry, here are the basic ingredients and proportions:

1 part clove, mustard seed and poppy seed, each
2 parts cardamom, nutmeg, fennel seeds and chile peppers, each
4 parts ginger and peppercorns, each
8 parts cummin, coriander and turmeric, each

Proportions vary geographically. Curries from northern India—Mahrati curries, for instance—are quite mild, but a Madrassi curry practically explodes with chiles and ginger. In the following recipe for a veal curry (serving six) I assume you will use the curry powder from the corner grocery:

2 pounds of veal steak, cut in 2 inch cubes
2 tablespoons of butter
2 tablespoons of flour
3 tablespoons of curry powder (2 tablespoons for those with tender palates)

1½ teaspoons of Worcestershire sauce
2 medium onions, chopped coarsely
2 plump cloves of garlic, finely chopped
1 10½-ounce can of beef bouillon, equal amount of water
1 tomato, quartered
1 cup of diced celery
½ cup of diced green bell pepper
3 tablespoons of grated coconut
Salt and pepper to taste

Melt half the butter in a large pot. An Indian chef would use coconut oil, sesame oil, or ghee, but since your supermarket may not have any of these and since ghee is clarified butter anyhow, we will use butter.

When the butter melts, throw in the veal and turn up the gas so that the meats sear quickly on all sides. While turning the veal, salt and pepper it. When well seared, remove it to a platter. Any liquid residue should be poured into a cup and added to the curry later.

Melt the rest of the butter and brown the onions and garlic. Then add the flour, stirring with a wooden spoon until the mixture is as smooth as fifty-year-old sherry. When the flour browns, add the bouillon, a little at a time, stirring constantly, then the water. While this is coming to a boil, make a paste of the curry powder with some of the liquid from the pot and the Worcestershire sauce, and add this, too. Now return your meat to the pot and add the rest of your ingredients. Let the whole business stew briskly for ¾ hour, uncovered.

Now taste the curry and correct the seasoning. If your guests have fireproof palates, you may want to add a little more curry powder. You will probably find you need more salt. Then re-cover the pot and simmer for another hour.

While the simmering is going on, prepare your condiments to be served either in a Lazy Susan or small vegetable dishes. I suggest some or all of the following:

Mango chutney (The Major Grey formula is packed by a number
of firms, most of them actually shipping from India.)
Peanuts and/or blanched almonds, toasted and coarsely ground
Grated coconut, toasted to a golden brown
1 green bell pepper, coarsely chopped
1 sweet red bell pepper (or tinned pimiento), coarsely chopped
Chopped radishes
Chopped scallions
Bombay duck

Bombay duck, I hasten to explain, is really not a duck,
but a small dead fish (phosphorescent while alive), dried
and shredded. You can buy it in the United States but it is
quite expensive and quite unfragrant. I suggest substituting
Mock Bombay Duck, which is shredded dried codfish,
lightly oven-toasted in a shallow pan.

Serve your curry on a mound of fluffy boiled rice, and
add what condiments appeal to your taste. A trickle of cold
beer is useful as first aid to the unsophisticated palate. It
is also a proper accompaniment to a properly pungent
curry.

With the Maoris in New Zealand

NOLA LUXFORD DOLBERG, O.B.E.

BECAUSE of her work "for international understanding" Nola Luxford Dolberg was the third woman in the United States to be awarded the Certificate of Merit by President Truman, and King George VI awarded her the Order of the British Empire. Author of a book entitled *Pattern for Peace*, this former foreign correspondent and commentator, lecturer, leading lady of the screen and radio, has become one of the outstanding experts on Australia, New Zealand and New Guinea and, as her contribution shows on the ceremonial dishes of the Maoris, the gentle, brown-skinned native Polynesian New Zealanders.

WE WERE seated on the grass in Hawkes Bay, New Zealand, listening to a Maori chief proclaim the good deeds of the warrior, whose body, wrapped in ancient-style flax cloth and surrounded by enormous photos of recently deceased relatives, lay in state before us. We were attending a Maori *tangi*, or as it would have been called in Ireland, a wake.

Nearby sat some fifty Maori women in their native costumes of flax skirts and capes of bird feathers. On their heads were the visible signs of mourning, wreaths of weeping willow, and as the orator majestically strode back and forth on the veranda, the women swayed in rhythm as they cried and moaned for their beloved leader.

Several hundred relatives and friends of the deceased stood or squatted in the area, attentive while other chiefs, friends and relatives exclaimed about the virtues of the deceased. Maoris are great orators: they have a Shakespearean way of dramatizing every word, and repeatedly we are told: "A great oak has fallen." The Maori does not believe there is any punishment after death, but that there are twelve heavens and that Io, the Supreme Being, is in the uppermost, and therefore there is only one God.

The oratory went on for hours and then, as if by magic, we were swept into the nearby hall where row upon row of long tables laden with food greeted us. The air was heavy with a strange odor, which I discovered was shark meat—a great delicacy at a *tangi*.

Besides roast pig, there were delicacies with surprising names, such as *pipi*, an elongated shellfish that lives in sandy mud and makes a delicious soup that tastes of oyster; *paua*, another shellfish that clings to rocks and provides a flat steak, tasting of turtle after it has been subjected to energetic scrubbings and special treatment; *huhu* beetle, which some brave Maoris consume live, despite its hard wing cases, though it can be fried in butter or made into fritters; mutton bird, which is somewhat like an oversized domestic pigeon; finally eel, hot and cold, and a stew made of *toheroa*, another shellfish that sports a long white tongue which it uses both for burrowing into the sand and for propulsion.

Some three days after the speeches and feasting had started, the several hundred guests said a final farewell and started for home, some to travel next door, others to go many miles to the far corners of New Zealand. Many would not meet again until some other outstanding chief died, and there would be another *tangi* and some more

SOUSED EEL

To prepare it take:

2 pounds of eel
2 onions
½ teaspoon of mixed herbs
Vinegar
¼ teaspoon of nutmeg
1 teaspoon of butter
Salt and pepper to taste

After the eel has been skinned, rub it with coarse salt and let it rest in this coating for a few hours. When ready to cook it, rinse thoroughly with very cold water and cut it into neat pieces. Lay them in a small baking dish with finely chopped onions, mixed herbs, nutmeg, pepper and salt and dabs of butter, and cover it with vinegar. (If the eel is to be served hot, use half vinegar and half water.) Cover the dish and cook the eel until it is tender. This dish may be served hot or cold.

TOHEROA STEW

6 *toheroas* (a type of clam of unusual flavor which is a great New Zealand delicacy)
1 onion
1 tablespoon of fat
Salt to taste
½ tablespoon of flour
½ cup of milk

Melt the fat and cook the onion in it until it is tender but not brown. Add salt, cut up *toheroas*, and water to cover them. Simmer the *toheroas* until they are tender.

Thicken the stew with flour and milk. Green peas and young carrots make a pleasing addition. (Four servings.)

I should like to add that the New Zealander eats a great deal of delicious lamb—it is the favorite dish—with green peas and new potatoes. The above recipes are the exotic foods eaten only on special occasions.

We Flew to Waziristan

ALLAN A. MICHIE

FEW MEN CONVEYED a more dramatic picture of the struggle in the Middle East and in India in the grim days of 1942 than Allan Michie in his *Retreat to Victory*. Together with the photographer George Rodger, he reported from that part of the world as a correspondent for *Time*, *Life* and *Fortune*. He tells of his memories of this experience:

A CAMEL-MOUNTED detachment of the Arab Legion's famed desert patrol had arranged a camel fantasia for us in the desert Fort El Mafrak, that had been the scene of exploits of Lawrence of Arabia in World War I. The camel corps maneuvered their ungainly beasts about on the sand, charged at the cameras again and again until we got the action we wanted, staging a mock battle for our benefit. Then we were invited to what was described as a "light lunch." Our hosts led us to a cement platform which had a goatskin Bedouin tent erected overhead and served a whole sheep cooked Arab-style with the white fat of the tail draped around the head, all covered with sticky sour goat's milk.

Later we requested a visit to a frontier post which was in constant action against the tribesmen (on the North-West Frontier) and our British Army friends selected Miram Shah, an advanced outpost in troublesome northern Waziristan. We took off in our DC-2 from Peshawar into a dust storm as thick as a London fog, and in a few moments were hedgehopping over mountainous crags, grim and inhospitable as any in the world. . . .

Our DC-2 neatly sideslipped into the saucer-small Miram Shah airdrome and we rolled to a halt next to antiquated R.A.F. biplanes which stood permanently loaded with bombs in case of trouble. Trouble was the daily fare for a handful of British officers and Indian troops who held this outpost. The last major operations against the tribesmen ended only three weeks before our visit, and native women were still busy scavenging among old food and petrol cans where the troops had camped. . . .

The obliging tribesmen called off their shooting for the day when they heard that American journalists were at Miram Shah and invited us to drive along the Tochi River valley road through their tribal strongholds. We didn't feel too happy when the political agent with us informed us that it was the first time in three years that cars had traveled the road without armed escort. On every hilltop stood tough-looking boys with rifles in the crooks of their arms. The agent assured us they were his *Khassadars* who'd turned out as a guard of honor for our benefit. Nevertheless, we were comforted at the sight of two British Lysander planes which shuttled back and forth overhead to make sure we weren't shot up.

Back at Miram Shah, Pathan soldiers had laid out a *tikala*—a native lunch—on the lawn of the officers' mess. Pathans, as Moslems, eat with the right hand only—the left is unclean—squatting on the ground so that the soles of their feet do not show toward their neighbors, and as Pathan guests we did likewise.

The meal consisted of huge plates of *chirg pilav* (chicken and rice), *keema* (mince curry), *chirg aloo* (chicken and potatoes), eaten simultaneously with the aid of *chipatis,* round pancakes which are used to scoop up the food. This was topped off with *feernie,* a sort of junket, covered with an incredibly thin layer of beaten silver called *varak,* which is a native aphrodisiac. I was persuaded to eat two helpings. I had stomach trouble for a week afterward.

Notes from the Editor and Cooking Specialists

This may be a warning to avoid *varak,* if it ever should come your way, but it might be interesting to try out a chicken pilaf, Waziristan-style. For four you will need:

2 medium chickens, that are a little plump
2 cups of rice, preferably the unpolished variety
½ teaspoon of powdered ginger
2 sticks of cinnamon
4 tablespoons of sesame or peanut oil
4 small onions, coarsely chopped
2 garlic toes
½ cup of shredded almonds
½ cup of seeded raisins
A few tiny sprigs of saffron

The chickens are cut into small pieces with the bones clinging to the meat to make sure that it retains its flavor. To secure neat-looking little bites, start cooking the chickens in salted water. Remove them before they are tender, when it is easier to cut them than when they are raw or cooked. Return the pieces to the broth in which the chickens started and cook a little more.

Remove the chicken stock and cook the rice in it for 6 minutes, together with the cinnamon and ginger. Fry the chicken pieces in the oil with the onions and garlic until they are nicely browned. Pack the rice and chicken into a casserole, mixing the almonds, raisins and the saffron. Cover with the chicken broth. Cook, covered, for 45 minutes in a medium oven (350°).

CHIPATIS

that go with the various Indian dishes can be bought in stores specializing in foreign foods. Do-it-yourselfers can mix whole wheat flour, water and a little salt into a stiff dough. Tear off little balls of the dough, of the size of pullet eggs, roll them on a floured board to ¼-inch thickness and bake on a griddle.

A Race Around the World for Birds'-Nest Soup

JAMES R. YOUNG

To MOST Americans the name of James R. Young conjures up memories of the dark days of World War II when the Japanese were preparing to attack our country. Because he dared to write a revealing series on Japan for International News Service, he was imprisoned by the Japanese in 1940. He survived this ordeal to write *Behind the Rising Sun,* which was made into a movie in 1943. His experiences were dramatized in the picture *Blood on the Sun,* in which James Cagney starred.

Today the old "Japan hand" is associate editor of the Anderson, S.C., *Daily Mail.*

For the readers of the O.P.C. cookbook he turns back to the days of adventure in the mid-twenties when he sailed the seas as aide to the famed, colorful E. W. Scripps and learned the secrets of a real Chinese birds'-nest soup. He shares it with us:

T HE FOUNDER of the United Press, the Scripps-Howard
newspapers, NEA, Science Service and other projects
of his era, E. W. Scripps, was a select eater aboard his
yacht *Ohio* where he lived as an ocean hermit for several
years.

On a diet, he had a few choice dishes, among them birds'-
nest soup. Scripps traveled alone but had a crew of twenty-
eight, and a private staff headed by James R. Young, now
of Anderson, S.C., who submits this recipe of The Chief.
On one of the yacht's world trips the eccentric publisher-
editor had a Chinese kitchen crew. They were paid off and
a new crew hired, headed by a Swiss chef. But Scripps
wanted birds'-nest soup like that the Chinese cooks had
made for him on the previous voyage.

He ordered me (we were then anchored in the Canary
Islands) to locate the Chinese at Hong Kong and have
them sent to Gibraltar, and to bring with them birds'-nest
soup ingredients. The order went through; the Chinese were
located. The yacht touched South Africa, then headed up
the west coast toward Gibraltar to pick up the Chinese.
The team of four traveled the trans-Pacific route, across
Canada and then across the Atlantic to reach Gibraltar. The
American consul had the four on his hands, with the birds'-
nest soup ingredients awaiting the yacht *Ohio*.

But despite this race around half the world, Scripps was
not to enjoy a last birds'-nest soup. Before the yacht reached
Gibraltar to pick up the Chinese team, Scripps died at
Monrovia, Liberia (in 1926). The Chinese were shipped
back to Hong Kong. I don't know what became of the soup
ingredients they had brought with them in boxes, but here's
the recipe for the favorite of E. W. Scripps:

Nests for birds'-nest soup, known as *nichee*, are made by
a special kind of seaside swallow, which gathers the flesh

of small fish and makes it into a nest by mixing it with saliva. It is rich in protein in its gelatinous state.

A bird's nest comes in the shape of a small dried transparent saucer about the size of a soup spoon bowl. It is boiled slowly in lightly salty water which separates it into strips resembling spaghetti.

There are two kinds of *nichees:* a fuzzy kind and a smooth kind, both of the same general shape.

Most birds' nests are made into gelatinous sweet dishes and some into soup. It is the soup, which E. W. Scripps enjoyed.

You can buy *Nichee de Mer* in dried, porous cakes made from ground, powdered (seaside swallow) birds' nests. This is the type used in making birds'-nest soup.

Birds'-nest soup has a faint, interesting flavor which is emphasized by proper seasoning and a chicken broth base.

½ box of dry birds' nests
4 cups of cold water
6 cups of chicken broth
⅓ pound of chicken
¼ pound of lean ham
1 teaspoon of salt

Place birds' nests in granite or iron pot and simmer slowly about 1 hour. Remove from fire and allow to cool. Shred the chicken and ham into the lightly salted 6 cups of chicken broth.

Cook until it boils. Combine the two and serve immediately. This is ample for eight portions.

This soup can be prepared ahead of time and kept in the icebox and warmed before serving.

Lightly beaten whites of 3 eggs can be added if desired. Place the beaten egg in the bottom of the soup (serving) dish and pour the hot soup over the eggs, stirring eggs as you pour, or it can be added to the soup in the pot just before serving.

Peking Duck Spiced with a Scoop

JUDGE N. F. ALLMAN

SOME LIKE to talk about the "ringside seat to history" as being part of the privileges enjoyed by correspondents. Judge N. F. Allman, an expert on Chinese economy and law, who was in the diplomatic service in China and a publisher in that country, has his own literal version of this saying as he recalls stormy days in Tientsin.

A JAPANESE colonel's penchant for good Chinese food unexpectedly netted a scoop for me and for the late George Woodhead, editor of the Peking and Tientsin *Times*.

Following the Boxer Rebellion in 1900 a dozen or so of the great powers posted military detachments to Tientsin. Among these were a regiment of Japanese soldiers and the U.S. 15th Infantry Regiment. Needless to say, not all was love and kisses among these units of varied nationalities. The boys made up for the dullness of daily military drill by enthusiasm. There was off-duty attendance in night clubs and bars. This provided perfect setups for clashes between the young fellows of many lands, seeking the favors of this or that Yamada San.

In March 1919 tension had built up to fever heat between the Japanese regiment and the U.S. 15th, leading to a fracas in one of the night clubs in the Japanese concession. As might be expected a Yamada San provided the *casus belli*.

Despite all the tension, and apparently with no premeditated connection therewith, the colonel of the Japanese regiment decided to give a Chinese dinner on March 12, 1919, to some two dozen European and American residents. George Woodhead and I were among the guests. We had a wonderful Chinese dinner including birds'-nest soup, sharks' fins and Peking duck, plus an abundance of *sake* and neat cognac of which the colonel was very fond. He drank it by the tumblerful.

After the dinner—the genial host was under the table— George Woodhead returned to his office to put the P. & T. *Times* to bed and I proceeded to the late show at the Empire Theater to enjoy a good look at the then-current vamp, probably Theda Bara. Hardly had we entered the theater when all hell broke loose in all the neighboring streets. The Empire was near the border of the Japanese and French concessions and this turned out to be the site where the American and Japanese soldiers had decided to fight out their differences.

The theater doors were quickly barred; we were reasonably safe inside and none of the Japanese or American civilians in the theater were anxious to volunteer and join in the fight.

For me this was a scoop made to order: I could follow every phase of the battle from the several windows in the veranda around the balcony, which provided a grandstand view right near a telephone. I rang up George Woodhead and I gave him a step-by-step description of the battle. It raged for two hours. There were many casualties. For this eyewitness scoop he pulled his front page off the press and substituted my reports.

About midnight the entire Tientsin police force was in action. Together with the M.P.s they restored order, ending up by escorting us out of the battle zone. In lieu of space rates, a case of scotch came my way which, plus the excellent Chinese dinner from the Japanese colonel, made the day a memorable one.

Oh yes. Now more about the dinner. Any host can delight his guests with birds'-nest soup, sharks' fins and Peking duck. He will require, however, a healthy bank balance. The recipe for birds'-nest soup is given elsewhere, so here are my recipes for sharks' fins soup and Peking duck:

SHARKS' FINS AND CHICKEN SOUP

3 cups of cooked sharks' fins
½ of a 3-pound chicken
4 cups of chicken stock
2 ounces of shredded Virginia ham
2 tablespoons of rice wine
2 teaspoons of water chestnut flour (for thickening)
1 small piece of crushed ginger root
1 tablespoon of fine-cut scallions
1 egg white
1 teaspoon of cornstarch
Gourmet powder, salt, pepper

Cut the chicken into shreds and roll it in the egg white and cornstarch.

Place the cooked sharks' fins into the chicken stock with the ginger, rice wine and scallions and simmer for 20 minutes. Add the chicken, pepper, salt, gourmet powder and bring to a boil. Mix the water chestnut flour into thin paste with a little stock. Stir into the cooking soup and cook another 2 minutes. When ready to serve add the Virginia ham.

To cook the fins: soak them first in warm water for at

322 *Overseas Press Club Cookbook*

least ½ hour with 1 tablespoon of bicarbonate of soda.
Simmer for 2 hours, or until the fins are soft. Remove from
the simmering pot and proceed as above. This will serve
six generously.

Sharks' fins and tails are made into gelatinous soups
which the Chinese consider highly palatable. They are usually served at big feasts and provide a fine foundation for
the dozen or more dishes that follow, such as, for instance:

PEKING DUCK—WITH BAOPING,
OR LOTUS LEAF PANCAKES

1 whole fresh duck, about 5½ pounds, dressed
Make a mixture of:
2 tablespoons of melted Chinese barley syrup
½ cup of water
1 teaspoon of salt
Have sufficient peanut or salad oil to smear duck all over when
ready to barbecue.
12 green onions frayed at the end

Dip duck in boiling water for 6 seconds. Sew stomach of
the duck leaving an opening that is big enough to insert
the hose of a hand air pump. Inflate duck into a balloon.
Fold opening with twist of hand and sew up to make air-
tight. Smear entire duck with peanut or salad oil and keep
at 76° temperature overnight.

When ready to barbecue the duck smear on the mixture
described above. Preheat the oven, and barbecue the duck
in the hot oven for about 55 minutes, or until golden brown.
When done, use sharp knife to strip off skin and cut into
pieces about 2 by 2 inches. The meat of the duck may be
removed from the frame and also cut into pieces for serving
with:

BAOPING, OR PANCAKES

½ cup of lard
2 cups of flour
1 cup of boiling water

Pour the water on the flour, stirring flour all the while. Knead into a fairly stiff dough, adding more flour if necessary. Roll into a sausage and cut into pieces 1-inch thick. Pat between hands into a small cake and press flat. Take two of these, brush lard between them and roll out into a thin pancake the size of a plate. Fry or bake in a griddle or frying pan with a small amount of fat. When done on both sides separate into two pancakes. Cover with a damp hot towel until ready to eat.

To serve, place pieces of the duck skin on a pancake, with 1-inch pieces of green onions frayed at each end; add *hoy sen chiang* (seafood sauce). Roll up pancake and eat. A delightful dish.

My Favorite Japanese Dish

E. WALLACE MOORE

FEW KNOW Japan and the Philippines as intimately as Mrs. E. Wallace Moore who wrote for the Japan *Times* of Tokyo and the *Japan Advertiser* in the days before World War II, who was director of public relations and publicity for the Philippine Government Tourist Bureau until she was taken prisoner of war in Manila. She also ventured deep into head-hunter country. In fact she can tell the story of a feast with the head-hunters that sends shivers down your spine and would discourage you from eating for some time, which is not the purpose of this book.

To give us an idea of Japanese cooking at its best, she has contributed her recipe for *Karuto Ago*, which she explains means "broiled armor" and refers to the lobster shell in which it is cooked. She writes:

I SHALL NOT set forth the quantities of some of the ingredients because they will depend on the size of the lobster to be cooked. Each vegetable should be equal in amount and their total should be about one third of the volume of the lobster meat.

KARUTO AGO

1 lobster body
Bamboo shoots, sliced thin in long strips
Shütake, sliced thin
Carrots, sliced thin
1 teaspoon of *shoyu* (the Japanese soya sauce)
1 teaspoon of *sake*
½ teaspoon of sugar
1 tablespoon of *dashi*
1 egg
Pinch of salt
⅛ teaspoon of *ajinomoto* (a seasoning powder)
¼ cup of bread crumbs
Green peas
Corn oil
Lemon slices

All above italicized items obtainable from any good Japanese food supply store.

Soak *shütake* before slicing.

Place fresh uncooked lobster body in boiling water, cook 12 minutes. Remove and cool quickly. Then remove meat from body and claws, discarding stomach, lungs, intestines but retaining green liver or red coral. Shred total.

Boil *Shütake,* bamboo shoots and carrots, only slightly.

Mix *shoyu, sake,* sugar and *dashi* and add to the vegetables.

Beat egg in bowl, add salt and *ajinomoto.* Put egg in lightly oiled saucepan and stir over low flame until egg thickens a little; add the cooked vegetables, the green peas and the lobster meat shredded. Mix well and replace in the properly cleaned half lobster shell with layer of bread crumbs over the top.

Spray if possible, or in some other way cover crumbs lightly with oil. Put in broiling oven until heated through. Top should be a golden brown. Serve with lemon wedges.

This recipe is for one person only. Multiply in accordance with number of shells to be filled.

I Remember Papa

MADELINE DANE ROSS

TRAVELERS heading for Japan may be grateful to Madeline Ross for the story about her coping with unexpected "delicacies" in the Far East. In her professional life she edited and published the *Team News* for UNRRA and later was special assistant to the U. S. Coordinator of Public Affairs at the Brussels World's Fair. Though few cuisines can rival the dishes of Brussels in its best restaurants, her memories of eating adventures in Japan impressed her most deeply. She explains why.

THIS IS NOT the story of my pshychoanalysis. My father died when I was a child and I do not think of him very often, but on a recent trip to Japan, his training which I had considered very strict, came to such urgent use that memories of him have been deeply refreshed. And because of his training, new paths were opened to me and I enjoyed glimpses of the real Japan and secured stories that would have escaped me without it.

I was brought up in the era when food that was placed before you, and *all* of it, had to be eaten. At the first signs of negation, the morality cliché, "Think of how those starving Armenian children would like to have this nice . . ." was uttered. Then if moral suasion failed, a gleam would appear in Papa's eyes which I learned early to translate: "Down the hatch, missy, or else."

The food in Japan is marvelous—if you choose it. My first important experience with it was at a formal lunch at Happo-En, an exquisite eating place in Tokyo. My wealthy hosts and I sat on silken cushions on the tatami-covered floor and were served on beautiful lacquer and porcelain ware by lovely maidens. My garden view as I sat in all this oriental perfection left nothing to be desired. I was asked a moment before the food was served if I ate raw fish. Recalling a piece that I ate at an Overseas Press Club regional dinner for Japan, I replied, "Oh, yes." The meal lasted more than two hours and there were thirty courses . . . twenty-six were raw fish. Thanks to Papa, I made it.

Another gracious host said, "I will take you to a place tourists don't get to. They telephoned me this morning to say they had been hunting." What do you do with an invitation like this when you are already in your host's car? We went to a tiny building harboring one of Japan's amazingly simple and efficient eating places. This one specialized in broiled wild game. We sat at a well-scrubbed counter arrangement near sizable charcoal braziers. The first course was broiled sparrows served with their heads on. Their glazed tiny eyes looked like accusing raisins. I struggled with them and then my host urged, "You *must* eat the heads, they're the best part. They're crunchy." I did—they were.

But when it came to enjoying baked Japanese lobster or Japanese salads, I did not have to remember Papa. The salad that goes under the name of *Kyuri Aka-Nasu Saradi Gomashi* has a delicious, slightly nutty flavor thanks to the ground sesame seeds and bits of bean curd that are in the sauce covering cucumber and tomato slices.

For four take:

1 big sliced tomato
1 peeled and sliced cucumber
½ teaspoon of salt
1 tablespoon of fried bean curd, finely shredded (obtainable in cans)
2 tablespoons of vinegar
1 teaspoon of *shoyu* sauce
1 teaspoon of ground, roasted sesame seeds

Mix the vinegar, sesame seed and *shoyu;* drain all juice from the tomatoes and the cucumber slices that have been sprinkled with salt. Mix in the bean curd and cover with the liquid mixture and turn like ordinary salad.

Part X

FROM AFRICA AND THE MIDDLE EAST, AND A REMINDER FROM SAUDI ARABIA

Little Ghana
Tests Cold War Leaders

MARGUERITE CARTWRIGHT

INSTRUCTOR at Hunter College, columnist of the Pittsburgh
Courier, Marguerite Cartwright has reported extensively from
Yugoslavia, the Asian-American Conference in Bandung, from
the Middle East, from Arab countries and from Africa, delving
deeply into race relations problems. She tells of a revealing
lunch in Accra.

THE FESTIVITIES to celebrate the newly won independence of little Ghana were in full swing in 1957, with
the eyes of the world—and specially of Africa—focused on
Accra, where prominent delegates from the United States,
Soviet Russia, Great Britain and many other countries had
assembled to pay homage to the newborn state and to court
its friendship.

One of the hosts was Ghana's Finance Minister, K. A.
Gbedemah, an old friend of mine, who gave a luncheon,
which certainly was one of the most striking that took place
in those days when the cold war was still at its coldest.

As diplomatic parties go, it was a small one, but after a look at my fellow guests, I had no doubt that my Puckish friend had arranged the party to see for himself just how the leading representatives of opposing ideologies would react when brought together at the same table. On the one side you had the Vice-President of the United States and Mrs. Nixon as well as Dr. Ralph Bunche of the United Nations. On the other was the chief Russian delegate, Mr. Ivan Benediktov. Slightly in the background were the delegates of Great Britain and Switzerland.

In a quiet, quick aside, I accused my host of displaying suspiciously neutralist-flavored sentiments, but he rejected my charge, stressing that as Prime Minister Nkrumah had said, Ghana was a small, new state that subscribed to no blocs.

Much of the conversation drifted toward agriculture since Mr. Benediktov had been Russian Minister of Agriculture and toured the United States to study our farming methods. Nixon made a point of speaking elaborately about the work of George Washington Carver in our country.

I hold that had it been a popularity contest between the American and the Russian, Nixon would have won because of the ease with which he spoke, while the Russian, though he tried to turn on the charm, remained tense and always on his guard. Marked was the difference between the representative of a free society and of a firmly controlled one.

The luncheon was not a lengthy one, as such things go— about 2½ hours. It started with drinks on the terrace of the luxurious, modern home and the following menu was all-African, with Mrs. Nixon delighting the heart of the hostess by taking two helpings of the national dish *Fou-Fou*. Small stuffed crabs were delicious hors d'ouevres followed by a ground nut soup (made of peanuts) and by the *Fou-Fou*. A mixed fruit salad, touched up with palm wine—a smoky-colored fermented drink—concluded the meal.

FOU-FOU

rivals cream of nuts soup in popularity in Ghana. A ball of *fou-fou* is placed in the center of a plate and surrounded by pieces of chicken, fricasséed in palm oil, hard-boiled eggs and fried "garden eggs," i.e., eggplants, all covered with the sauce from the fricassée which is bright red, thanks to vast quantities of red pepper. The story goes that if you take a ball of *fou-fou* and throw it up to the ceiling and it sticks there, it is good.

In order not to keep you in suspense, may I reveal that it is made of yams, boiled in water, that are pounded in a mortar and seasoned with red peppers, grated nutmeg, salt and cayenne with a little palm oil or sesame oil added to ensure the desired consistency.

Most Americans will prefer the:

CREAM OF NUTS SOUP

To make a small portion of it for four, take:

⅔ cup of browned and crushed peanuts, or almonds
2 tablespoons of cream
2 tablespoons of butter
2 tablespoons of arrowroot or cornstarch
4 cups of meat or chicken stock
Salt and pepper

After crushing the nuts in a mortar, mix with the cream. Melt the butter and pour it into the broth into which the arrowroot or cornstarch has been blended. Heat thoroughly until the mixture reaches the desired consistency and blend in the cream and nuts; add salt and pepper.

Not too far from Ghana, up the coast where French chefs have taken over some of the local recipes and adapted them to European taste, the traveler may, if lucky in his choice of hosts, make the acquaintance of:

CHICKEN IN LEMON SAUCE

which is served with fluffy rice.
To make it the chef takes:

2 pounds of frying chicken
½ cup of butter
1 tablespoon of sherry
1 tablespoon of white wine
Grated rind of 1 small, undyed orange
Grated rind of 1 small lemon, also undyed
2 teaspoons of lemon juice
1 tablespoon of arrowroot
¾ cup of light cream
Salt, pepper

Cut up the chicken into serving pieces, discarding the skin. Roll them first in a little of the lemon juice, then dust with a little flour. Sauté in the butter until the pieces are golden brown. Cover with a tight lid and cook over a low flame until tender.

Take the chicken from the pan and keep it warm. Stir wine and sherry into the drippings. Add the lemon and orange rind, the remaining lemon juice, salt and pepper. Mix a spoon of this sauce and a little cold water. Dissolve the arrowroot and add it to the sauce. Cook over low fire until the sauce thickens. Then return the chicken pieces to it and heat for 5 minutes. Stir in the cream. If you like Parmesan, put chicken and sauce in a fireproof dish and pass under the broiler for just 1 minute.

Secrets from the Kitchen of Gamal Abdel Nasser

CHARLES P. ARNOT

As A CORRESPONDENT for the American Broadcasting Company
Charles P. Arnot served extensively in Africa and especially in
Egypt. In Cairo he was able to glean secrets from the kitchen
of Egypt's chief of state besides important news.

WHEN President Gamal Abdel Nasser of the United
Arab Republic dines at home, or entertains Egyptian
guests, his little-known, publicity-shy wife, Tahia, invariably prepares their favorite Egyptian dish: green *molokia*
with chicken (or rabbit).

This is not served, however, when President Nasser entertains foreign visitors unless it is known that they have a
taste for such a seasoned oriental dish. Mrs. Nasser, almost
unknown to the Egyptian public, never appears at her husband's official dinners or functions. She has only entertained
officially—even then privately and quietly—when Mrs. Tito,
first lady of Yugoslavia, visited Egypt with her husband,
Premier Josip Broz Tito, in February of 1959.

A strange meeting indeed: the sheltered shy, young Arab wife and mother and the daring, bright-eyed Yugoslav who had fought side by side with her countrymen against the German invaders.

The recipe for the dish that ranks as favorite in the first family of the United Arab Republic was garnered from Mrs. Nasser's sister.

It is *molokia* (pronounced "moo-loo-key'-ah"), a flavorful green soup made from the leaves of a green spinach-like plant called *molokia* which grows in Egypt. The fresh *molokia* leaves are washed thoroughly and dried in a clean cloth. Then they are cut into tiny pieces with a special sharp knife requiring the use of both hands. The tiny pieces emerge crescent-shaped. Two chickens or rabbits, as desired, are placed in boiling water and cooked until tender, then removed. The green-cut *molokia* leaves are then put into the broth together with finely chopped garlic, oriental herbs (to suit the taste), salt and pepper. This is cooked slowly until it becomes a thick, green soup. The chickens (or rabbits) are cut, fried until brown in butter and served with boiled rice—together with the *molokia* soup as a side dish. Two or three pounds of *molokia* and two chickens or rabbits will serve a family of six.

Potted in Persia

ANTHONY CHAPELLE

As MAY BE gathered from Anthony Chapelle's spiced chicken, he strayed far away from Mom's kitchen. Navy photographer in both world wars, he specialized in documentary motion pictures in the Middle East, Southeast Asia and postwar Europe.

IN ONE of Rex Stout's books, the famous and well-fed Nero Wolfe solves a murder to get a recipe—for *saucisson,* as in boloney. Famous chefs have been decorated by kings and governments for other cleverly contrived variations on an old dish, diplomatically renamed.

Now all of this may be commendable, but when most of us enjoy a little gastronomic normalcy between attacks of dyspepsia and ulcers, we usually develop a "Mom" complex. Nothing seems as wonderful in retrospect as the way she threw a beef stew together, and even her morning eggs grow a nostalgic flavor.

Maybe Mom did add something that wasn't a conditioned reflex or just plain juvenile hunger. But the chances are that we just miss the simplicity of home cooking.

For her menu, you remember, you needed no glossary, nor were you ever left to appear an ignorant lout because your college French, applied to the menu of a Hungarian restaurant, left you only frustrated.

(You know what I mean—I said to the waiter, "What's that?" And he said, "I don't know but I think it's some kind of chicken—I'll go back and ask." And the sweet young thing I was endeavoring to impress immediately marked me down to ninety-eight cents.)

My point is that life can be beautiful and so can a platter of ham and eggs, sans parsley, insolence and the moment of indecision about the size of the tip. It matters not if your china is chipped and left over from Grandma, and if the silver proves that your name at one time ended in "Hotel." There is still no food like that prepared with your own mental expectations. And once you've shown even verbal promise as a home cook, it doesn't matter whether she will come up "for a drink." For a meal, she's probably already there.

By then there is no time to start consulting competent guides on how to cook an octopus, a rattlesnake, a lizard or a locust, even though, with the appropriate box-top and a few *rial* to cover mailing charges, you could master the preparation of all of them. It is a good time, though, to Look East, young man, and to look to the chicken of the poultry species.

Much of what's outstanding in the preparation of rice, chicken and lamb originates in the Middle East. Within this seemingly narrow choice of staples, the whole Arab world creates an almost infinite variety of delectable eatables.

Not the least of these is their spiced chicken, appropriate to any display of your culinary talents. First forget whatever you've heard about the rare spices of the Orient; they are all in little tins at the supermarket.

To prepare spiced chicken, we have to make only one digression from the Asian original. I do not find essential a plump sheep's tail to provide the fat. Butter or olive oil does as well or better.

You start with a dismembered roasting chicken, or, if your city boasts a shop that sells "poultry in parts," you can put the emphasis on breasts, legs or wings as you prefer. For quantity, let's say five pounds.

Having washed the pieces under running water and toweled them dry again, I suggest that you give the necks and backs, if any, to the cat, along with the other minor accessories. They are hardly worth the trouble to fix. (*Editor's Note:* Anthony Chapelle, that is wasteful. They make a fine base for soup.)

The parts of your chicken are then salted and peppered, and browned in about a quarter pound of butter, or four ounces of olive oil.

Now take a half pint of heavy cream. Add:

1 level teaspoon of powdered cinnamon
½ teaspoon of powdered ginger
½ teaspoon of nutmeg
Pinch of paprika
A little more salt and pepper, as your taste dictates

Stir together, and add the whole cream business to your chicken in the pan. Cover, and let it simmer until the chicken is soft and tender. Then take the cover off the pan, and continue the simmering until the gravy thickens.

The whole job should take just under an hour.

One variation on this recipe is to add a finely chopped onion while browning the chicken.

A second is to eliminate the cream, and substitute a dry white wine.

Spiced chicken should be served with rice, and you can't beat the cooking instructions on whatever package of rice you buy. Follow them implicitly, and you won't go wrong.

Of the million possibilities to add to the rice, my favorite is never believed until tasted. But it's a perfect complement to spiced chicken; add a cup of drained pie cherries from a can into the rice after it's cooked, and let the dish stand over a very low flame, stirring a few times until the cherries are warmed and the rice has absorbed some of the pink juice.

Fresh fruit, dates and coffee provide the traditional finish to this meal. If you want to be daring, add a level teaspoon of ground cardamom seed to your coffee while it's brewing. You'll find a new zing! to the coffee—but only if you serve it strong and black. (You can't use the spice with milk or cream.)

But why not serve it black? You've got your whole evening ahead of you.

Surprise in Saudi Arabia

JOHN P. LEACACOS

As a correspondent for the Cleveland *Plain Dealer*, John P. Leacacos has reported from Europe and the Middle East since the middle thirties. He tells of his interview with one of the richest men in the world whose choice of a chef will surprise many of us.

IN JUNE 1951, with Aramco pull, I managed to get to Riyadh in Saudi Arabia, the first correspondent to be allowed in since Ed Curtis of the A.P. four years before.

King Saud was then Crown Prince but regent in effect, as old Ibn Saud was in his last decline. The climax of my visit was a banquet in the gardens of the new palace at which I sat on the Prince's right.

We talked about the new role of Saudi Arabia in the Middle East, his Haroun al Rashid hopes to "do good" for his people and modernize the country, during which he broke the news to me of the first military aid agreement made between his country and the U.S.A.

We were eating several courses, which tasted like blue

plate specials except for one delectable Arab pilaf and some wonderful watermelon from his oasis.

I thought I'd do the usual and asked to give my compliments to the chef for the "wonderful" repast, etc.

So the head chef showed up. He was a Clevelander—from Cleveland Bible College (Charles B. Ernst, '46).

I asked him how he held his job with the Arab future king. Ernst said: "Oh, he likes my shredded-cheddar-cheese-on-pineapple salad."

We Discovered the Nigerian "DODO"

JAMES H. SHELDON

JAMES SHELDON, free lance correspondent and adviser to the Democratic National Committee, belongs to the ranks of the men who foresaw the awakening of Africa and studied its problems before they hit the international front pages. Like others, he likes to tell of the surprises the new countries have in store for us. He writes:

WHEN I was in Nigeria in 1960 we had an unexpected layover at Kano, a thousand-year-old city, 550 miles inland. The plane to Khartoum had developed engine trouble and I found time on my hands. I decided to use it to call on the editor of the *Northern Star*, an eight-page daily that had just been threatened with all kinds of reprisals by a government official whom it had attacked. Like most Americans, I felt that freedom of the press was our special possession and I was ready to give the threatened editor a friendly greeting, plus a pep talk about the rights of newsmen. He surprised me: he was one of the least-worried men I had ever seen—in fact, he was busy writing another editorial to carry on his battle with the official. Thus I realized in far-off Kano that the freedoms we deem so important are not restricted to our side of the Atlantic. Nigeria enjoys them too.

Nigerians are wonderful hosts who believe in ample food supplies. The menu of the Kano Hotel included: sunrise tea, a four-course breakfast, a seven-course luncheon, afternoon tea, a seven-course dinner, and finally a bedtime "snack" with good Scotch at about fifteen cents a glass. And how good the regional dishes are we learned in Lagos, when we had the good fortune to dine at the home of some old friends. Here is one Nigerian recipe that I feel will appeal to most palates from New York to Hong Kong. It is called Dodo—but, unlike the Mauritian bird of that name, is far from extinct.

NIGERIAN DODO

    1 large ripe plantain
    1 small finely chopped onion
    1 medium finely chopped tomato
    1 small can of crayfish or baby shrimp
    Vegetable oil, salt, pepper

Peel plantain, cut in diagonal slices about ¼-inch thick. Fry in shallow oil until golden brown. In another pan start cooking the onion and tomato in a little vegetable oil, add the crayfish or shrimp, and cook for 7–10 minutes. Pour mixture over the plantain. This makes a generous portion for two.

Plantains may be purchased in any stores catering to our Spanish or Puerto Rican groups.

Part XI

LOOK HOMEWARD, CHEFS!

Buffet Supper with Major and Mrs. John Eisenhower

JACK HARRISON POLLACK

LET THERE be no doubt in anybody's mind: though correspondents are glad that on occasion their hunt for news and knowledge in foreign lands helped them discover new flavors and new dishes, no group relishes sound American cooking and the long list of our own regional specialties more than we do. In fact, we go in for what you might call parochial pride. Arguments about which state of the Union has the best waffles and hot breads, the best strawberry shortcake, the best chowders or abalones, the best turkey stuffing or what-have-you, crop up whenever some member of the crew on duty overseas suffers from a touch of homesickness.

What kind of home dinners would tempt them? Jack Harrison Pollack believes he has an answer to this question. One of the founders and former president of the Society of Magazine Writers, who has written literally hundreds of stories to delight and enlighten American readers, he thinks many would enjoy the kind of meal which the son of President Eisenhower and his young wife would be serving to their guests on a Saturday night:

IN FEBRUARY 1954 I was in Fort Benning, Georgia, sitting in the kitchen of the modest Army post home of Major and Mrs. John Eisenhower. I was interviewing Barbara Eisenhower for a story for *Good Housekeeping* and enjoying the unique privilege of getting to know refreshing Barbara Eisenhower long before millions of people observed her natural friendliness on her December 1959 eleven-country Asia-Africa-Europe tour with President Eisenhower.

So here I was with an open notebook in the young Eisenhowers' home not far from where Major Dwight Eisenhower had lived in 1926. It was Friday afternoon and Barbara was busy preparing the food for her sit-down buffet supper that she was having the following night for eight Army post friends. Like many busy young mothers, she wanted to make her dinner ahead of time, freeze it, so that she could have time to enjoy her own party. "I like to have Saturday free to lay out the silver and clean up the house," she explained. Barbara had already made the chicken suprême and the lime cottage-cheese mold salad and was now making her dessert of chocolate angel nut pie from meringue crust, pecans, coffee and whipped cream.

I was asking her questions which would have rattled a lesser woman but Barbara took them all in stride until she observed the fluffy pie filling. A snag arose! Barbara's first batch of cream wouldn't whip. It threatened to become butter. Barbara sampled it quickly and her suspicions were confirmed. Yes, it was sour.

I could see she was troubled and stopped my chatter. "What shall I do?" she seemed to ask herself.

I looked out the window and saw the ever-present Secret Serviceman near his car watching the three Eisenhower children. When their grandfather was elected President of the United States, three Secret Service agents were assigned to guard David, Anne and Susan around the clock as prescribed by law. Newsmen kidded them as the "Diaper Detail." But the Secret Serviceman was now powerless to help Barbara without neglecting her children. Since she was in the middle of her culinary mobilization and didn't want to leave the house herself, I volunteered, "Could I drive over to the post store and buy you some fresh whipping cream?"

"Would you?" she gratefully inquired.

In my rented car I felt honored to save the day. I was back a half-hour later with a fresh supply of whipping cream. This time it spun along to creamy perfection in Barbara's electric mixer.

It was now too late to return to our interview, so I started to leave when John marched in. Barbara hustled him into the kitchen and told him about my errand. She returned quickly and asked me if I'd like to stay to dinner that night to have a preview of their Saturday night buffet.

Would I? Naturally I accepted and got my best material for the story that night. We discussed everything from the West Point Honor Code to the late Senator McCarthy's antics. We talked about how John and Barbara had met on a blind date at another dinner party in Vienna in October 1946. We all laughed at how John burned the dinner rolls at their first party after they were married. We all laughed at how John attended Fort Benning's Cooks and Bakers School, to learn how to handle a slick mess sergeant in his company. We all laughed at their children romping in the White House.

After dinner John played for us on the piano "The Dog-Faced Soldier," the Third Division's song which has become a kind of unofficial song of the entire Infantry. He also loaned me his scholarly master's degree thesis called "The Soldier as a Character in Elizabethan Drama," in which he contrasted such soldier-characters as Tamburlaine, Henry V, Falstaff and Othello with the heroes of such then popular plays and movies as *Mister Roberts, South Pacific, Command Decision, Battleground,* and the *Story of GI Joe.* He also contrasted such commanders as Generals Bradley, Patton, Hodges, Eichelberger, Doolittle and Spaatz with their Elizabethan counterparts.

Later in the evening hard-working Major John Eisenhower invited me to drive over with him to inspect his troops at the post. When his men appraised this sloppy-looking "friend" of Major Eisenhower, they must have wondered if he were an investigating congressman or something!

In any case, I'll never forget that evening. And it all began—luckily for me—with some whipping cream which wouldn't whip!

CHICKEN SUPRÊME

1 stewing chicken—5 or 6 pounds
Carrots
Salt
Onions
Celery tops
Bay leaves
1 cup of chicken broth
1⅛ cups of rice
2 cups of toasted slivered almonds
1½ cups of minced pimentos (8 tablespoons)
4 cans of sautéed sliced mushrooms
Buttered bread crumbs

Cook the chicken together with carrots, salt, onions, celery tops and bay leaves. Pour 1 cup of chicken broth over 2 cups of cooked rice (1⅓ cups uncooked rice makes more than 2 cups cooked rice). Make 3 cups of creamy chicken gravy and 3 cups of cooked chicken. Place in separate layers in greased casserole—rice, 2 layers of chicken. Sprinkle over each layer 1 cup of toasted almonds, ¾ cup of minced pimentos and 2 cans of sliced mushrooms. Top with buttered bread crumbs. Bake at 350° for 45 minutes. Serve hot.

CREAMY CHICKEN GRAVY

12 tablespoons of chicken fat
12 tablespoons of flour
1 teaspoon of salt
⅛ teaspoon of pepper
Stir in 4 cups of seasoned chicken broth
2 cups of cream

Boil 1 minute, stirring constantly. Pour over layers in casserole. P.S. You have to make adjustments in this recipe according to taste.

LIME COTTAGE-CHEESE MOLD SALAD

Drain and reserve syrup and fruit from 1 can (9 oz.) of crushed pineapple. Add to the syrup ¼ cup of lemon juice and boiling water to make 1½ cups of liquid. Pour hot liquid over 1 package of lime-flavored gelatine. Stir until gelatine dissolves. Chill until syrupy.

Stir into half of the chilled gelatine the reserved drained pineapple, ½ cup of chopped shelled walnuts and 1 tablespoon of grated lemon rind. Pour into loaf pan, 9 by 5 by 3 inches, rinsed with cold water. Chill until firm. Keep remaining gelatine at room temperature.

When mixture in mold is firm, beat the reserved gelatine until foamy. Blend in a mixture of 1 cup of cottage cheese, ½ cup of finely diced celery, 1 teaspoon of prepared horseradish, and ¼ teaspoon of salt. Pour on top of firm gelatine in mold and chill until firm. Unmold on serving platter and garnish with sliced bananas and lettuce.

Serve with banana-nut dressing.

BANANA-NUT DRESSING

1 cup of mayonnaise
1 mashed banana
½ cup of nuts

Add a bit of cream to mayonnaise and squeeze of lemon.

CHOCOLATE ANGEL NUT PIE

½ cup of sugar
⅛ teaspoon of cream of tartar
2 egg whites
½ cup of chopped pecans
¾ cup of Nestlés bits
3 tablespoons of strong coffee
1 teaspoon of vanilla
1 cup of heavy cream

Make meringue crust by beating egg whites until stiff, not dry. Add sugar gradually. Beat until smooth and glossy. Line well-buttered 9-inch pie plate with this mixture. Sprinkle with nuts. Bake at 275° for 1 hour.

Melt chocolate bits, stir in coffee and cook 5 minutes until thickened. Cool and fold in whipped cream. Turn it into meringue shell and chill 2 or 3 hours. This pie may be kept several days in the refrigerator.

For the sake of political neutrality, let us turn from the home of the young couple whose name is tied in with Republicans to the ranch of a leading Democrat, Lyndon B. Johnson. Our guide is the Press Attaché of the United States Embassy in Mexico, Arthur V. Diggle, who was accompanying the President of Mexico on a state visit to our country in 1959.

A Texas Barbecue for the President of Mexico

ARTHUR V. DIGGLE

I T WAS the last stop of Mexico's President Adolfo Lopez
Mateos on his tour of the United States. The locale: the
LBJ Ranch of Senator Lyndon B. and Lady Bird Johnson
in the rolling hill country near Johnson City, Texas, not far
from Austin.

President Lopez Mateos, as he had promised, was repay-
ing a visit made him by Senator Johnson a year before in
Acapulco. The visit of the Mexican president was something
of an historic occasion. His stopover in Johnson City at the
LBJ Ranch was one of the very rare times when a Mexican
president had visited Texas. And there was certainly no
record of any previous time when the Mexican president
had stayed overnight as a Texan's house guest.

At the old-time Texas barbecue for some 300 guests that
Sunday afternoon, the roster of speakers was an impressive
one.

There was ex-President Harry Truman, Speaker of the
House Sam Rayburn, Secretary of Treasury Robert Ander-

son, U. S. Ambassador to Mexico Robert C. Hill, Mexican Ambassador to U.S. Antonio Carrillo Flores, Senator Johnson and, of course, the Mexican president.

The theme was the understanding and friendship which united Mexico and the United States.

Harry Truman jocularly threatened to go down to Mexico some day and run for president himself, he liked the country so much. Senator Johnson paid tribute to two peoples living side by side, sharing the same ideals of peace, freedom and justice.

When the Mexican president rose, he smiled at Truman and Johnson and the other honored guests on the improvised speaking stand, then turned to face an acre or so of picnic tables.

He spoke briefly and sincerely along the same theme of friendship and understanding. Then he turned again to his platform companions and added in measured and significant tones:

"We are friends, and where there are friends, there can be no need for borders."

There was a pause and then from the audience roaring applause. Senator Johnson jumped up, shook the Mexican president's hand and gave him a big *embrazo*. Harry Truman grabbed his hand and pumped it.

And then, at a word from Johnson, the crowd pitched in on the barbecued beef, barbecue beans, cole slaw and cold beer.

The barbecue beans, a recipe used by Lady Bird Johnson and her mother before her, are called barbecue beans, not because they are actually barbecued, but because they are served in Texas with barbecued meats—beef, pork, sausage and goat. This is the recipe in Mrs. Johnson's own words:

TEXAS BARBECUE BEANS

4–5 cups of pinto beans
Chili powder, amount depending on degree of seasoning desired,
  as explained below
1 whole medium onion
5 pods of garlic
¼ pound of salt pork
Salt

Wash beans and bring them to a boil. Let them simmer and add boiling water when necessary to add water. Slice ¼ pound of salt pork to the rind and add the salt pork to the beans when first putting them on to cook.

After beans have cooked for about 2 hours, add salt to taste and add chili powder dissolved in hot water. Add 1 rounded tablespoon of chili powder for each cup of beans if you desire hot, highly seasoned beans. Also add at this time the garlic pods and the one onion, cither sliced or diced.

Cook 2 to 3 hours more, adding boiling water when necessary, and remove onion if desired (if it is sliced, it will be easier to remove) and also garlic pods if they are still whole.

The thing you must remember about adding chili powder is that once you have got too much in, you can't take it out—so add the chili powder slowly and keep adding it until it suits your taste.

To point to the infinite variety of foods that can turn our continent into an epicure's delight, Fred Kerner, correspondent-author-editor, sounds the call:

"Come to Alaska"

FRED KERNER

I WAS ONE of the early correspondents and world travelers who sallied forth on assignment to Churchill, Manitoba, in the days before flying eased the traveler's lot. I think I may boast of a "curious palate," thanks to which I can tell about fricassée of Arctic hare, polar bear steak, seal casserole and muktuk.

The fricassée was especially delicious and I don't think I really ever appreciated the problem of catching Arctic hares. They are a very well-camouflaged animal—both winter and summer.

ARCTIC HARE FRICASSÉE

The hare was cleaned and cut into serving portions and well browned in butter. Then it was placed into a casserole along with:

¼ teaspoon of garlic powder
2 tablespoons of olive oil
1 cup of red wine
1 cup of stock
The entire mixture was well sprinkled with salt and pepper, covered and then baked for an hour and a half at 325°
1 can of cream of mushroom soup
1 teaspoon of parsley flakes

Then, with the oven still at the same temperature, the dish was placed back in the oven for another half-hour without its lid.

And if you think Arctic hares are hard to catch, then you ought to try to catch a polar bear. The Eskimo claims that the best way is to stand out on an ice floe and when a polar bear joins you, you start talking to him until he gets around to seeing your point of view. This is very important, because if he refuses to see your point of view, he has very definite ways of making you see his.

POLAR BEAR STEAK

The polar bear meat makes a delicious steak, but all the excess fat must be removed; otherwise the meat will taste far too sweet. It can be broiled over a hot fire, or tastes very delicious boiled in a pot with onions. For the sake of variety, bear steak can also be ground into bearburger.

SEAL CASSEROLE

In preparing seal casserole, it's most important that the fat should have been removed from the young seal soon after killing. Young seal is quite tender, but if any fat remains after killing, there is likely to be a very fishy taste.

2 pounds of seal steak, cut into 2-inch-square chunks
3 tablespoons of flour mixed with salt and pepper
3 tablespoons of butter or bacon fat
½ cup of dehydrated onions
3 cloves
1 teaspoon of thyme
1½ cups of water

Brown the chunks of steak that have been coated with the flour in the butter or bacon fat. Transfer them to a casserole, sprinkle with the onion flakes and thyme, bury the cloves, and pour over the water. Cover and bake in a 300° oven for 1½ hours.

MUKTUK

Muktuk is nothing more than whale skin. It has a rubbery texture and it tastes much like fried eggs. It can be eaten raw or fried. Once you get beneath the skin—and the blubber—there is quite a sizable amount of meat on a whale and this is best served in steaks, making sure to remove every bit of fat first.

Mrs. Cilley's Vermont Doughnuts

ROBERT CONWAY

WITH profound apologies to the regions and specialties of our country which we by-passed, let us turn to Vermont and share a memorable experience of Robert Conway of the New York *Daily News*. He covered crises in Poland and Germany, wars in the Middle East and reported from many parts of the United States:

I REMEMBER them as Calvin Coolidge's sour milk and sour cream doughnuts; but they weren't, of course, for Calvin Coolidge, the thirtieth President of the United States, was dead. We'd just watched his coffin lowered into the hillside burying ground at Plymouth, Vt., beside five generations of his ancestors, while hailstones bounced off the bare heads of the little group of mourners. We'd trudged from the still open grave over muddy lanes to the little country store where facilities had been set up for filing our stories; originally it was the farmhouse where Calvin Coolidge was born sixty years earlier.

And we were a cold and wet and hungry mob of reporters, photographers and telegraph operators as a three-day blizzard developed freak lightning that nightfall.

Then it was that Mrs. Florence Cilley's (pronounced Silly's) wonderfully hot, golden, crisp and fragrant doughnuts, mixed before our eyes from sour milk and sour cream and flour scooped out of a barrel, revived our spirits. She dropped the dough, shaped into rings, into a great iron pot of sweet-smelling natural deep fat sizzling on top of an old-fashioned wood-burning range. After she fished out the finished product and handed it to us, she would pause for a moment to dip into a milkpail for the freshest and creamiest cow's juice to fill the tumblers we held out to her.

Strange, but that simple meal on that snowblown night of January 7, 1933, stands out as one of the most memorable in my thirty-six years of newspaper work.

Why?

Mainly, I think, it was the inherent New England—and typically Vermont—honesty of Mrs. Cilley and of all the folks in Calvin Coolidge's native village in the sequestered Green Mountains. She stood there over the hot wood fire, beads of perspiration running down her pink cheeks, wiping her face dry with her apron so as not to sully the food, and flatly refusing to take an extra nickel from any of us.

"My doughnuts," she said, "have always been two for a nickel and they remain two for a nickel, and in Vermont we don't take tips. The milk has always been five cents a tumblerful and that's what it is going to remain tonight."

And when some of us walked away without picking up our change she followed us, anger in her blue-gray eyes, and we flushed with embarrassment as we pocketed the little left over.

I suppose it was Mrs. Cilley's—and Calvin Coolidge's—innate integrity which, in a fashion, made for what Vermonters call "the good" in so simple a product as the doughnut. The ingredients were "all real"—real sour milk, not the synthetic "store kind" recommended in modern cookbooks; real animal fat, culled out of many renderings and drippings of pork to fry the doughnuts in, and the real flour was the plain sort, ground without the bleaching additives which are commonplace nowadays.

Besides, we were feeling starved, the result of long hours and hard work and lungs full of clean mountain air. Many a fine meal is judged so, in part at least; according to the appetite of the trencherman.

That morning we'd attended the memorial services in Northampton, Mass., not far from the colonial-type white house, overlooking the Connecticut River, where Silent Cal's lips had unexpectedly been sealed forever two days before, during the winter's first severe snowstorm.

Then, after the services we'd crowded into cars and followed the slow-moving cortege along the narrow and winding highway, finding it rutted and uncomfortable.

For the Depression was with us and the New Deal's public works programs, which improved so many roads, hadn't even been dreamed about.

Our funeral procession passed through Deerfield, Mass., long ago the scene of an Indian massacre. Then through Brattleboro and Bellows Falls, Vermont, through the clean farmlands and into the pine and hemlock-studded wilderness above White River Junction, Vt. And so to the hamlet of Plymouth.

On that sad trip I carried the image of a great divide in American history: the end of the Old Order and the beginning of the New Order or, if you choose, the New Deal. For we'd watched, among the striped-trousered mourners at the church services, the gray faces of President Herbert Hoover, who had only two more months to serve as the nation's Chief Executive, and Chief Justice of the Supreme Court Charles Evans Hughes, his once red beard almost white with age. Into this austere Republican setting had come long-striding Mrs. Franklin Delano Roosevelt on the arm of her son, James, representing the President-elect who was too crippled from the old attack of polio to brave the wintry weather for a personal appearance. And all the way to Plymouth we'd watched silent New Englanders along the roadside—some arriving in horse-drawn buggies or in farm carts with their families, but most of them on foot in their work clothes—standing bareheaded in quiet tribute to the physical passing of a man who was, perhaps more than any before or after, the incarnation of their stern tradition.

Even the burial had been Biblical in its simplicity and setting.

Winter lightning had streaked the evening sky, as one might expect in a Greek tragedy, and rain and hailstones had fallen on the bald head of Calvin Coolidge's oldest friend, Frank Stearns, the Boston merchant. The mourners had stood on the grave's edge, near a canvas stretched to protect Mrs. Grace Coolidge, a youthful-looking widow, and her tall son, John.

Mrs. Dwight W. Morrow, the mother-in-law of Charles Lindbergh, was there, together with other notables, silhouetted against the clouds like so many figures in a primitive Italian painting. We, the members of the press, standing below the open pit, had this perspective of the last scene in the life not merely of an individual but of an era.

And it was from all this that we'd come into Mrs. Cilley's country kitchen.

After we'd completed our writing chores, I looked for Mrs. Cilley. I found her in her kitchen, cleaning up, with the assistance of her cheerful adopted daughter, now Mrs. H. Pelkey. Mrs. Cilley showed me the spot where the bed used to stand in which Calvin—he was baptized John Calvin Coolidge, she believed but was always known there as Cal—was born. Then, because the flavor of her doughnuts and of the fresh milk still lingered on my taste buds, I asked her for the recipe. I wrote it down. But over the years the slip of paper was lost. Only recently, speaking to Mrs. Pelkey, who succeeded Mrs. Cilley as postmistress when

Mrs. Cilley died in 1945, was this gap in my culinary knowledge corrected.

"Of course," said Mrs. Pelkey, "Mother always claimed that there was a mysterious ingredient which made them so good. But I watched her make doughnuts every day of her life from the time I came here to live when I was nine years old. And I'm pretty certain there wasn't anything mysterious, except that sometimes she'd add a little nutmeg or spice or use maple sugar instead of cane sugar, if one was plentiful and the other was not. And she'd add a little soda and cream of tartar or what we know as baking powder, for that makes them lighter and fluffier. You know, a really good cook doesn't always make everything exactly the same; sometimes you want it a little different."

So I wrote down Mrs. Cilley's recipe again. Like most good things in Vermont, it isn't complicated.

The first thing is to remember that you mix things in the following proportions—more or less, since eggs vary in size and some sour milk and sour cream is richer than others. First you beat the eggs, then add the sour cream or sour milk, or, best of all, half and half of each, and you melt a couple spoonfuls of unsalted butter to add richness (a little less if you use sour cream without any sour milk), and stir into this the sugar and salt and nutmeg, and then thicken with flour to the right consistency. And the less flour you use (but it must be enough to enable you to roll out the dough), the lighter the doughnuts or twists will be. The quality of the fat you boil or sizzle—that's how Mrs. Cilley referred to frying—is important, the best being sweet pork lard. But other fats used in frying will do.

The proportions are:

For each 2 eggs—
1 cup of sour cream or half-and-half sour cream and sour milk
2 tablespoons, more or less, of fresh unsalted butter
1 generous pinch (½ to ¾ of a teaspoon) of salt
1 teaspoon of freshly grated nutmeg
3–4 cups of flour, remembering that some flour must be used when
    rolling out the dough, and that this may thicken it too much
    if you use 4 cups to start with.

Immediately after stirring these ingredients together, roll out and cut or shape into rings or, if you wish, into twists. Mrs. Cilley used a large tumbler for the outside circle and then cut out the center with a small whisky glass.

Then she dropped the rings into sizzling deep fat; actually it was boiling fat. She fished them out when they were light brown or golden, for she was careful not to overcook.

She placed them on brown paper to drain or "dry," using plain grocery bags for that purpose. Then she served them while still hot, or very warm. Vermonters like them best when served with fresh rich milk, but coffee or tea may be substituted.

Refreshed with such hot doughnuts, and milk, Cal Coolidge's ancestors could chop cordwood all day and stuff it into fireplaces and chunk stoves through the bitter cold of a Vermont night without excessive fatigue.

That was the Vermont stamina and that was the Vermont way.

And may we add, it helped to build a tradition of which we have a right to be proud!

Index

PEOPLE AND PLACES

RECIPES